Francis Bacon's *New Atlantis*

# TEXTS · IN · CULTURE

SERIES EDITORS
Jeff Wallace and John Whale

FOUNDING EDITORS
Stephen Copley and Jeff Wallace

ADVISORY EDITORS
Lynda Nead, Birbeck College, London
Gillian Beer, Girton College, Cambridge
Roy Porter, Wellcome Institute for the History of Medicine
Anne Janowitz, University of Warwick

This series offers specially commissioned, cross-disciplinary essays on texts of seminal importance to Western culture. Each text has had an impact on the way we think, write and live beyond the confines of its original discipline, and it is only through an understanding of its multiple meanings that we can fully appreciate its importance.

ALREADY PUBLISHED

Charles Darwin's *The Origin of Species*
David Amigoni, Jeff Wallace (eds)

Adam Smith's *The Wealth of Nations*
Stephen Copley, Kathryn Sutherland (eds)

Niccolò Machiavelli's *The Prince*
Martin Coyle (ed.)

Simone de Beauvoir's *The Second Sex*
Ruth Evans (ed.)

Sigmund Freud's *Interpretation of Dreams*
Laura Marcus (ed.)

*The Great Exhibition of 1851*
Louise Purbrick (ed.)

Edmund Burke's *Reflections on the Revolution in France*
John Whale (ed.)

## TEXTS · IN · CULTURE

# Francis Bacon's
# NEW ATLANTIS

## New interdisciplinary essays

BRONWEN PRICE
*editor*

Manchester University Press
*Manchester and New York*
*distributed exclusively in the USA by Palgrave*

*Published by* Manchester University Press
Oxford Road, Manchester M13 9NR, UK
*and* Room 400, 175 Fifth Avenue, New York, NY 10010, USA
http://www.manchesteruniversitypress.co.uk

*Distributed exclusively in the USA by*
Palgrave, 175 Fifth Avenue, New York, NY 10010, USA

*Distributed exclusively in Canada by*
UBC Press, University of British Columbia, 2029 West Mall,
Vancouver, BC, Canada V6T 1Z2

*British Library Cataloguing-in-Publication Data*
A catalogue record is available from the British Library

*Library of Congress Cataloging-in-Publication Data applied for*


ISBN 0 7190 6051 6 *hardback*
     0 7190 6052 4 *paperback*

First published 2002

10  09  08  07  06  05  04  03  02     10  9  8  7  6  5  4  3  2  1

Typeset in Apollo
by Koinonia, Manchester
Printed in Great Britain
by Bell & Bain Ltd, Glasgow

# Contents

# Series introduction

Texts are produced in particular cultures and in particular historical circumstances. In turn, they shape and are shaped by those cultures as they are read and re-read in changing circumstances by different groups with different commitments, engagements and interests. Such readings are themselves then re-absorbed into the ideological frameworks within which the cultures develop. The seminal works drawn on by cultures thus have multiple existences within them, exerting their influence in distinct and perhaps contradictory ways. As these texts have been 'claimed' by particular academic disciplines, however, their larger cultural significance has often been obscured.

Recent work in cultural history and textual theory has stimulated critical awareness of the complex relations between texts and cultures, highlighting the limits of current academic formations and opening the possibility of new approaches to interdisciplinarity. At the same time, however, the difficulties of interdisciplinary work have become increasingly apparent at all levels of research and teaching. On the one hand the abandonment of disciplinary specialisms may lead to amorphousness rather than challenging interdisciplinarity; on the other, interdisciplinary approaches may in the end simply create new specialisms or sub-specialisms, with their own well-guarded boundaries. In these circumstances, yesterday's ground-breaking interdisciplinary study may become today's autonomous (and so potentially circumscribed) discipline, as has happened, it might be argued, in the case of some forms of History of Ideas.

The volumes in this series highlight the advantages of interdisciplinary work while at the same time encouraging a critical reflexiveness about its limits and possibilities; they seek to stimulate consideration both of the distinctiveness and integrity of individual disciplines, and of the transgressive potential of interdisciplinarity. Each volume offers a collection of new essays on a text of seminal intellectual and cultural importance, displaying the insights to be gained from the juxtaposition of disciplinary perspectives and from the negotiation of disciplinary boundaries. The volumes represent a challenge to the conception of authorship which locates the significance of the text in the individual act of creation; but we assume that no issues (including those of interdisciplinarity and authorship) are foreclosed, and that individual volumes drawing contributions from a broad range of disciplinary standpoints, will raise questions about the texts they examine more by the perceived disparities of approach that they encompass than by any interpretative consensus that they demonstrate.

All essays are specially commissioned for the series and are designed to be approachable to non-specialist as well as specialist readers: substantial editorial introductions provide a framework for the debates conducted in each volume, and highlight the issues involved.

We would, finally, like to dedicate the series to the memory of our colleague Stephen Copley, whose insight and energy started it all.

Jeff Wallace, University of Glamorgan
John Whale, University of Leeds
GENERAL EDITORS

# Acknowledgements

I would like to thank all of the contributors to this volume for their patience, efficiency and hard work.

My thanks also go to the following people for their advice and support: Jeff Wallace, Martin Coyle, Jon and Jocelyn Donlon, Stephen Copley (*in memoriam*), my colleagues from the English and History department at Portsmouth, especially to Robbie Gray, who sadly died before this project was completed, Sue Harper and Simon Wortham. I am also very grateful for the administrative assistance of Lyn Kerr and the help of our librarian, David Francis. I am particularly indebted to Tom Cooper, for his tender loving care, and to my dog, Chloe, who slept faithfully and soundly during much of the process of putting this volume together.

This book is dedicated to my father, Israel Price (1929–78).

# Chronology

Bacon sentenced by the House of Lords for taking bribes

Robert Burton's *Anatomy of Melancholy*

First Parliament since 1614

1622    Bacon's *The History of the Reign of King Henry the Seventh*

Bacon's *A Natural and Experimental History* Part I

Parliament dissolved

1623    Bacon's *A Natural and Experimental History* Part II

Bacon's *History of Life and Death*

Bacon's *De Dignitate et Augmentis Scientiarum* (an expanded version of *The Advancement of Learning*)

Shakespeare's First *Folio*

Tommaso Campanella's *The City of the Sun* (publd in Latin)

c1624    Bacon begins the *New Atlantis*

1625    Bacon's *Essays or Counsels, Civil and Moral* enlarged; rpt. 1625, 1629, 1632

James I dies; accession of Charles I

1626    Bacon dies

1627    Bacon's *Sylva Sylvarum: or a Natural History* and the *New Atlantis*

Details of Bacon's life and works are indebted to Brian Vickers (ed.), *Francis Bacon: A Critical Edition of the Major Works* and Jerry Weinberger (ed.), *New Atlantis and The Great Instauration*.

# 1

# Introduction

BRONWEN PRICE

> if a man could succeed ... in kindling a light in nature – a light which should in its very rising touch and illuminate all the border-regions that confine upon the circle of our present knowledge; and so spreading further and further should presently disclose and bring into sight all that is hidden and secret in the world, – that man should be the benefactor indeed of the human race, – the propagator of man's empire over the universe, the champion of liberty, the conqueror and subduer of necessities.[1]

Francis Bacon produced his final draft of the *New Atlantis* around the years 1624/5.[2] He was then nearing the end of his life and had printed the majority of the (often incomplete) works for which he is most renowned – *The Advancement of Learning* (1605); nearly all of his *Essays* (1597, 1612, 1625); and *The Great Instauration* and *Novum Organum* (1620). The *New Atlantis* itself was written in semi-exile, when Bacon was physically weak and focusing on intellectual pursuits. By this stage in his career Bacon had been ousted from the centre of power after admitting to accepting bribes while at the height of public office as Lord Chancellor and Viscount of St Alban.[3]

This sense of marginality has an important application both to the text and the context of the *New Atlantis* which extends beyond its relation to Bacon's own career. Standing at the threshold of early modern thought, Bacon's text operates at the interstices of its contemporary culture and does indeed signal a desire to 'illuminate all the border-regions that confine upon the circle of our present knowledge'. The essays in this volume show

how the *New Atlantis* negotiates a variety of contexts – literary, philosophical, political, religious and social – in order to achieve this. It frequently draws on traditional modes of understanding so as to provide fresh perspectives upon them, revising and often challenging expectations.

The 'in between' quality of the text is apparent in its very form. It has often been regarded as an apotheosis of the ideas outlined in Bacon's works on natural philosophy, projecting an advanced society in which 'science' is awarded central status and is subsidised by the state.[4] However, the *New Atlantis* is also a 'fable' and Bacon's first entry into fictional writing. It draws on, mixes and reworks a range of genres, most particularly, as Paul Salzman points out in Chapter 2, the utopian fantasy and the travel narrative. It implicitly alludes to, rethinks and questions the societies represented in both Plato's *Republic, Timaeus* and *Critias* and More's *Utopia* (1516).[5]

Despite such fictional richness, however, the text is often thought to be incomplete. This is primarily the result of the Preface to the *New Atlantis* by William Rawley, Bacon's secretary and editor, which suggests that Bacon's original intention was 'to have composed a frame of Laws, or the best state or mould of a commonwealth',[6] and that, as Rawley notes at the end, 'The rest was not perfected' (488). However, some critics consider the *New Atlantis*'s apparent fragmentariness to be part of its overall design:[7] its identity lies between part and whole. Significantly in this regard, Bacon's fable is appended to the much larger work of natural history, *Sylva Sylvarum*, which comprises a compendium of hundreds of experiments both conducted by Bacon and ones about which he had read (see Chapters 2, 3 and 5 of this volume). Though this work relates to the core of Bacon's fictional narrative – the functions, operations and instruments of Salomon's House, the scientific institution that lies at the heart of New Atlantis – it also in some senses overshadows it through its length and basis in practical science.

However, as this volume demonstrates, the scientific enterprise of the *New Atlantis* is only one aspect of the work. Rather, Bacon's fable stands on the cusp between the fictional and factual, the visionary and practical, utopia and utility, unknown and known. It unsettles a whole range of areas central to Bacon's contemporary culture, from 'science' to censorship, gender to Judaism. Moreover, the text's provisionality provides much of its resonance, allowing it to speak beyond the limits of its own time and to continue to intrigue and challenge its readers. As a number of the following essays reveal, the complex repositioning of the reader throughout the narrative is key to the ambivalent interpretations the text arouses and opens it up to a range of possible meanings. In order to have a sense of these subtle manoeuvres, it is necessary to explore the intricacies of Bacon's fable in some detail.

## I

The narrative begins with a standard literary device. Lost in a remote part of the Pacific Ocean, a European crew arrive at the unknown, reclusive island of New Atlantis, or Bensalem, '(for so they call it in their language)' (463). The narrator, a crew member, describes how they are greeted with a scroll in different languages inscribed with the sign of the cross. Before disembarking they must affirm their adherence to the Christian faith; they are then placed in 'the Strangers' House' (459) where they are treated humanely and their sick are cured. At the end of their quarantine period the visitors' movements are still restricted and they later learn that there are 'laws of secrecy' governing travellers and that strangers are rarely permitted entry into Bensalem (463). They also find Bensalem to be an orderly, hierarchical and largely patriarchal society whose inhabitants profess to be happy and contented.

The Governor of the Strangers' House, who is 'a Christian priest' (462), offers the mariners his services and invites a group of them to ask him questions. They request to know how New Atlantis converted to Christianity and are told that it was brought about by 'a true Miracle' (464), which was confirmed by one of the Fellows of Salomon's House.

In response to further enquiry, the governor explains why Bensalem knows and yet is unknown to the rest of the world. Relating Bensalem's ancient history, he describes how the island lost contact with the outside world following a 'deluge or inundation' of great Atlantis, a form of 'Divine Revenge' wrought on the Americas for attempting to invade New Atlantis (468). The island's knowing but unknown position was consolidated, however, by their lawgiver, King Solamona, who 'reigned in this island, about nineteen hundred years ago' (469). It was he who introduced the current immigration legislation by ordaining 'the interdicts and prohibitions ... touching entrance of strangers' (470). This he did because he wished to avoid the 'conmixture of manners' such exchanges would bring (470).

It is at this point that the governor introduces the first detailed reference to Salomon's House, or, as it is also called, the College of the Six Days' Works, which was established by King Solamona and stands as 'the noblest foundation (as we think) that ever was upon the earth; and the lanthorn of this kingdom' (471). The description acts as a preliminary to the governor's explanation of Solamona's laws restricting travel abroad with the exception 'That every twelve years there should be set forth out of this kingdom two ships, appointed to several voyages' by three Fellows of Salomon's House (471). The explorers must remain *incognito*, their mission being to obtain, not material goods, but knowledge, or '*Light*' (472).

After this account the mariners are allowed free access to Bensalem. Two of the crew are invited to the Feast of the Family, a semi-religious celebration of lineage and fertility which pays homage to any man with thirty descendants over the age of three, and whose rituals are described in detail. The narrator then introduces his acquaintance with Joabin, a Jew, and outlines Bensalem's toleration of Jewish people, while noting that 'they are of a far differing disposition from the Jews in other parts' (475–6). Joabin continues the subject of familial relations by explaining Bensalem's marriage and sexual customs.

A messenger, however, interrupts and we learn that one of the Fathers of Salomon's House is to visit, none of them having been seen for a dozen years. There follows a description of the lavish ceremony that accompanies the Father's arrival, after which the Father meets the mariners and chooses to have 'private conference' with the narrator (479). It is in this discourse that the Father discloses 'the true state of Salomon's House', identifying 'the End of our Foundation', its 'preparations and instruments', 'the several employments and functions whereto our fellows are assigned. And ... the ordinances and rites which we observe' (480), concluding by permitting the narrator to publish what he has related 'for the good of other nations' (488). Appended to the end of the *New Atlantis* is a '*Magnalia Naturae*', a list of Salomon's House's discoveries.

As Davis shows, this narrative comprises two key sections: the first part concerns New Atlantis's relation to the outside world, the second its internal workings.[8] Both parts may be divided into two again: the arrival of Christianity and Bensalem's immigration and foreign policies; the familial and marriage customs of the island and the operations of Salomon's House. The form of the narrative, then, signals the borderland relations between the external and internal, each stage recounting a seemingly gradual movement from outside interests, narrated to a group of strangers, to what appears to be the core of New Atlantis, discussed in 'private conference' (479). At the same time, the crew shift from being offshore, to quarantine, to gradually gaining more freedom of movement and, in turn, more access to the inner workings of Bensalem (for a detailed account of the narrative structure see Chapter 8 of this volume).

There are, however, other aspects to the narrative structure. Each section bears a parallel relation to the whole, fragmentary text. Both stages, while seemingly self-contained, include an interruption within the discourse: the governor is called away when describing the miracle, Joabin's discussion is broken off by a messenger's arrival.[9] This gives the impression that each section is in some sense incomplete and that, though the mariners (and the reader) are allowed some access to the island, they remain positioned as outsiders, never quite penetrating its heartland.

## II

This troubled relationship between part and whole, outside and inside, is a key feature of the text and can be identified further within the texture of the *New Atlantis*. The island lies at the edge of the rest of the world, 'beyond both the old world and the new' (461), in a place which is 'utterly unknown' (457). Its apparently enlightened society resides 'in the midst of the greatest wilderness of waters' and is covered by 'thick cloud' in a land 'full of boscage'

(457). New Atlantis presents a self-contained world within the world which is both part and whole, willing to undertake, but not reliant on, its espionage expeditions. Bensalem society exhibits features that lie between the familiar and the strange;[10] they are in some sense recognisable without necessarily being explicable to its European visitors. For example, the 'reverend man' who receives them wears a turban 'not so huge as the Turkish turbans' (458), but reverses expectations by at once manifesting New Atlantis's Christianity.

By contrast, the mariners and their manners do not seem unfamiliar to the Bensalemites who, on the crew's arrival, greet them 'in so civil a fashion, as if it had been not to wonder at us but to welcome us' (460). They understand the visitors' gesture of offering them material gifts in exchange for their kindness, even though they civilly refuse to participate in this social custom.

Furthermore, Bensalemite society seems continually to signal the incompleteness of the culture from which the travellers come, and, by contrast, to have a 'more than' quality when the narrator describes details of food and clothing. The drink of grain they are given is like ale 'but more clear' (461); the reverend man's gown is 'of a kind of water chamolet', but 'far more glossy than ours' (458). This later points to the deficiencies of European culture more broadly. During his description of the utilities of Salomon's House, the Father punctuates his statements with references to what is lacking or fragmentary in European knowledge: '"We have also divers mechanical arts, which you have not ... We have also precious stones of all kinds ... to you unknown ... We have also engine-houses ... There we imitate and practise to make swifter motions than any you have"' (484–5). Repeatedly he thus points to the deficiencies of European culture.

Yet Bensalem looks to the past in order to provide its European visitors with a vision of the future. While we learn about its importation of knowledge and development of experiments, this apparently progressive society seems strangely static.[11] It is locked in the ancient laws and traditions established by King Solamona, whose values are enshrined in the Old Testament discourse of Solomon's wisdom.[12] However, as elsewhere in the text, this link with the familiar is only partial, for Salomon's House, though named after the Hebrew King, 'famous with you, and no stranger to us' (471), is designed for a primarily utilitarian, scientific purpose, not a specifically sacred one. The major changes that occur take place within the travellers whose thresholds of understanding are reframed by their encounter with New Atlantis.

Bensalemite society itself remains largely free from the interference of external agents. In this regard, the rhetoric of addition noted above is simultaneously one of negation. Joabin, for example, defines the 'chaste' sexual and marriage customs of New Atlantis in reference to their exclusion of European malpractices. Just as Bensalem is unpenetrated by the contaminating influences of outside forces in other areas, so it is 'free from all pollution or foulness' in this one. As 'the virgin of the world' it is innocent without being ignorant (476). While New Atlantis apparently pushes forward the frontiers of European understanding, its integrity is founded on a tight and containing grip of border control.

Indeed, Bensalemite society contains all kinds of boundaries and exclusion zones, from its laws on travel to the secrecy surrounding the practices of Salomon's House (see Chapter 9 of this volume). These separate what might be regarded as its inner and outer communities. Bensalem as a whole is characterised as knowing but unknown, observing but unobserved, something which one of the crew members identifies with 'a condition and propriety of divine powers and beings' (466). Most citizens, though, lie outside the inner sanctum of Salomon's House, reaping the countless material benefits it brings without having access to its processes of production. From its god-like position, Salomon's House stands as both 'the very eye of this kingdom' and its source of light, or 'lanthorn' (464, 471), surveying and sustaining the island. Yet, in spite of its apparent centrality, it also lies on the edge of Bensalemite society: the Fathers of the House are rarely seen, the information they divulge is sketchy, their activities are carefully self-regulated and safeguarded from the public arena, unknown to all but a select few. In this sense, Salomon's House is at one remove from the society to which it is integral. The collaborative task of its members to achieve a complete understanding through 'the enlarging of the bounds of Human Empire, to the effecting of all things possible' (480) excludes the majority of Bensalem's citizens, let alone the rest of humanity.[13]

When investigating the inner workings of Bensalemite society more broadly Salomon's House is not the only area in which information is fragmentary. There is a sense of incompleteness about what is disclosed, especially, as numerous commentators have noted, concerning Bensalem's underlying power structures (see Chapter 4 of this volume).[14] The relationship between the activities of Salomon's House and the political and economic arrangements of Bensalem are not imparted; the monarch is mentioned (474), but remains unnamed and does not appear; we hear of 'the state' without learning about its form. As Innes argues, 'We see the effects of government but not the mechanics, the agents but not the authority'.[15] Some things are revealed to the mariners, but not others. Indeed, we are made continually aware of different levels of knowing in operation throughout the narrative, from the members of Salomon's House, to 'the state', which is not told everything about the scientists' activities (486), to Bensalem's citizens and finally to the strangers, who 'knoweth least' at the outset (463), and whose understanding still remains patchy at the end.

These gradations of knowledge are also apparent when examining the perspective through which events are conveyed. Information is delivered, of course, through the focus of one of the mariners, who is at first identified closely with his crew companions. The first word in the narrative is 'We', representing an integrated group united by their borderland position: they are 'between death and life' (461), hope and despair, drifting in a sea of confusion as they lose control over the direction of their ship. They become, it seems, objects of the natural elements and the controlling force of God's hand.

In their first encounters with Bensalemite society the crew continue to form a collective position, now defined by their identity as 'strangers', not least through their literal physical location on the island. They invariably respond as a group to their experiences of the Bensalemite people and customs. Initially, they are 'much perplexed' (458), both fearful for their lives and yet touched by the Christian charity and 'parent-like usage' they receive from their hosts (462). When the narrator addresses the crew to advise them 'to behave ourselves', he finds that they are all in agreement, 'Our company with one voice thanked me for my good admonition' (462).

Shortly, however, the mariners are broken up into different types of knowers. The Governor of the Strangers' House speaks only 'with some few of us: whereupon six of us only stayed' to have their questions answered (462); two of the crew alone are invited to the Feast of the Family. By the time the narrator meets Joabin and learns about Bensalem's marriage customs, the pronoun 'we' that dominates the first part of the narrative gives way to 'I'. The narrator's discussions with the Father of Salomon's House are still more intimate. They take place 'in a fair chamber' in 'private conference', where, after instruction, he has been selected by one of the mariners to hear 'the greatest jewel' of information the Father has chosen to 'impart unto thee' (479–80). By the end of the meeting the narrator has surely become a special knower with the implication that he has indeed been taken 'into their bosom' (472), fast transforming from being a stranger to becoming a member of Bensalemite society.

However, this impression of the privileged disclosure of exclusive Bensalemite knowledge mutates to one of general, inclusive understanding when the Father concludes by giving the narrator 'leave to publish' this relation 'for the good of other nations' (488). Presumably the text before us signals the narrator's attempts to do just this. The insider information he has apparently received has indeed been disseminated outside the clandestine boundaries of Bensalem, as well as beyond the limits of individual knowledge. Precisely why the Father permits the narrator to do this, however, given that Salomon's House lies at the heart of Bensalem's codes of secrecy, remains unclear.

## III

At this point we may wish to consider how the *New Atlantis* positions its reader. Initially, there is a sense of inclusion with the mariners as a result of being party to 'so strange things so probably told' (472). Like the crew, we begin in the position of strangers, our viewpoint and understanding gradually identified with the narrator's as we gain more privileged access to the inner

workings of New Atlantis. Or so it seems. The cryptic, elliptical
quality of the text is actually unsettling, and works counter to
the journey of discovery we appear to undertake. The reader is
kept on the borderland of the text, allowed only partial entry
into the world it constructs. But this, in turn, seems to ask us to
look beyond and in between what is spoken and unspoken, and
to investigate the boundaries of what we are told.

One striking feature of the narrator's discourse is its lack of
data about Bensalem's natural environment. While the study of
the natural world lies at the heart of Salomon's House, and we
learn that the 'rare fertility of soil' enables Bensalem to be self-
sufficient (469), the narrator says virtually nothing about the
type of terrain, vegetation, animal life or climate of New Atlantis.
This may, of course, signal his physical restriction within Bensalem's city limits. Much of the information he recounts is
imparted indoors, but such omissions seem strange nonetheless.

Instead, the narrator focuses his attention on cultural matters.
The highly precise recording of time, food, dress, ritual, ceremony
and the use of number and colour within Bensalem's customs is
especially notable.[16] Some of the particulars the narrator relates
contain an obvious symbolic value. For example, the significance
of number often seems to carry a Biblical resonance which ties in
with the references that underscore the entire narrative, signalling the Christian basis of Bensalemite society. The number three,
which may refer to the trinity, is central to its customs, while the
'College of the Six Days' Works' alludes to the six days of
Creation described in Genesis, and is a number that recurs in a
whole range of Bensalemite practices. The mariners arrive at the
Strangers' House at six o'clock, where they are attended to by six
people and are initially licensed to stay for six weeks, and it is
after six days that the narrator's sense of time, which has been
very precise up to that point, begins to become hazy. The reader,
along with the narrator, comes to grasp certain key Bensalemite
habits: we quickly learn that they do not take material payment
in return for their hospitality; we soon discover that the
Bensalemite gesture of putting 'their arms a little abroad' is a sign
of welcome (460).

However, while such specific detail provides the narrator's
account with a sense of authenticity, it is not necessarily

accompanied with understanding. Information seems full, but is in fact fragmentary. Many of the details recorded by the narrator remain enigmatic, or at least ambiguous. The attention paid to the colours of the attire of the various Bensalemite officials, and also discrepancies in their headgear and hair arrangements, imply significance of status, but in what specific ways they do so remain obscure. Similarly, the precision given to number throughout the narrator's account suggests that there is, for example, a possible relationship between the twelve-year intervals of the scientists' missions abroad and the visit of one of the Fathers of Salomon's House after a dozen years to the city where the travellers reside. But this, too, is not made clear. Such intricate details demand interpretation, belying transparency.

In spite of these (and many more) unexplained particulars, the narrator nonetheless shapes much of what he sees and hears. Indeed, it is precisely a sense of mystery that informs his reading of Bensalemite customs and causes him 'to think there was somewhat supernatural in this island; but yet rather as angelical than magical' (466). Unveiling the secrets of Bensalem is like revealing divine provenance: it cannot be completely contained or known because it lies on the borders of human understanding. The narrator gives the emphatically Christian foundation of Bensalemite society an extra dimension: to him and his companions it appears as a kind of paradise. For example, on receiving Bensalemite hospitality at the Strangers' House, 'It seemed to us that we had before us a picture of our salvation in heaven' and that 'God surely is manifested in this land' (461–3). They hope that they 'may find grace in the eyes of this people', believing they have 'come into a land of angels' and a nation 'compounded of all goodness' (462–3, 472). The entire process of the crew's encounter with New Atlantis contains a Biblical register: they arrive out of a 'wilderness' and, after praying to God, are saved by 'a kind of miracle', whereby they are 'cast on land, as Jonas was out of the whale's belly'; their identities are transformed and renewed through the revelations of the island, which make them desire to stay in 'this happy and holy ground' and to 'forget all that was dear to us in our own countries' (457, 461, 463, 472).

Yet we are aware from the outset that the narrator's account of New Atlantis is partial: it arises in the first instance from relief

after great fear and physical danger.[17] The point, however, is not
so much whether the narrator is right or wrong in his interpretations, but that he presents events from a very particular
perspective which is continually foregrounded for the reader.
Information is delivered after which a gloss is frequently placed
upon it, usually punctuated by phrases that underline the process of interpretation: 'it seemed to us', 'we thought', 'we found
[it] wonderful strange', 'it was a thing we could not tell what to
make of' (465–6). While noting that they are 'cloistered' in the
Strangers' House, the narrator chooses to focus on the 'courtesy',
'piety and humanity' of their captors, and concerns himself with
suppressing the 'vices and unworthiness' his companions may
possibly possess when he suspects they are under the surveillance of the Bensalemite authorities (461). The narrator reports,
but does not question, why thirteen of the previous visitors left
Bensalem, nor the governor of the Stranger's House's ambiguous
hypothesis that their accounts of New Atlantis would be taken
'but for a dream' in their native lands (470). Perhaps Bensalem is
not quite as able to contain its societal boundaries as it appears.

In various ways, then, the reader is made aware of a gap
between information and interpretation, and the narrator's viewpoint of events does not investigate fully all aspects of what he
observes and is told. Indeed, the potential for the narrator to mis-
read what he is shown is highlighted at the end of the narrative
by the Father of Salomon's House, who decides not to recount the
'excellent works' of Bensalem's inventors, for 'in the right
understanding of those descriptions you might easily err' (487).[18]

The very term 'descriptions' is worth attention, for in depic-
ting the activities of Salomon's House, as in other aspects of
Bensalemite society, the narrator relies primarily on discursive
information for his understanding, rather than immediate observation or empirical evidence. For all the experimental, inductive
method that Salomon's House seems to uphold in its quest for
'*Light*', its activities are 'revealed' to the narrator in a largely
conversational, rather than practical, form. Apart from the medicine and nourishment the mariners receive at the outset, they
hardly experience the products of Salomon's House directly.
Moreover, the Father of Salomon's House invites the narrator to
turn what he tells him into further discourse by publishing what

he imparts, rather than transforming it into practical application or instrumental use.

While the narrator claims to have 'continually … met with many things right worthy of observation' (472), throughout the text he relies on reported information, which is often filtered through a number of sources, so that he is at one or more removes from the events themselves. It is, for example, unclear as to whether he has first-hand experience of the Feast of the Family's rituals. The invitation for 'two of our company' to attend the ceremony may or may not include the narrator (472). But whether or not he attends, he seems straightforwardly to accept what he observes or is told, defining the occasion simply as 'A most natural, pious, and reverend custom' (472) when it is presented primarily as a celebration of fertility. The only reporter whose judgement he questions is, significantly, Joabin's, whose explanation of Bensalem's origins the narrator dismisses as being 'Jewish dreams' (476). He nonetheless accepts Joabin's account of Bensalem's marriage customs and their superiority to those of Europe without ever witnessing them.

There is, though, another point to be made about the form in which the narrator acquires knowledge, and that is that it runs counter to the empirical, experimental, inductive approach Bacon promotes in his works on natural philosophy. For example, in affirming a new practical approach to learning, *The Advancement of Learning* argues that 'the first distemper of learning' is 'when men study words and not matter … for words are but the images of matter',[19] while in establishing its programme for the renewal of scientific study, *The Great Instauration* recommends 'a true and lawful marriage between the empirical and the rational faculty' and 'a form of induction which shall analyse experience and take it to pieces, and by a due process of exclusion and rejection lead to an inevitable conclusion'.[20] The revelations of *New Atlantis*, however, do not seem to have taught the narrator to engage in these practices. He neither analyses nor interrogates the information he is given, but bases his knowledge largely on the words of others, rather than on a rigorous investigation of practical experience.

It is perhaps the central contradiction between the methods employed by the members of Salomon's House and the way in which the narrator disseminates information about Bensalem that makes the text so ambiguous and open-ended. It ensures that the reader remains active and alert, being encouraged to examine the different positions from which knowledge is presented, rather than simply accepting them. Indeed, the Father of Salomon's House's concluding request for the narrator to disclose his findings 'for the good of other nations' does not necessarily mean that they should be imitated and followed. Neither wholly inside nor outside the text we are invited to enter, the reader is placed in an interrogative position, prompted to investigate its hidden recesses and to venture beyond the limits of what we are told.

## IV

Not surprisingly, the *New Atlantis*'s contradictions, gaps and ambivalences have allowed it to be read for different meanings and different interests. The history of the text's reception makes this manifest. The *New Atlantis* was appended to all of the seventeenth-century volumes of *Sylva Sylvarum* and together they ran into more editions than any other of Bacon's works, being printed at least fifteen times during the course of the century, besides appearing in French and Latin.[21] In particular, Bacon's imaginative concept of Bensalem was invoked in practical terms as a model for a collaborative, scientific research community across the political, religious and social spectrum. In the 1640s and early 1650s the puritan reformer Samuel Hartlib and his circle drew upon the utilitarian, utopian and religious register of the *New Atlantis* to provide an image of the 'redeeming power of science' and its capacity to produce 'earthly salvation'.[22] Charles Webster notes that 'the medical reform tracts of the Puritan Revolution carried a marked imprint of the utopian ideals of *New Atlantis*.'[23] This was also apparent in works such as Gabriel Plattes' *Macaria* (1641), which coincided with the opening of the Long Parliament and advocated 'a Colledge of experience' that would support 'the health or wealth of men', and Gerard Winstanley's *Law of Freedom* (1652), which proposed that its communes' citizens should reap the rewards of experimental philosophy.[24]

Writing in 1657 from a different political perspective, the royalist Walter Charleton identified the more socially conservative

London College of Physicians (whose founder members were mainly Royal Physicians) as 'Solomon's House in reality'[25] when, in being threatened by political events, they 'deliberately consolidated themselves as a self-conscious community of Baconian experimentalists'.[26] Most famously, though, Salomon's House is connected to the more fully fledged institutionalisation of natural philosophy with the founding of the Royal Society in 1660. Joseph Glanvill's dedication in *Scepsis Scientifica* (1665) makes this link direct, echoing the discourse of the *New Atlantis* in promoting 'the *Empire* of *Man* over *Nature*' and regarding Salomon's House as 'a Prophetick Scheam of the ROYAL SOCIETY'.[27] In establishing such a connection, however, Pérez-Ramos notes that royalist historians, like Thomas Sprat, were keen to disguise the achievements of Republican Baconianism 'so that experimental science could be made politically unobjectionable',[28] while Hunter and Wood highlight the Royal Society's 'rival strategies based on differing intellectual outlooks',[29] which bear an ironic relationship to the image of homogeneity, harmony and like-mindedness of the fellows of Salomon's House.[30] Nonetheless, the sanctioning of a collective scientific community by the State through royal charter, and the Royal Society's aims to compile comprehensive data on the works of nature and art, and to develop practical and experimental knowledge for the benefit of mankind, are broadly akin to the goals of Salomon's House. Indeed, the workability of Bensalemite society is stressed throughout the period. For example, John Evelyn writes to the Earl of Clarendon, 'There is certainly nothing more expedient than … to set upon a Design no way beneath that of … *Solomons House*; which, however lofty, and to appearance *Romantic*, has yet in it nothing of Impossible to be effected'.[31] Multhauf signals the still broader appeal of the *New Atlantis*'s influence in suggesting that 'From the 1660s it was widely held in France and Germany, as well as England, that Bacon was the fountainhead of inspiration of the scientific society'.[32]

However, the *New Atlantis* was also employed for more eclectic and idiosyncratic purposes during the seventeenth century. In 1660 R. H., most likely Robert Hooke, produced a continuation of the *New Atlantis*, 'Wherein is set forth a Platform of Monarchical Government. With a pleasant intermixture of divers rare Inventions, and wholsom Customs, fit to be introduced into all Kingdoms, States, and Common-Wealths'. Preceded by a eulogy by George Herbert, this work highlights the public benefits of Bensalem's material comforts and specifies New Atlantis's 'Frame of Laws', supposedly omitted from Bacon's work.[33] In 1676 another 'Continuation of the *New Atlantis*' appeared with Glanvill's 'Anti-fanatical Religion and Free Philosophy'.[34] More curiously still, in the 1650s Thomas Bushell, a mineralogist and alleged disciple of Bacon, planned to construct a 'foundation or building, which is designed for the execution of my Lord Verulam's *New Atlantis*' in Lambeth Marsh and later to build 'Solomon's House in all its dimensions' in the city of Wells so as to gain publicity and potential patronage for his mining exploits.[35]

During the centuries that followed, such specific references to and uses of the *New Atlantis* decreased, though the ideas behind the scientific community represented in Bacon's fable and elsewhere in his work continued in various shapes and forms. The French *philosophes* of the Enlightenment highlight the social and humanitarian function of scientific knowledge in Bacon's writings,[36] and his ideas were implicitly regarded as being central to the Encyclopedists' focus on the mechanical arts, practical science and classificatory schemes.[37] Immanuel Kant dedicated his *Critique of Pure Reason* (1781) to Bacon and refers to the 'fresh vigour' 'wise Bacon' gave to the seventeenth century's 'new direction' of 'physical studies' in the preface to the second edition of that text,[38] while in the next century Karl Marx praised 'the celebration of work and technical skill' in the *New Atlantis*.[39] However, in the latter part of the nineteenth century Bacon's work was discredited for what was perceived as its failure to combine hypotheses with its inductive approach. In this respect, the influence of Baconian methods on scientific innovators, such as Newton, was questioned, and from this period the significance of Bacon's contribution to modern science was challenged.[40]

The extent to which the *New Atlantis* (and Bacon's work more generally) represents the claims of social progress based on a seminal form of modern science has also occupied twentieth-century critics. Writing in 1949, Farrington regards the *New Atlantis* as representing 'Bacon's fullest and clearest expression of his ideal of organized scientific research' in enabling 'the marriage between natural philosophy and industrial production'.[41] For Rossi, too, in the next decade, it is Bacon's identification of the scientific community's form and function within society that is most significant in establishing an ideal of scientific progress, for it projects 'an awareness of the social importance of scientific research, an amelioration of the conditions of human existence, and organised scientific collaboration'.[42] Some twenty years later, in describing the activities of Salomon's House's fellows, Vickers goes so far as to suggest that 'The world of the *New Atlantis* is no fantasy, but the world of modern science and technology' in which 'All is done to make human life easier to bear, and enjoy.'[43]

More recently, Zagorin presents the *New Atlantis* as 'an imaginary picture of an ideal or an advanced society', highlighting once again its humanity, benevolence and the philanthropic aims of Salomon's House.[44] However, Zagorin also comments on how Bensalem's secrecy signals a 'lingering allegiance to the principle of esotericism'.[45] Moreover, far from indicating a tension between religion and science, the *New Atlantis* depicts a society in which science 'almost resembles a religious vocation' and may reverse the consequences of original sin.[46] Similarly, albeit in a more complex fashion, Briggs suggests that Bensalem's 'science grows from archaic roots and modern prophecy.'[47]

Nor are these the only areas in which the *New Atlantis* is regarded as adopting traditional value systems in order to promote its vision of an advanced society. Zagorin points out that the sketchy details about Bensalem's political organisation indicate that it is founded on a carefully graded hierarchical system not unlike those existing in seventeenth-century Europe.[48] Where Zagorin suggests that Bensalem presents 'an aristocracy of intellect',[49] though, Achinstein argues that its hierarchical foundation is built on more traditional pro-genitive, patrilineal lines. In this reading succession and inheritance, celebrated at the Feast of the Family, provide both a metaphor for and means of deradicalising progress.[50] However, while Box, too, identifies the *New Atlantis*'s reconciliation of 'a conservative and Christian social order with … a progressive and sceptical science', he suggests that this is the result of its 'generally apolitical character', where 'the fruits of science and technology have made political rule superfluous.'[51] In this sense, the fable does not engage with the

pressing, historically specific concerns with advancement outlined in Bacon's philosophical work, nor with the contradictions
they imply between scientific progress and social stability, but
rather takes on a curiously timeless quality.[52] By contrast, Innes
and Renaker suggest that the *New Atlantis* is a peculiarly modern
text, both critics highlighting the way in which science predates
and marginalises Christianity.[53]

Recent criticism has often tended to question the benevolent
and ideal nature of the society presented in the *New Atlantis*.
Feminist readings have frequently focused on the exploitative
aspects of Salomon's House's activities, presenting its technological proficiency as signalling the dominion of a masculine
society of knowers over feminine nature, the object of enquiry,
and treating Bacon's work more generally as representing a new
set of discursive practices that attempt to naturalise the relationship between knowledge and power (see Chapter 8 of this
volume).[54] Other readings have highlighted what are regarded as
being the colonialist ideology underscoring the Bensalemites'
activities. Whitney, for example, presents Bacon's fable as 'a
political allegory' offering 'a vision of science linked inseparably
to external and even internal colonialism'. It demonstrates, he
argues, 'a prospective model' of 'a British colony planted among
aliens' whose 'covert form of colonization', figured in the
Merchants' of Light espionage expeditions, 'is also an apt analogy
for an ideally exploitative class relationship between scientists
and the artisans and mechanics whose inventive skills and useful
devices Bacon would harness'.[55]

Other critics, too, identify the problematics of the internal
workings of New Atlantan society from a range of viewpoints
informed by post-modernist theories. In exploring Bensalem's
sexual customs, Bruce argues that the *New Atlantis* presents a
case for eugenics, for Bensalemites seek to eradicate physical
desire in favour of producing healthy children who will further
the progress of 'an objective state of scientific perfection'.[56]
Weinberger approaches the tricky area of desire from a slightly
different perspective. He points out the implicitly dark under-
tones which underscore the description of Bensalem's erotic
practices (as well as other areas of society), noting that without
confronting the problems of political life, Bensalem's science and

Christianity, for all their surface beneficence, cannot be safe-guards against excessive desire, erotic or otherwise.[57] Similarly, for Innes it is the hidden, undisclosed nature of Bensalem's politics that belies New Atlantis's apparent benevolence and piety. Behind the scenes, Innes suggests, lurks 'an unknown knower', whose function may simply be one of control rather than virtue, and whose mechanisms produce not so much spiritually enlightened as totally submissive, well-regulated citizens who, in exchange for their docility, reap the thoroughly earthly rewards of bodily comfort, preservation and security.[58] Box, too, pays attention to the somewhat sinister compliance of Bensalem's inhabitants. Far from demonstrating a lively, dynamic community of science, New Atlantis's affluence and plenty produces a society that remains 'content but inert, healthy perhaps, but passive', where desire does not form a threat and is replaced by complacency. Indeed, 'There are no life sciences in Bensalem,' he argues, 'because there is no life.'[59] Also concentrating on the double-edged features of the text, Faulkner regards the New Atlantis as a specifically rhetorical work, which, in seeking to provide a persuasive case for its 'seminal vision of progressive society' 'exaggerates the goods to come', while concealing 'the repulsive features (such as dangerous inventions, pervasive control, and the overthrow of European faith, morals, and monarchy)'.[60] Once again, the utopian register merges with a dystopian one.

In their various ways, the above readings foreground the complex texture, ambiguities and resonant silences of the New Atlantis. They signal a text which is both generically hybrid and mixed in terms of its modes of thought. Residing on the border-line between Renaissance and early modern ideas, its vision of progress is tentative. In turn, the perspectives of post-modernity encourage a revaluation of the New Atlantis's provisional projection of the future.

## V

This volume is informed by and develops recent critical reas-sessments of Bacon's work. The essays reflect a concern to locate the New Atlantis in reference to Bacon's oeuvre specifically, and to the broader cultural and historical context in which it intervenes. The range of disciplinary approaches provided by the volume underlines the variety of particular contexts pertinent to our understanding of this work. Most of the readings here mediate their discussions about such contextual details through reference to contemporary theoretical debates. However, they also reveal how the *New Atlantis* moves beyond its own specific context to complicate and raise questions about theory, so as to form an ongoing dialogue with current critical ideas.

The first three essays of this volume show how the *New Atlantis* represents more than a clear-cut model of an ideal society, highlighting instead the important complexities of its form. Paul Salzman's opening essay examines the significance of the *New Atlantis*'s uses of literary forms and also its relation to *Sylva Sylvarum*. Exploring its interaction with and impact on the emergence of a range of narrative genres during the period, Salzman argues that the *New Atlantis* provides a particularly striking example of narrative hybridity, shifting between utopian vision, travel narrative and genres designed for political and social commentary. In turn, the *New Atlantis* is fundamentally linked to *Sylva Sylvarum*, for together these works form 'an intersecting genre', combining 'natural history/fable, treatise/fiction, which readers were encouraged to see as inseparable'.

Sarah Hutton's essay is also concerned with the *New Atlantis*'s form and the importance of its appendage to *Sylva Sylvarum*. However, Hutton focuses on the rhetorical features of the text, arguing that these have been underestimated in most interpretations of the *New Atlantis*. Locating her reading in the context of Bacon's assertions on the nature and function of language, she challenges the received view that Bacon's fable is merely 'a blueprint' for his scientific programme. Instead, she treats the *New Atlantis* as 'a carefully crafted' piece of persuasion 'designed to engage the involvement' of its contemporary audience 'in the grand project for which *Sylva Sylvarum* lays the ground'.

David Colclough considers the importance of the concept of reading and the reader's position in the *New Atlantis* in further detail, particularly with regard to the political and ethical concerns which Salzman signals in his essay. Colclough contends that the pragmatic aims of the text are expressed less through a transparent representation of a model society (the details of whose moral and political aspects are notably absent) than through the demonstration of a model of reading and thought as 'it might be practised.' The type of reading and thought the *New Atlantis* recommends, Colclough suggests, are directly related to Bacon's ideas about the reform of knowledge and are character-ised by a process of 're-use and re-appropriation', where past knowledge is 'deployed to new ends'. In addition, the text offers a set of reading practices with which they themselves may engage, ones which are 'open and exploratory' and that revise the expectations with which the reader enters the text. Colclough's argument complements those of Claire Jowitt and Kate Aughter-son in this respect, for their essays also highlight the text's inver-sion of narrative expectations and standard modes of thought, showing how it thus provides an implicit critique of contem-porary European customs and norms.

Whereas the first three essays focus on extra-scientific con-cerns, Richard Serjeantson's essay closely examines the nature of the 'science' represented in the *New Atlantis*. Locating Bacon's work in its specific historical context, Serjeantson finds that Bensalem's scientific interests are not as advanced as they are often thought to be. Rather, they have much in common with the contemporary preoccupations of what Serjeantson terms 'natural knowledge', while also being linked to Bacon's own method-ological writing. In a way that converges with Colclough's argu-ment, Serjeantson shows, however, that traditional modes of knowledge are given different possibilities by being placed in the imaginative form of Bacon's fable and the new institutional context of Salomon's House it represents.

Jerry Weinberger's, Claire Jowitt's and Kate Aughterson's essays highlight, in their different ways, the allegorical and rich allusive register of the *New Atlantis*. Like Serjeantson, Weinber-ger is interested in the role of religion in reference to New Atlantan science. In contrast to Serjeantson, however, Weinberger argues that Bensalem represents a thoroughly technological society, whose project for the mastery of nature places religion's function in an ambiguous position. In particular, Weinberger explores Bacon's account of miracles, so central to the text, providing a very different view of the implicit ethics and politics underlying New Atlantis from Colclough's. Placing his discussion in close reference to Bacon's other writings on morality, Weinberger's investigations lead him to consider the ways in which 'the *New Atlantis* suggests the problem, as much as the promise, of technology.'

Claire Jowitt relates the politics of the *New Atlantis* more directly to the immediate context of Jacobean England, exploring in particular its implicit messages about colonial expansion and Jewish toleration. At a specific level, Jowitt suggests that Bacon's text provides a covert critique of James I's domestic and foreign policies, which is closely connected to Bacon's relation to the Court at the time of writing. However, she goes on to show that in its equivocal attitude towards the effects of travel and ambiguous representation of Joabin the *New Atlantis* also reproduces some of the social and political contradictions existing in Bacon's own cultural context.

Ambivalence and contradiction also underscore Kate Aughterson's and Simon Wortham's readings of the *New Atlantis*. Aughterson's essay provides an analysis of the complex formulation of gender in Bacon's text, arguing against the tendency of feminist criticism to view Bacon as the founding father of a thoroughly masculinised science. Instead, she shows how concepts of sexual difference and gender in the *New Atlantis* are connected to the 're-visioning' across a range of areas that takes place in the text. By closely analysing its rhetoric, metaphors and allusions, Aughterson argues that Bacon's fable questions clear-cut sexual hierarchies and articulates a version of scientific endeavour and its relation to nature that is both more equitable and ambiguously gendered than is generally acknowledged.

Like Aughterson, Simon Wortham suggests that the *New Atlantis* troubles straightforward binary oppositions. Where Aughterson's essay problematises feminist readings concerning the repressive features of Bacon's sexual politics, Wortham challenges the tendency of some Renaissance Studies critics to treat the politics of censorship in purely negative terms. In particular, Wortham examines the silences and interruptions so central to the *New Atlantis*, investigating the highly ambiguous quality of the concealment upon which Bensalem's knowledge rests and its refusal to be a simple counterpart to what is present, visible and known. Operating 'in a space between pre-modern and modern types of legitimation', Wortham contends that 'Bensalem's secrecy does not constitute a form of institutionalised repression, but rather enacts a kind of "productive" censorship.'

From their disparate perspectives, all of the essays in the volume stress the open-ended and in-between quality of the *New Atlantis*. They show how it unsettles categories and troubles clear-cut identification, allowing the text to be read for a variety of purposes and range of possibilities, which pass beyond the 'border-region' of its own particular context, enabling it to participate in contemporary discussions as well as to generate new ones.

## Notes

1 Francis Bacon, Proem to *Of the Interpretation of Nature* (*De Interpretatione Naturae*), *The Works of Francis Bacon*, ed. James Spedding, Robert Leslie Ellis and Douglas Denon Heath, 14 vols (London, Longman, 1857–74), vol. X, p. 84.

2 Most critics agree that the *New Atlantis* was written at around this date (see Brian Vickers (ed.), *Francis Bacon: A Critical Edition of the Major Works* (Oxford, Oxford University Press, 1996), pp. 786–7). However, some suggest that an initial draft exists from as early as 1614 (see Ian Box, *The Social Thought of Francis Bacon: Studies in the History of Philosophy*, vol. 10 (Lewiston, The Edwin Mellen Press, 1989), p. 126). J. C. Davis follows Joseph Anthony Mazzeo (*Renaissance and Revolution: The Remaking of European Thought* (London, Pantheon Books, 1965), p. 221) in arguing 'that Bacon first drafted the work in the period 1614–17 and revised it for publication in, or about, 1623' (*Utopia and the Ideal Society: A Study of English Utopian Writing 1516–1700* (Cambridge, Cambridge University Press, 1981), p. 122). The initial appearance of the *New Atlantis* is also a moot point. Some commentators suggest that it first came out in 1626. This volume follows the British Library Catalogue in proposing a publication date of 1627.

3 For a recent authoritative account of Bacon's life see Lisa Jardine and Alan Stewart, *Hostage to Fortune: The Troubled Life of Francis Bacon* (London, Victor Gollancz, 1998).

4 Vickers, for example, suggests that 'this work sums up a lifetime's concern with the reformation of natural philosophy' (*Francis Bacon*, p. 787), while John E. Leary establishes more general links between the *New Atlantis* and Bacon's other writings, especially its conception 'of scientific inquiry as a collective, collaborative, and social enterprise' (*Francis Bacon and the Politics of Science* (Ames, Iowa State University Press, 1994), pp. 231–8, 258). Bacon's own attempts to gain patronage from James I for a scientific institute were unsuccessful (see Perez Zagorin, *Francis Bacon* (Princeton, NJ, Princeton University Press, 1998), p. 124).

5  See Jerry Weinberger, *Science, Faith, and Politics: Francis Bacon and the Utopian Roots of the Modern Age* (Ithaca and London, Cornell University Press, 1985), pp. 28, 32–4; and Howard B. White, *Peace Among the Willows: The Political Philosophy of Francis Bacon* (The Hague, Martinus Nijhoff, 1968), pp. 112–34. Plato's *Timaeus* and *Critias* provide the first description of the ideal, mythical society of Atlantis before it was destroyed in a natural disaster. For a comparative account of More's *Utopia* and the *New Atlantis* see Susan Bruce, 'Virgins of the world and feasts of the family: sex and the social order in two renaissance utopias', in Neil Rhodes (ed.), *English Renaissance Prose: History, Language and Politics* (Tempe, MRTS, 1997), pp. 125–46.

6  Vickers (ed.), *Francis Bacon*, p. 785. All further references to the *New Atlantis* come from this edition and are given in parentheses in the text.

7  See, for example, Jerry Weinberger's 'Introduction' to his edition of Francis Bacon, which suggests that 'the *New Atlantis* may only *appear* to be incomplete and thus impossible to grasp in its entirety' because of Bacon's view that political science is '"secret and retired"' and 'can be discerned only with difficulty' (*New Atlantis and The Great Instauration* (Wheeling, Illinois, Harlan Davidson, 1980, revised edn 1989), pp. xii–xiii). Writing from a different perspective, Davis argues that Bacon's failure to believe in human perfectibility means that he is unable to present a complete and unambiguous vision of a utopian society (*Utopia*, pp. 106–37 and esp. pp. 118ff.). Robert K. Faulkner, by contrast, regards the *New Atlantis*'s 'apparent incompleteness' as being 'a literary device' which enables Bacon to 'conclude with an exhortation to world-wide scientific enlightenment' (*Francis Bacon and the Project of Progress* (Maryland, Rowman and Littlefield, 1993), p. 234).

8  *Utopia*, pp. 106–18.

9  Amy Boesky describes the *New Atlantis* as 'a collection of broken or incomplete prose kinds – aphorisms, dialogues, experiments, fables' ('Bacon's *New Atlantis* and the laboratory of prose', in Elizabeth Fowler and Roland Greene (eds), *The Project of Prose in Early Modern Europe and the New World* (Cambridge, Cambridge University Press, 1997), p. 143).

10  See *ibid.*, pp. 147–8 and also Chapter 8 of this volume.

11  Box points out the 'ahistoric quality' of Bensalemite society, which appears to exist 'in a seemingly timeless present' without appearing to be 'oriented to the future' (*The Social Thought*, p. 128). Box links this temporal quality to the relative inactivity of Bensalem's citizens, who seem to want for nothing and so do not need to work for a better future (pp. 129–33).

12  See Sharon Achinstein, 'How to be a progressive without looking like one: history and knowledge in Bacon's *New Atlantis*', *CLIO*, 17:3 (Spring 1988), 249–64. Achinstein argues that Bacon locates his ideas in this traditional Biblical source in order to de-radicalise them, 'relying on a myth of the past for his scheme of historical progress' (p. 257). See also Chapter 4 of this volume which provides a different reading of Bacon's use of past texts.

13  See Box, who argues that instead of presenting 'an authentic community of science', Bensalemite society is 'divided between those who know and

those who don't' (*The Social Thought*, p. 147). Box also rightly notes that Bensalem's 'idea that knowledge must be kept secret is at odds with Bacon's scientific programme' where 'the co-operative aspect of inquiry imposes an important democratic aspect on the instauration' (pp. 133–4).

14  See Weinberger, 'Introduction' to *New Atlantis*, pp. xiii–xxxiii and note 6 above. See also Davis, *Utopia*, pp. 117–37; David C. Innes, 'Bacon's *New Atlantis*: the Christian hope and the modern hope', *Interpretation*, 22:1 (Autumn 1994), 3–37; Leary, *Francis Bacon*, p. 256; Weinberger, *Science, Faith, and Politics*, 32–5. Leary departs from the other critics listed in this note in choosing not to read the *New Atlantis*'s silences as being filled with extra meaning. Instead, he suggests that the text 'conforms to what we already know of [Bacon's] views on organised science' (pp. 231, 256–8). Faulkner suggests that in spite of its 'secretive handling of matters of government', the politics of the *New Atlantis* is more comprehensive than is often acknowledged (*Francis Bacon*, pp. 234–5 and Chapter 11).

15  See Innes, 'Bacon's *New Atlantis*', p. 13. See also Faulkner, *Francis Bacon*, pp. 245–9.

16  See White, *Peace*, for a detailed analysis of the significance of number and colour in the *New Atlantis* (Chapter 10).

17  See Innes, who takes the unreliability of the narrator and his companions even further, suggesting that 'They mistake provision of necessities and comforts for kindness, and they mistake kindness for godliness' ('Bacon's *New Atlantis*', p. 8).

18  Susan Bruce also notes the discrepancy between the narrator's and reader's perspectives in her introduction to S. Bruce (ed.), *Three Early Modern Utopias: Utopia, New Atlantis, The Isle of Pines* (Oxford and New York, Oxford University Press, 1999), pp. xxxiv–v.

19  Vickers (ed.), *Francis Bacon*, p. 139.

20  Weinberger (ed.), 'Introduction' to *New Atlantis*, pp. 15, 23.

21  R. W. Gibson, *Francis Bacon: A Bibliography of his Works and of Baconiana to the Year 1750* (Oxford, The Scrivener Press, 1950), pp. xv, 147–58, 184–7. See also Vickers (ed.), *Francis Bacon*, p. 789.

22  Antonio Pérez-Ramos, 'Bacon's legacy', in Markku Peltonen (ed.), *The Cambridge Companion to Bacon* (Cambridge, Cambridge University Press, 1996), p. 315. See also Rose-Mary Sargent, 'Bacon as an advocate for cooperative scientific research', in the same volume, pp. 164–5. Stephen Clucas importantly notes that, while Bacon's ideas are significant to the Hartlib circle, their sources of influence are more disparate than is generally acknowledged ('In search of "The True Logick": methodological eclecticism among the "Baconian reformers"', in Mark Greengrass, Michael Leslie and Timothy Raylor (eds), *Samuel Hartlib and Universal Reformation: Studies in Intellectual Communication* (Cambridge, Cambridge University Press, 1994), pp. 51–74).

23  Charles Webster, *The Great Instauration: Science, Medicine and Reform 1626–1660* (London, Duckworth and Co., 1975), p. 250.

24  *Ibid.*, pp. 48, 368.

25  Cited in *ibid.*, p. 315.

26  Theodore M. Brown, 'The rise of Baconianism in seventeenth-century England', in *Studia Copernicana: Science and History: Studies in Honor of Edward Rosen* (Warsaw, the Polish Academy of Science Press, 1978), pp. 516, 509.

27  Cited in Vickers (ed.), *Francis Bacon*, p. 789. See also Gibson, *Francis Bacon*, p. 261.

28  Pérez-Ramos, 'Bacon's legacy', p. 315.

29  Michel Hunter and Paul B. Wood, 'Towards Solomon's House: rival strategies for reforming the early Royal Society', *History of Science*, xxiv (1986), 49–108, p. 50.

30  Box significantly notes, however, that the *New Atlantis*'s orderly, peaceful and contented society runs counter to the concept of a dynamic, active community of science so central to Bacon's other works, especially his *Essays* (*The Social Thought*, pp. 128–44).

31  Cited in Richard Foster Jones, *Ancients and Moderns: A Study of the Rise of the Scientific Movement in Seventeenth-Century England* (2nd edn, St Louis, Washington University Studies, 1961), p. 317, n. 86.

32  Robert P. Multhauf, 'Copernicus and Bacon as renovators of science', in *Studia Copernicana*, p. 492. It is important to acknowledge, however, that some scientific societies, most notably Rome's *Accademia dei Lincei* (1603), were established before the *New Atlantis* appeared (Vickers (ed.), *Francis Bacon*, p. 785).

33  Jones, *Ancients and Moderns*, p. 319, n. 103, p. 174. See also Gibson, *Francis Bacon*, p. 263.

34  Gibson, *Francis Bacon*, p. 260.

35  Cited in Webster, *The Great Instauration*, p. 366. The above cases are also noted by Vickers (ed.), *Francis Bacon*, p. 788.

36  See Pérez-Ramos, 'Bacon's legacy', pp. 320–1.

37  See Anthony Quinton, *Francis Bacon* (Oxford, Oxford University Press, 1980), pp. 19, 79–80, and Paolo Rossi, 'Baconianism', in Philip P. Wiener (ed.), *Dictionary of the History of Ideas*, vol. 1 (New York, Scribner, 1968–74), pp. 177–8. Rossi rightly shows how this represents a very partial reading of Bacon (p. 177), while Pérez-Ramos, 'Bacon's legacy', suggests that specific reference to Bacon's work is vague in Encyclopedists' writings (pp. 320–1).

38  Immanuel Kant, *Critique of Pure Reason*, ed. Vasilis Politis (London, Everyman, J. M. Dent, 1993), p. 13.

39  See Rossi, 'Baconianism', p. 179.

40  See Pérez-Ramos, 'Bacon's legacy', pp. 324–7; Quinton, *Francis Bacon*, p. 80 and Rossi, 'Baconianism', p. 178.

41  Benjamin Farrington, *Francis Bacon: Philosopher of Industrial Science* (1949, rpt. London, Macmillan, 1973), pp. 16–17.

42  Paolo Rossi, *Francis Bacon: From Magic to Science* (1957), trans. Sacha Rabinovitch (London, Routledge and Paul Kegan, 1968), p. xiii.

43  Brian Vickers, *Francis Bacon* (Harlow, Longman, 1978), pp. 28–9.

44  Zagorin, *Francis Bacon*, pp. 170, 173.

45  *Ibid.*, p. 44. Cf. Weinberger, who suggests that this feature of the *New Atlantis* retains 'the ancients' "enigmatical method"' found in classical utopianism (*Science, Faith, and Politics*, p. 35). See also Box, *The Social Thought*, pp. 134–5.

46  Zagorin, *Francis Bacon*, pp. 173, 45.

47  John Channing Briggs, 'Bacon's science and religion', in Peltonen (ed.), *The Cambridge Companion*, p. 192.

48  Zagorin, *Francis Bacon*, p. 225.

49  *Ibid.*

50  Achinstein, 'How to be a progressive', pp. 249–64. See also Leary, who emphasises the way in which ceremony is used throughout the narrative to support the social order (*Francis Bacon*, pp. 238–47).

51  Box, *The Social Thought*, pp. 125, 127. Weinberger also notes that Salomon's House 'seems to have no place for the study of politics' so that 'neither the scientific elite nor the political establishment can claim comprehensive wisdom about policy and government' ('Introduction' to *New Atlantis*, pp. xxx–i).

52  Box, *The Social Thought*, pp. 128–9.

53  Innes, 'Bacon's *New Atlantis*', pp. 3–37 and David Renaker, 'A miracle of engineering: the conversion of Bensalem in Francis Bacon's *New Atlantis*', *Studies in Philology*, 87:2 (Spring 1990), 181–93. See also Briggs, 'Bacon's science', p. 193 and Weinberger (ed.), 'Introduction' to *New Atlantis*, pp. xviii–ix.

54  See, for example, Carolyn Merchant, *The Death of Nature: Women, Ecology and the Scientific Revolution* (San Francisco, Harper and Row, 1980), pp. 180–90.

55  Charles C. Whitney, 'Merchants of light: science as colonization in the *New Atlantis*', in William A. Sessions (ed.), *Francis Bacon's Legacy of Texts: 'The Art of Discovery Grows with Discovery'* (New York, AMS Press, 1990), pp. 256–7. See also Boesky, who also indicates the close alliance between Bacon's scientific and imperial goals, but shows how his fable complicates a straightforward colonialist reading by inverting the conventional relationship between the European explorers and the native island they discover ('Bacon's *New Atlantis*', pp. 138–53).

56  Bruce, 'Virgins of the world', p. 146 and pp. 139–46.

57  Weinberger (ed.), 'Introduction' to *New Atlantis*, pp. xiii–xxxiii.

58  Innes, 'Bacon's *New Atlantis*', p. 13 and pp. 3–37. See also Faulkner, *Francis Bacon*, pp. 248–9.

59  Box, *The Social Thought*, pp. 143, 158.

60  Faulkner, *Francis Bacon*, pp. 229, 244, 230, and Chapter 11.

# 2

## Narrative contexts for
## Bacon's *New Atlantis*

### PAUL SALZMAN

When Bacon wrote the *New Atlantis,* he clearly had More's *Utopia* in mind as a model, offering a small homage to it in a comment made by the 'good Jew': 'I have read in a book of one of your men, of a Feigned Commonwealth, where the married couple are permitted, before they contract, to see one another naked'.[1] With great acuity, Susan Bruce has pointed out the significance of the family, and of desire, as a link between the two utopias.[2] Bruce argues that in Bacon's utopia of Bensalem, More's male gaze of desire is replaced by a scientific elaboration of the value of male potency and procreation as a kind of state enterprise (in Bensalem a friend of each party views the naked potential partner). Bacon's vision does seem to me to be a deliberate counter to More's, in so far as it offers a world in which scientific knowledge structures society, as opposed to More's vision of a society structured by humanist ethics. I will argue later in this essay that Bruce's reading is particularly suggestive if we take into account the way that a later writer, Margaret Cavendish, unsettles the hierarchy of the patriarchal family in a utopia that, like Bacon's, is presented to the reader as an afterpiece following a scientific treatise. As a whole, this essay points to the way that the *New Atlantis* is richly allusive at the level of genre, gathering together, as it does, a range of reference to a wide variety of narrative possibilities.

If Bacon saw the *New Atlantis* as belonging to a fictional genre, it is not enough to say that the acknowledgement of More's *Utopia* means that this genre is 'the utopia'.[3] While the date of composition of the *New Atlantis* is uncertain (probably 1624), the 'utopian' works preceding and surrounding it are extremely disparate in nature. More's *Utopia* itself seems to have been interpreted in the early seventeenth century not so much as a particular kind of prose fiction as a particular kind of concept. This is most evident in Robert Burton's utopian musings in the preface ('Democritus Junior to the Reader') to *The Anatomy of Melancholy*, first published in 1621. Burton quotes extensively from *Utopia*, usually in reference to issues of moral reformation; for example, he writes 'our Trades generally ought to be reformed, wants supplied' and footnotes a quotation from *Utopia* Book One.[4] In addressing these issues of reform, Burton was arguing his thesis that social abuses help to engender melancholy, and that society itself was a primary cause of the ailment that he analysed at such length in his treatise. In a famous quotation from the preface (spoken by Democritus), the manifold abuses of the world are outlined:

> Judges give judgement according to their own advantage, doing manifest wrong to poore innocents, to please others. Notaries alter Sentences, and for money loose their Deedes. Some make false moneys, others counterfeit false weights. Some abuse their Parents, yea corrupt their own Sisters, others make long Libells and Pasquils, defaming men of good life, and extoll such as are lewd and vitious, some robbe one, some another; Magistrates make lawes against theeves, and are the veriest Theeves themselves. Some kill themselves, others dispaire not obtaining their desires. Some dance, sing, laugh, feast, and banket, whil'st others sigh, languish, mourne and lament, having neither Meat, Drinke, nor Cloathes. Some pranke up their bodies, and have their mindes full of execrable Vices.[5]

Burton's response to a diseased society is what might be called a utopian musing in which, again inspired by More as a model of argument rather than a creator of a genre, he imagines a place which is his fantasy of a more ideal society. This occurs in direct response to the thought that the evils of society cannot be redressed: 'there is no remedy'.[6] Burton writes:

> I will yet to satisfie & please my selfe, make an Utopia of mine owne, a new Atlantis, a poeticall commonwealth of mine owne, in which I will freely domineere, build Citties, make Lawes, Statutes, as I list my selfe. And why may I not?[7]

The reference to 'a new Atlantis' did not appear until the 1628 edition of *Anatomy of Melancholy*; in 1621 Burton began only by evoking *Utopia* as the poetical commonwealth. In the year following the publication of the *New Atlantis*, Burton, as was his habit, engaged in the process of accretion which characterised each successive edition of *The Anatomy of Melancholy*. The *New Atlantis* therefore forms a kind of pivot around which the notion of utopia shifts, in Burton's revision, from being a concept to something more approaching a genre. As Burton goes on, he evokes other precedents for his speculations: 'For the site, if you will needs urge me to it, I am not fully resolved, it may be in *Terra Australis Incognita*, there is roome enough (for of my knowledge neither that hungry *Spaniard*, nor *Mercurius Brittanicus*, have yet discovered halfe of it).'[8] In this sentence Burton points to the significant intersection of the utopian tradition and the travel narrative (both 'imaginary' and 'real'), which further complicates the generic context for the *New Atlantis*. Pedro Fernandez de Quiros' *Terra Australis Incognita* is his account of a Portuguese voyage which reached Vanuatu, but Quiros was convinced that he had reached the Great South Land and campaigned constantly for a colonising expedition. *Terra Australis Incognita* was translated from Latin into English (and French) in 1617. Mercurius Britannicus is the purported author/protagonist of Bishop Joseph Hall's *Mundus Alter et Idem* ('A World Different and Yet the Same'), published in Latin in 1605 and in an English translation in 1609. I will return to Hall's work in detail below; it is important to note here that *Mundus Alter et Idem* is fiercely satirical, rather in the manner of *Gulliver's Travels*, and is quite different from the musings of Burton about an idealised world which will contrast with the diseased world of reality. Burton sees himself as *creating* his utopia, not discovering it: 'I will chuse a site.'[9]

Burton's utopia is essentially a purged and reformed version of his own society: it will be orderly and regulated but not radically different, simply purified. Burton particularly favours hierarchy: 'Utopian parity is a kinde of government, to be wished for, rather than effected, *Respub. Christianopolitana*, *Capanella's* city of the Sun, and that new *Atlantis*, witty fictions, but meere *Chimera's*, and *Platoes* community in many things is impious, absurd and ridiculous, it takes away all splendor and magnificence.'[10] The three 'modern' examples coming before Plato were added to the text by Burton for the editions of 1628 and, in the case of Campanella, 1638. Johann Andreae's *Christianopolis* (1619) is, like the *New Atlantis*, in part a vision of a science-oriented society.[11] Tommaso Campanella's *City of the Sun* was written in Italian in 1602 but published in Latin in 1623. Ironically, both these utopias, like Bacon's, would be seen by most readers as clearly evoking hierarchical societies. Perhaps the key difference, for Burton, is that his utopia sustains a hereditary elite, though individuals are also to be elevated by election and by gift. Burton's government will, of course, be monarchical, but, as J. C. Davis has pointed out, the monarch is more of a figurehead, and real power is concentrated on a carefully structured social system which would, through various officials, ensure in particular an orderly economy.[12] Burton writes:

> If it were possible, I would have such Priests as should imitate Christ, charitable Lawyers should love their neighbours as themselves, temperate and modest Physitians, Politicians contemne the world, Philosophers should knowe themselves, Noblemen live honestly, Tradesmen leave lying and cosening, Magistrates corruption &c. but this is unpossible, I must get such as I may.[13]

The line of irony that runs through Burton's fancy constantly draws our attention to the fact that this is a utopian projection with a clear sense of how individuals will always fail to live up to an ideal society.

Like Bacon, Burton envisages a society which values the pursuit of knowledge above all else: scholars are ranked above soldiers, and 'he that invents any thing for publike good in any Art or Science, writes a Treatise, or performes any noble exploit, at home or abroad, shall be accordingly enriched, honoured, and preferred.'[14] But Burton offers no real detail for this aspect of his utopia; indeed, he soon segues into his meditation on the fact that everyone is, in fact, mad, including himself (or at least himself in the persona of Democritus): 'I am as foolish, as mad as any one.'[15] Burton always turns towards the narrator/meditator's self. Unlike Burton's self-reflexive text, Bacon's notion of narration owes more to the travel narrative, which offers another intersecting generic context for the *New Atlantis*.

Bacon turns his back on the multiple, ironising frames within which More places his narrative. The reader of *Utopia*, by the edition of 1518, moves from an address by Erasmus to John Froben, one by Budé to Thomas Lupset, maps of Utopia, its alphabet, Peter Giles's narration to Jerome Busleyden 'verifying' Raphael Hythlodaeus' account of Utopia, John Desmarais to Peter Giles, Busleyden to More, and More to Giles. We then reach the narrative 'of' Raphael Hythlodaeus. The actual narrative of the *New Atlantis* simply begins: 'We sailed from Peru, (where we had continued by the space of one whole year), for China and Japan, by the South Sea; taking with us victuals for twelve months; and had good winds from the east, though soft and weak, for five months' space and more' (457). Here we have the typical beginning of many a travel narrative. For example, 'The Discovery of Guiana', by Sir Walter Ralegh, in Richard Hakluyt's influential collection of English voyages, opens: 'On Thursday the 6. of February in the yere 1595. we departed England, and the Sunday following had sight of the North cape of Spaine, the winde for the most part continuing prosperous: we passed in sight of the Burlings, & the Rocke, and so onwards for the Canaries, and fel with Fuerte ventura the 17 of the same moneth, where we spent two or three dayes, and relieved our companies with some Fresh meat.'[16] The plain style of the travel narrative accorded well with Bacon's own ideal prose. The early modern travel narrative was intended not just to inform but also, frequently, to persuade. For example, de Quiros' *Terra Australis Incognita* is part of his scheme to persuade the King of Spain to colonise the great South land. What might be called the dry, factual description, particularly of places encountered, is a common component of this style; for example (from the same account):

> The great river of Orenoque or Baraquan hath nine branches which fall out on the North side of his owne main mouth: on the South side it hath seven other fallings into the sea, so it disemboqueth by sixteene armes in all, between Ilands and broken ground, but the Ilands are very great, many of them as bigge as the Isle of Wight, and bigger, and many lesse. From the first branch on the North to the last of the South, it is at least 100 leagues, so as the rivers mouth is 300 miles wide at his entrance into the sea, which I take to be farre bigger then that of Amazones.[17]

Where de Quiros advocated a colonial venture, Bacon uses New Atlantis to advocate a scientific paradigm for the pursuit of knowledge. John Gillies has pointed to Bacon's interest in the idea of travel as a parallel to his notion of scientific advancement.[18] This is part of Bacon's attack on the reliance upon the ancients for scientific knowledge. In *Novum Organum* (1620), Bacon states:

> Nor must it go for nothing that by the distant voyages and travels which have become frequent in our times, many things in nature have been laid open and discovered which may let in new light upon philosophy. And surely it would be disgraceful if, while the regions of the material globe – that is, of the earth, of the sea, and of the stars   have been in our times laid widely open and revealed, the intellectual globe should remain shut up within the narrow limits of old discoveries.[19]

Gillies notes how:

> Bacon fully recognised the importance of the voyager myth to his age and made a concerted effort to transform it into a metaphoric vehicle of the experimental method. The frontispiece to the *Instauratio Magna* (1620) shows a ship sailing out through the Pillars of Hercules.[20]

In the *New Atlantis*, the voyage allows Bacon to incorporate his scientific ideal within the society of Bensalem.

As a travel narrative, the *New Atlantis* is full of allusions to the significance of colonial endeavours by England and its competing European powers in the quest for possession, as well as knowledge. The travellers are met by a 'delegation' from New Atlantis and are spoken to in Spanish. They are offered an elaborate explanation when they ask why 'this happy island where we now stood was known to few, and yet knew most of the nations of the world; which we found to be true, considering they had the languages of Europe, and knew much of our state and business' (466). Under the provisions by the great and wise Solamona, the island has deliberately set out to exclude those who might attempt to assimilate it into colonial enterprise, yet a carefully controlled series of explorations (every twelve years) ensure that the flow of knowledge into the island will be constant: 'in either of these ships there should be a mission of three

of the Fellows or Brethren of Salomon's House; whose errand was
only to give us knowledge of the affairs and state of those countries to which they were designed, and especially of the sciences,
arts, manufactures, and inventions of all the world' (471). Bacon's
vision of the *New Atlantis* entails an incorporation of colonial
endeavours as part of the general expansion of knowledge.

However, the techniques of the travel narrative also form
part of the satirical tradition of imaginary voyages, utopias and
dystopias; the ready evocation of verisimilitude lends itself to
parody and manipulation. (One could argue that this ambiguity
is present from the very start, as both imaginary and 'real' travel
narratives overlap in so many ways, from classical times through
the conduit of someone like Sir John Mandeville to the early
modern period.) Joseph Hall's *Mundus Alter et Idem* is a satirical
account (complete with detailed maps) of the journey of Mercurius Brittanicus to a world of vice and excess. It begins with the
lure of armchair travel: 'Contrary to expectation, dear Reader,
driven neither by storms nor by the never-ending tossings of
waves, without winds, without sails, you have been driven to a
new world.'[21] The readers of travel narratives are teased into a
satire directed both at travel itself and the imaginings of travellers, and also at the vices of the contemporary world. As Richard
McCabe notes, 'In Hall's eyes the wanderlust of his contemporaries was indicative of their vanity, idleness and greed. Their
desire for the marvellous – whether marvellous wealth or marvellous experiences – was a symptom of their moral decline.'[22] In
the preface our attention is drawn to the journey to Ophir by
Solomon and Hiram (see Kings 9.26–8). This points to *Terra
Australis Incognita*, or at least to the imaginings associated with
it. Then the satire commences, the first place reached being
Crapulia. As Hall's satiric account of Mercurius Brittanicus's
journey proceeds, the travel narrative becomes the vehicle for a
fairly broad sweep at a variety of vices (such as gluttony).

Milton famously condemned Hall for offering, in *Mundus*,
self-indulgent satire which revelled in the vices it described, as
opposed to the sober virtues of true utopias:

> That grave and noble invention which the greatest and sublimest
> wits in sundry ages, *Plato in Critias*, and our two famous country-
> men, the one in his *Utopia*, the other in his *new Atlantis* chose, I

may not say as a field, but as a mighty Continent wherein to display the largenesse of their spirits by teaching this our world better and exacter things, then were yet known, or us'd, this petty prevaricator of *America*, the zanie of *Colombus*, (for so he must be till his worlds end) having rambl'd over the huge topography of his own vain thoughts, no marvell, if he brought us home nothing but a meer tankard drollery, a venerous parjetory for a stewes. Certainly he that could indure with a sober pen to sit and devise laws for drunkards to carouse by, I doubt me whether the very sobernesse of such a one, like an unlikour'd *Silenus*, were not stark drunk.[23]

Milton's attack may be part of a general polemic against Hall, rather than Milton's final thoughts on the utopian form, but it points to some of the tensions (as well as interconnections) between utopia and dystopia. Hall's narrative is satirical throughout, but the voyage that Mercurius Brittanicus describes is a geographically detailed voyage (however much it is at the same time a satirical one), complete with detailed maps of the lands he visits. Indeed, one interesting comparison with the *New Atlantis* is the somewhat perfunctory way in which Bacon sets up his account of his imaginary land: there are no maps provided (although it is true that the *New Atlantis* remained incomplete, so we cannot be absolutely certain that Bacon did not intend to provide one). *Mundus Alter et Idem* satirises the idealising imagination which calls a utopia into existence in the first place, and this is done via a satire on the travel narrative's tendency to revel in both the marvellous and the potential wealth of the new world being described. Hall also satirises the claims for geographical knowledge exemplified in a work like Peter Heylyn's *Microcosmus* (1621), a typical example of the comprehensive geographical description available in the seventeenth century. Heylyn claims that 'Historie without Geographie like a dead carkasse hath neither life nor motion at all.'[24] For Hall, geographical knowledge, like the travel narrative, is a particular example of worldly pride and accordingly it is a fitting target for his satire. In contrast, Bacon offers Bensalem as an ideal society and the voyage to it as a fortuitous discovery of an ideal.

The intersection between travel narrative, dystopia and imaginary voyage in relation to the *New Atlantis* can be illustrated by turning to the kind of source criticism now completely

unfashionable, but once the mark of true scholarship. It can serve
to indicate the sorts of links that suggest themselves to 'empirical' scholars who look back at a work like the *New Atlantis*. In
his study of the influence of voyagers on Elizabethan literature,
Robert Cawley points to two 'sources' for the *New Atlantis*:
William Adams' voyage to Japan and de Quiros.[25] In the case of
Adams, Cawley is able to point to some interesting parallels with
the opening of the *New Atlantis*. Adams' voyage begins in 1598,
and during the first part many sailors become ill, and are put off
ship at 'the coast of Gynny'.[26] The voyage, like that of the *New
Atlantis*, moves from Peru towards Japan for five months via the
Straits of Magellan. Adams arrives to a welcome not dissimilar to
that meted out by Bensalem:

> the King of Bungo, the place where we arrived, did us great friend-
> ship. For he gave us an house on shore for our sick men, having all
> refreshing that was needfull. We had when we came to anchor in
> Bungo foure and twentie men, sicke and whole, of which number
> the next day three dyed, the rest for the most part recovered,
> saving three which lay long time sicke, and in the end also died.[27]

Adams is sent for by the Emperor, and offers an account of English
merchant enterprise. The Emperor orders the mariners to remain
in Japan, making provision for them. Japan, like Bensalem, is
carefully shielded from outside influences.

For a source-hunter like Cawley, the sole issue here is whether
or not Bacon read Adams' account. However, for what we might
call generic considerations, what is interesting is the desire to
relate the 'realist' detail at the beginning of the *New Atlantis* to
an actual voyage narrative like Adams'.[28] (It is worth noting that
Adams' account is in the form of two letters sent from Japan: one
general letter 'To my unknowne Friends and Countrey-men', the
second to his wife.[29] This produces a very strong sense of transparency and directness in the narrative.) Cawley also cites *Terra
Australis Incognita*, again looking for details which mesh with
Bacon's account of the initial voyage which ends up at Bensalem,
but also pointing to de Quiros' idealistic view of the great Southern
continent. Cawley emphasises the Spanish connection here (given
that Spanish is the European language spoken by the Bensalem
representatives). Again, this raises the issue of the colonial spirit
behind the *New Atlantis*, given that de Quiros is principally

concerned to hawk Terra Australis to the King of Spain as a suitable place to settle: 'If vpon a bare suspition Christoferus Columbus did pursue his designe with so much obstinacie, you are not to account it strange in me if the things which I haue beheld with mine eyes, and touched with mine hands, doe put some kind of constraint vpon me to be importunate'.[30]

With the travel narratives in mind, we perhaps need to ask when the utopian part of the *New Atlantis* actually begins. 'Our' voyage from Peru is curiously anonymous compared to an account like Adams', which carefully establishes the narrator's identity and bona fides to begin with:

> I am a Kentish-man, borne in a Towne called Gillingham, two English miles from Rochester, one mile from Chattam, where the Kings ships lye: and that from the age of twelve yeares, I was brought up in Lime-house neere London, being Prentise twelve yeares to one Master Nicholas Diggines, and have served in the place of Master and Pilot in her majesties ships, and about eleven or twelve yeares served the Worshipfull Company of the Barbarie Marchants, untill the Indian Trafficke from Holland began, in which Indian Trafficke I was desirous to make a little experience of the small knowledge which God had given me. So in the yeare of our Lord God 1598. I was hired for chiefe Pilot of a Fleete of five sayle.[31]

Bacon's narrative may use similar voyage details, but his narrator is without any clear identity; indeed, he is something of a cipher. Bacon's interest in verisimilitude is, therefore, more a matter of narrative detail than of anything we might call characterisation. In fact, he shows no real interest in the Bensalemites as individual characters (or even as types); they are more like mouthpieces for the social and scientific aspect of the narrative. The speeches of the narrator are exemplary in the same way that the Bensalemite speeches tend to be: 'I thought good to call our company to-gether; and when they were assembled said unto them; "My dear friends, let us know ourselves and how it standeth with us."' (461). When it begins, the account of Bensalem is not greatly dissimilar to Adams' description of Japan: '"We of this island of Bensalem (for so they call it in their language), have this; that by means of our solitary situation, and of the laws of secrecy which we have for our travellers, and our rare admission of strangers, we know well most part of the habitable world, and are ourselves

unknown"' (463). Of course the 'history' of Bensalem is narrated
back to 'three thousand years ago'. Plato's account of Atlantis is
cited: while it is 'all poetical and fabulous: yet so much is true,
that the said country of Atlantis, as well that of Peru, then called
Coya, as that of Mexico, then named Tyrambel, were mighty and
proud kingdoms in arms, shipping and riches' (467–8). The
destruction of Atlantis impacts upon Bensalem's trade and this
brings the history forward to the edicts of the wise king who,
'about nineteen hundred years ago' (469), decided that Bensalem
should stay out of the world's eyes.

Throughout this stage of the narrative we are in the province
of 'true' history and geography. When does this pass into utopia? I
would argue that this transition does not occur until about half
way through the text of the *New Atlantis* (as we have it), when
Salomon's House is first mentioned (471). At this point the narrative
still resembles the travel account, but when Bacon begins to describe the society which stems from the creation of Salomon's House,
the utopian vision becomes incorporated with the travel narrative.
The two remain intertwined when we are informed of the careful
regulation of traffic with the outside world (this is the section
which Cawley sees as reminiscent of Adams' account of Japan):

> When the king had forbidden to all his people navigation into any
> part that was not under his crown, he made nevertheless this
> ordinance; That every twelve years there should be set forth out of
> this kingdom two ships, appointed to several voyages; That in
> either of these ships there should be a mission of three of the
> Fellows or Brethren of Salomon's House; whose errand was only to
> give us knowledge of the affairs and state of those countries to
> which they were designed, and especially of the sciences, arts,
> manufactures, and inventions of all the world; and withal to bring
> unto us books, instruments, and patterns in every kind. (471)

Here Bacon links the history of Bensalem's attitude towards
travel with its idealised society – a society that is carefully
protected from the outside world but not insular.

As Bacon moves into an analysis of the society created in
Bensalem, which has at its heart the institution of Salomon's
House, the narrative glances at more peripheral genres which
touch upon political commentary. The most interesting example
of these is the kind of political and didactic commentary that

seeped into fiction early in the seventeenth century. None of this material can be described as utopian, but it may be allied with the utopian mode in so far as it sees fiction as a vehicle for serious social or political commentary. In *Censorship and Interpretation*, Annabel Patterson has traced the complex methods by which literature in the early modern period searched out ways of making political comment beneath a general blanket of censorship.[32] In particular, she notes the way that the romance form became politicised in the early seventeenth century. This is most evident in the work of John Barclay. Barclay grew up in France, the son of a Scottish father and a French mother. Around 1603 he became a quite important figure in the court of James I, having already made a name for himself in Europe with the publication of *Euphormio's Satyricon*, in Latin, in 1605. This work is generally classified as belonging to the rather ill-defined genre of Menippean satire: a mix of allegory, picaresque narrative and satirical commentary.[33] Barclay dedicated Part One to James and Part Two (which was published in 1610) to Robert Cecil, Earl of Salisbury. In the dedication to James, Barclay stresses the satirical nature of his book: 'my bitter attack in this book against the crimes of the world'.[34] *Euphormio's Satyricon* shares the satirical impulse of Hall's *Mundus Alter et Idem*, which also has the characteristics of Menippean satire.[35] Barclay begins with the narrator Euphormio's paean to his utopian country Lusinia:

> Here no one worships fancy furniture, jewels, power, wealth, or any of those things on which the sterile lust of men sets a high price. Here, if anyone is at all enthusiastic about the pursuit of virtue, he is immediately raised to a magistracy in an honest election; and he inspires all with envy of his way of life, none with envy of his position.[36]

Euphormio then immediately launches into an attack on the 'depraved inhabitants of earth' who are venal and corrupt.[37] The narrative in fact details Euphormio's picaresque journey through the 'real' world, enumerating vices en route. The narrative offers thinly disguised accounts of the Spanish Netherlands and Paris. In Part Two, he visits Italy and then the court of Henry IV, but finally arrives at the court of James (named King Tessaranactus in the narrative) in London and concludes with a glowing account of James's country and character. Euphormio's travels through

Europe, while very much in the picaresque mode, evoke the travel narratives discussed above and also the accounts by individual travellers through Europe, the most famous in England being *Coryate's Crudities* (1611), Thomas Coryate's account of a journey (mostly on foot) from England to Venice and back.

Barclay's editor, David Fleming, points out the significance of Barclay's use of allegorical references to current events and people in *Satyricon*: a technique that was taken up by other writers during the seventeenth century.[38] These direct references are a change from the way some forms of fiction, such as Philip Sidney's *Arcadia*, may have offered glancing portraits of contemporary situations or general political commentary. They point towards a growing sense that prose fiction is an appropriate medium for social and political commentary and thus provide a further context for the *New Atlantis*, gathering up elements from an increasingly varied mixture of genres and modes.[39] In particular, Bacon uses the combination of voyage/utopia to encapsulate an account of England's social failings as well as a picture of the ideal society to which it might aspire. In *Satyricon*, Barclay offers a portrait of England (Scolimorrhodia = thistle/rose, a compliment to James for uniting Scotland and England) which is both admiring and critical: 'I was in wonder at this happy region … But the people (as happens often) were fattened by excessive fortune and had replaced the resourceful initiative that results from poverty by a proud laziness.'[40] But the aristocratic inhabitants (according to Euphormio) are another matter: 'When I considered the conversation of the great men and the good-breeding of their daughters, they somehow seemed to me more blessed than heaven itself.'[41] At this point the narrative ends rather abruptly with a poem in praise of James, and we don't receive many details about Scolimorrhodia, but we do glimpse a (politically astute) comparison between an idealised England and a satirised Europe.

Barclay's second major prose work was a political romance called *Argenis*, first published in Latin in 1621. James asked Ben Jonson to translate it into English, but after his translation was apparently lost in the infamous fire of 1623, Kingesmill Long published an English translation in 1625, followed by another by Robert Le Grys in 1628.[42] (*Argenis* was also translated into a number of European languages and was widely reprinted in Latin

during the seventeenth century.) *Argenis* is quite different from
*Euphormio's Satyricon*: it works with the romance tradition, but
uses an allegorical method to depict both contemporary and
historical individuals and events. *Argenis* is actually set in France
at the time of Henry III and Henry IV, but it also includes more
contemporaneous events, such as the Overbury scandal. At the
same time, Barclay offers a purely fictional narrative through
which he examines more abstract political issues.

Annabel Patterson has pointed to the significance of Barclay's
use of fiction for political purposes.[43] She notes in particular the
philosophical discussion led by Nicopompus (Barclay's self-
portrait), which revolves around the way that fiction might
(through disguised representation) take up political and historical events. Nicopompus offers a description of the kind of
literature of which *Argenis* itself is an exemplar:

> I will compile some stately Fable, in manner of a History: in it will I
> fold up strange events ... The Readers will be delighted with the
> vanities there shewne incident to mortall men: and I shall have
> them more willing to reade mee, when they shall not find me severe,
> or giving precepts. I will feed their minds with divers contempla-
> tions, and as it were, with a Map of places ... because I seem to tell
> them Tales, I shall have them all: they will love my Booke above
> any Stage-play, or spectacle on the Theater ... While they reade,
> while they are affected with anger or favour, as it were against
> strangers, they shall meete with themselves; and finde in the glass
> held before them, the shew and merit of their owne fame ... he may
> be as much deceived, that would draw all in my writing, as he that
> would nothing, to the truth of any late or present passage of State.[44]

*Argenis* exemplifies these precepts of Nicopompus, containing, as
it does, an account of European events and an analysis of significant individuals fictionalised in such a way that general moral
doctrines may be discerned by the reader. Barclay's narrative is
not simply a *roman à clef*, but a fictional re-creation of historical
events for a specific political purpose.

Patterson stresses that *Argenis* represents a particular moment
in the use of literature to circumvent censorship and open up a
political dialogue which will simultaneously reach the reader and
protect the writer.[45] I am not arguing that these works of Barclay
are a direct influence on the *New Atlantis*, but rather that they

establish a particular context for the intersection between fiction and social comment. Bacon in disgrace and enforced retirement did not simply perfect his scientific writings, he also turned to a mode of writing that might at first sight seem quite different from all his other works, however varied they might be. In their recent biography of Bacon, Lisa Jardine and Alan Stewart offer a particularly interesting description of how Bacon:

> tacitly erased all signs that his 'thought' and his 'life' (in the political arena) had hitherto been intimately linked. Instead he constructed a 'before' and an 'after': before, Francis Bacon was an active politician, caught up in the hurly-burly of court and parliamentary affairs, his outlook inevitably coloured (not to say tarnished) by the times; after, he was a patrician thinker, selflessly pursuing his scientific endeavours for posterity.[46]

Just as Jardine and Stewart point to this divide as an artful construct, so I would want to argue that *New Atlantis* is a perfect fictional negotiation of the shift between active political comment and 'neutral' speculation. As a narrative, the *New Atlantis* operates in the space between direct political intervention and private political musing: the space that various quite disparate forms of fiction helped to create in the early seventeenth century. From this perspective, the *New Atlantis* can be linked to Bacon's non-fictional writing in what we might at a stretch call other narrative forms, such as the history, or the dialogue. Having played the complicated Jacobean political game for the highest stakes and lost, Bacon uses the *New Atlantis* to offer a vision of a society dedicated to scientific advancement, but he also uses it indirectly to convey a political vision of an ordered society (in which, in various ways, a Francis Bacon would receive his just desserts).

With this in mind, I want to conclude by looking at one last generic issue for the *New Atlantis*: the specific way in which the narrative is actually situated. The modern reader who encounters the *New Atlantis* as part of an anthology (such as the Brian Vickers' collection, or the old World's Classics edition of *The Advancement of Learning and New Atlantis*) has a quite different experience of the text from the seventeenth-century reader.[47] In 1627 Bacon's chaplain William Rawley oversaw the publication of *Sylva Sylvarum: or, A Natural History in Ten Centuries*. This is what might be called a miscellany of scientific curiosities, experiments and information. Much of the material was gathered by Bacon from ancient sources, such as Aristotle, but Bacon also made considerable use of Sandys' *Travels* (1615) for material about Greece, the Middle East and Italy. *Sylva Sylvarum* is broken up into one thousand brief, numbered paragraphs (arranged in ten 'centuries'). Here is an entirely random example:

> Experiment solitary touching cements and quarries.
> 850. There have been found certain cements under earth that are very soft; and yet, taken forth into the sun, harden as hard as marble: there are also ordinary quarries in Somersetshire, which in the quarry cut soft to any bigness, and in the building prove firm and hard.[48]

At the conclusion of *Sylva Sylvarum*, a new title page announces *New Atlantis. A Work unfinished*. There is then a note from Rawley headed 'To the Reader' in which both the genre and the placement of the *New Atlantis* are carefully explained:

> This fable my Lord devised, to the end that he might exhibit therein a model or description of a college instituted for the interpreting of nature and the producing of great and marvellous works for the benefit of men, under the name of Salomon's House, or the College of the Six Days' Works. And even so far his Lordship hath proceeded as to finish that part. Certainly the model is more vast and high than can possibly be imitated in all things; notwithstanding most things therein are within men's power to effect. His Lordship thought also in this present fable to have composed a frame of Laws, or of the best state or mould of a commonwealth; but foreseeing it would be a long work, his desire of collecting the Natural History diverted him, which he preferred many degrees before it.
>
> This work of the *New Atlantis* (as much as concerneth the English edition) his Lordship designed for this place; in regard it hath so near affinity (in one part of it) with the preceding Natural History.[49]

So this work is a fable, but it nevertheless belongs with *Sylva Sylvarum* because, through the fable, Bacon offers an exemplary scientific society. The two works accordingly form an intersecting genre of natural history/fable, treatise/fiction, which readers were encouraged to see as inseparable. The *New Atlantis* was included in all the seventeenth-century editions of *Sylva*. It was included in Bushell's *Abridgement* of 1659. It was also published

separately in Latin in the 1638 *Operum Moralium* and, significantly, paired with Hall's *Mundus* in an edition of 1643.[50] The
*New Atlantis* and *Sylva Sylvarum* form an implied commentary
on each other. Given Rawley's stress on the word fable as a
description of the *New Atlantis*, it is worth noting the way he
concludes his Preface to *Sylva Sylvarum*: 'I will conclude with an
usual speech of his lordship's; That this work of his Natural
History is the world as God made it, and not as men have made it;
for that it hath nothing of imagination'.[51] So the *New Atlantis*
might be seen as the vision of the natural history with the addition of imagination. It is also, in many ways, a kind of reaching
forward in time for Bacon, who, if he is unable to perfect his
scientific work, is able at least to imagine a world in which a
whole society would be devoted to such perfection. Bensalem is
also, of course, shot through with other forms of Baconian wish-
fulfilment, such as the obsessive, luxurious social ceremony of
the Feast of the Family (472–5).

This intersection of scientific treatise and utopia might be
viewed as a late version of the general Renaissance interest in
mixed modes.[52] The result is not so much a specific form of fiction
as a specifically productive yoking of fiction with something
else. Recently, scholars working on Margaret Cavendish have
noticed the parallel between Cavendish's utopian *Blazing World*
and the *New Atlantis*.[53] In 1666 Cavendish published *Observations Upon Experimental Philosophy*, an attack on Robert Hooke's
*Micrographia* of 1665. Cavendish attached to *Observations*, with a
separate title page, *The Description of a New World Called The
Blazing World*. She states in a preface to the reader, 'If you wonder
that I join a work of fancy to my serious philosophical contem-
plations, think not that it is out of a disparagement to philosophy.'[54] Like the *New Atlantis*, *Blazing World* creates a society
in which the author's scientific ideas are taken up by a proto-
Royal Society (in Cavendish's case composed of a number of
beast-like creatures, rather than human beings). Cavendish also
answers Bacon's celebration of patriarchal authority with a
vision of a female society, ruled by an Empress who is joined by
Cavendish's own spirit in the *Blazing World*. In this sense,
Cavendish argues against the male potency and dominance of a
patriarchal family structure which Susan Bruce sees as essential

to Bacon's purpose in the *New Atlantis*.[55] Cavendish offers an antidote to Bacon's masculine society by way of a society in which the Emperor is a cipher who allows the Empress complete domination over his world. Just as Bacon envisages a society oriented both towards his dreams of science and full of ceremony and degree, Cavendish imagines a world in which both her dramatic and her scientific writing is appreciated. Of course it is Bacon who provides a context for Cavendish, rather than the other way round, but Cavendish's *Observations/Blazing World* diptych draws our attention to the way that Bacon's *Sylva*/the *New Atlantis* is a particularly hybrid example of a particularly hybrid genre.

## Notes

1  Brian Vickers (ed.), *Francis Bacon: A Critical Edition of the Major Works* (Oxford, Oxford University Press, 1996), p. 478. All further references to *New Atlantis* are from this edition. More's *Utopia* was first published in Latin in 1516, followed by many other editions and an English translation by Raphe Robinson in 1551.

2  Susan Bruce, 'Virgins of the world and feasts of the family: sex and the social order in two renaissance utopias', in Neil Rhodes (ed.), *English Renaissance Prose: History, Language and Politics* (Tempe, MRTS, 1997), pp. 139–46.

3  J. C. Davis argues that, during this period, 'utopian thought itself is not a tradition', *Utopia and the Ideal Society* (Cambridge, Cambridge University Press, 1981), p. 3.

4  Robert Burton, *The Anatomy of Melancholy*, ed. Thomas Faulkner *et al.* (Oxford, Clarendon Press, 1989), vol. I, p. 80; the copytext is the greatly augmented 1632 edition; in this instance the quotation is in the 1621 edition. For the actual *Utopia* quotation see *Complete Works of St Thomas More*, ed. Edward Surtz and J. H. Hexter (New Haven, Yale University Press, 1965), vol. IV, p. 70.

5  Burton, *Anatomy*, pp. 36–7.

6  *Ibid.*, p. 85.

7  *Ibid.*

8  *Ibid.*, p. 86.

9  *Ibid.*

10  *Ibid.*, p. 89.

11  For a good account see Frank and Fritzie Manuel, *Utopian Thought in the Western World* (Cambridge, Mass., Bellknap Press, 1979), Chapter 11.

12  See Davis, *Utopia*, pp. 97–8.

13  *Anatomy*, p. 91.

14  *Ibid.*, p. 92.

15  *Ibid.*, p. 109.

16  Richard Hakluyt, *Principal Navigations, Voyages Traffiques and Discoveries* (Glasgow, Glasgow University Press, 1904), vol. X, pp. 348–9.

17  *Ibid.*, p. 382.

18  John Gillies, *Shakespeare and the Geography of Difference* (Cambridge, Cambridge University Press, 1994), p. 223.

19  Francis Bacon, *The New Organon*, ed. Fulton Anderson (New York, Liberal Arts Press, 1960), p. 81.

20  Gillies, *Shakespeare*, p. 223, n. 98.

21  *Another World and Yet the Same: Bishop Joseph Hall's Mundus Alter et Idem*, trans. John Miller Wands (New Haven, Yale University Press, 1981), p. 3.

22  Richard A. McCabe, *Joseph Hall: A Study in Satire and Meditation* (Oxford, Clarendon Press, 1982), p. 76.

23  *Complete Prose Works of John Milton*, ed. Don M. Wolfe (New Haven, Yale University Press, 1953), vol. I, p. 881. I should note here that this is from 'An Apology Against a Pamphlet' (1642), a direct attack on Hall. The editor points out that Milton offers a quite different view of Utopias in *Areopagitica*, where he writes 'To sequester out of the world into Atlantick and Eutopian polities, which never can be drawn into use, will not mend our condition; but to ordain wisely as in this world of evill, in the midd'st whereof God hath placed us unavoidably,' *Complete Prose Works*, ed. Ernest Sirluck (New Haven, Yale University Press, 1959), vol. II, p. 526.

24  Peter Heylyn, *Microcosmus* (Oxford, 1621), p. 11.

25  Robert Ralston Cawley, *Unpathed Waters: Studies in the Influence of the Voyagers on Elizabethan Literature* (1940, rpt. New York, Octagon, 1967), pp. 44–7.

26  'William Adams his Voyage by the Magellan Straights to Japon', in Samuel Purchas, *Hakluytus Posthumous or Purchas his Pilgrims* (Glasgow, Glasgow University Press, 1905), vol. II, p. 327; Adams' account was published by Purchas in 1625.

27  *Ibid.*, p. 332.

28  Cawley concludes that Bacon's knowledge of Adams can only be conjectural, because Adams' account was published after the likely composition date of *New Atlantis*. See Cawley, *Unpathed Waters*, pp. 44–5.

29  Purchas, *Hakluytus*, p. 339.

30  Ferdinand de Quiros, *Terra Australis Incognita* (1617), p. 27.

31  Purchas, *Hakluytus*, p. 327.

32  Annabel Patterson, *Censorship and Interpretation: The Conditions of Writing and Reading in Early Modern England* (Madison, University of Wisconsin Press, 1984).

33 John Barclay, *Euphormionis Lusinini Satyricon*, ed. and trans. David A. Fleming (Nieuwkoopp, de Graaf, 1973), p. xvi.

34 *Ibid.*, p. 3.

35 See McCabe, *Joseph Hall*, p. 76 and my discussion above.

36 *Euphormionis*, p. 5.

37 *Ibid.*, p. 5.

38 *Ibid.*, p. xx.

39 I have argued this case at greater length in *English Prose Fiction 1558–1700: A Critical History* (Oxford, Clarendon Press, 1985), Chapter 11.

40 *Euphormionis*, p. 349.

41 *Ibid.*, p. 351.

42 For full details see Salzman, *English Prose Fiction*, pp. 149–55.

43 Patterson, *Censorship*, p. 180.

44 John Barclay, *Barclay His Argenis*, trans. Kingesmill Long (1625), p. 109.

45 See Patterson, *Censorship*, pp. 181–3.

46 Lisa Jardine and Alan Stewart, *Hostage to Fortune: The Troubled Life of Francis Bacon* (London, Victor Gollancz, 1998), p. 475.

47 Vickers (ed.), *Francis Bacon; Advancement of Learning and New Atlantis*, ed. Thomas Case (London, Oxford University Press, 1906).

48 *The Works of Francis Bacon*, ed. James Spedding, Robert Ellis and Douglas Denon Heath, 14 vols (London, 1857), vol. II, p. 620.

49 *Ibid.*, vol. III, p. 127.

50 See R. W. Gibson, *Francis Bacon: A Bibliography* (Oxford, Scrivener Press, 1950).

51 Bacon, *Works*, vol. II, p. 337.

52 See Rosalie Colie, *The Resources of Kind* (Berkeley, University of California Press, 1973).

53 See especially Bronwen Price, 'Journeys beyond frontiers: knowledge, subjectivity and outer space in Margaret Cavendish's *The Blazing World*', *Literature and History*, 7 (1998), 21–50: Price specifically discusses Cavendish's argument with Bacon's view of science, pp. 25–31; see also Marina Leslie, *Renaissance Utopias and the Problem of History* (Ithaca, Cornell University Press, 1998), p. 123; as yet unpublished work on this issue has been done by Sarah Hutton, Rebecca Totaro and Debra Taylor-Pearce; I am grateful to them for drawing their work to my attention.

54 *An Anthology of Seventeenth-Century Fiction*, ed. Paul Salzman (Oxford, World's Classics, 1991), p. 251.

55 For Bruce's reading see above, note 2.

# 3

# Persuasions to science: Baconian rhetoric and the *New Atlantis*

## SARAH HUTTON

For all his strictures on the use of language for rhetorical effect,
it is now well established that Francis Bacon was thoroughly
grounded in the Renaissance art of rhetoric and that he consciously
drew on his rhetorical skill in his writings, adapting his style as
occasion demanded. The nature and extent of Bacon's use of
rhetoric has been extensively, though not exhaustively, explored.[1]
Gone are the days when Bacon was regarded as a dysfunctional
writer, or a 'dissociated sensibility', in T. S. Eliot's phrase. Nevertheless, Bacon's impatience with stylistic affectation is well known
from his own comments: 'eloquence and copie of speech' is, he
writes in *The Advancement of Learning*, 'the first distemper of
learning, when men study words and not matter'.[2] In conjunction
with this repudiation of ornamental excess, Bacon's preference
for an unadorned style of writing for the communication of natural
philosophy, in particular his recommendation of the aphorism
for the purpose, apparently confirms his antipathy to fictional
flights of fancy. His one excursus into narrative fiction employs a
genre, the utopia, where fiction is presented as fact. So successful
was Bacon's use of the genre in the *New Atlantis* that the tale has
come to be interpreted as a simple allegory or a thinly disguised
blueprint for a society where science flourishes under state control.[3] The *New Atlantis* is, then, not just a curiosity as a Baconian
fiction, but an interpretative paradox: the only excursion into
narrative fiction by a writer who repudiated the charms of
language; a work of imagination that is read as a virtually factual

document of Bacon's project for the advancement of learning, and especially of science. Although an apparently unfinished narrative, it is treated as the epitome of his life's work as a whole, its apparently unfinished state a fit emblem for the incompleteness of his project at the time of his death.[4] However, to read the *New Atlantis* as an unfinished allegorical narrative belies the literary complexity of the work and the intricacy of its web of cross-reference to Bacon's oeuvre as a whole. In this essay I argue that the *New Atlantis* is less an epitome of Bacon's ideas than a means of persuading others to support his projected reform of scientific endeavour. The *New Atlantis* amply illustrates Bacon's understanding of rhetoric, or the 'art of elocution or tradition', as the art of communication – a 'transitive' art, the scope of which is 'the expressing or transferring our knowledge to others'.[5] But the *New Atlantis* is, above all, an *instrumental* text. Although it is designed to communicate Bacon's ideas, it is not so much a descriptive or a prescriptive text, but a *persuasive* one. This is consistent with Bacon's own view of rhetoric as having a key motivating function in active life, where 'the duty and office of rhetoric is to apply reason to imagination for the better moving of the will.'[6] In all Bacon's writings, style is not incidental: eloquence, for him, has a key part to play 'for the winning and persuading' of an audience. In what follows, I shall discuss ways in which the *New Atlantis* exemplifies his understanding of the role of rhetoric and what we can discern from its relationship to other works, especially *Sylva Sylvarum*, with which it was first published.

The combined edition of *Sylva Sylvarum* and the *New Atlantis* appeared in 1627, having been seen into print by Bacon's secretary, William Rawley. It is from Rawley that we derive the information that both works are incomplete. The *New Atlantis* is described on the title page of the 1627 edition as, 'A Worke unfinished'. It ends with a brief editorial epilogue, 'The rest was not perfected.' Rawley corroborates this by noting in his preface that Bacon had intended to supply his imaginary society with 'a *Frame of Lawes*', but had not been able to do so, because his time had been taken up with 'Collecting the *Naturall History*'. The impression of incompletion is underlined by Rawley's presentation of the companion piece of the volume, *Sylva Sylvarum*, as imperfect. In his preface, he introduces *Sylva Sylvarum* as uncrafted and unpolished – 'an Indigested Heap of Particulars', an unpolished piece of writing which lacks 'that Lustre which Bookes cast into Methods have'. Rawley takes credit for such organisation that the book has, namely the subdivision into chapters called 'Centuries'. Bacon did, apparently, live to complete *Sylva Sylvarum*.[7]

It was also Rawley who set the mould for regarding the *New Atlantis* as a blueprint for his scientific programme. Its truncated state notwithstanding, he introduces the *New Atlantis* as a 'Fable' showing 'a *Model or Description* of a *College*, instituted for the *interpreting of Nature*, and the Producing of *Great and Maruellous Works*, for the *Benefit of Men*'. He also suggests that there is a practical objective for the *New Atlantis*, which cannot 'be imitated in all things; Notwithstanding most Things therein are within Mens Power to effect'. Even if incomplete, the *New Atlantis* is a carefully crafted text. In contrast to the haphazard 'unmethodzed' appearance of *Sylva Sylvarum*, the *New Atlantis* gives the impression of being a highly controlled piece of writing.

Bacon's description of rhetoric as 'ornament', in contrast to the 'judgement' of logic, belies the importance of both eloquence and imagination in his philosophy. Not only does Bacon couple rhetoric with logic as 'the gravest of sciences', but he repeatedly reminds us in *The Advancement of Learning*, that rhetoric, or the art of eloquence, is 'a science excellent, and excellently well laboured'.[8] His criticism of humanistic style is directed at stylistic affectation and excess (*copia*). He condemns 'speech that is uttered with labour and difficulty, or speech that savoureth of the affectation of art and precepts'.[9] There is plenty of evidence, however, that Bacon regarded figurative language and imaginative fiction as more than mere ornament. He shares Sidney's view that poetry is more effective than history, because poets are free from the constraints of realism and fact:

> The use of this Feigned History hath been to give some shadow of satisfaction to the mind of man in those points wherein the nature of things doth deny it … Therefore, because the acts or events of true history have not that magnitude which satisfieth the mind of man, poesy feigneth acts and events greater and more heroical; because true history propoundeth the successes and issues of actions not so agreeable to the merits of virtue and vice, therefore

poesy feigns them more just in retribution, and more according to
revealed providence; because true history representeth actions and
events more ordinary and less interchanged, therefore poesy
endueth them with more rareness, and more unexpected and alternative variations. So as it appeareth poesy serveth and conferreth
to magnanimity, morality, and to delectation.[10]

Furthermore, as Bacon explains at a later point in *The Advancement of Learning*, fables and figurative language have a key role
in conveying new ideas. Being by definition unfamiliar, these
ideas are difficult to express, and require the aid of 'similitudes',
that is, similes and other analogies:

For that knowledge which is new and foreign from opinions
received, is to be delivered in another form than that that is agreeable and familiar; ... those whose conceits are beyond popular
opinions, have a double labour; the one to make themselves
conceived, and the other to prove and demonstrate; so that it is of
necessity with them to have recourse to similitudes and translations to express themselves.[11]

This is a situation which obtains when a topic is new, 'in the
infancy of learning', as was the case in ancient times, when fables
were used for communicating new science and philosophy.
Abstruse mysteries of religion, likewise, are suitably conveyed
by 'similitudes':

And therefore in the infancy of learning, and in rude times, when
those conceits which are now trivial were then new, the world was
full of Parables and Similitudes; for else would men either have
passed over without mark or else rejected for paradoxes that which
was offered, before they had understood or judged. So in divine
learning, we see how frequent Parables and Tropes are: for it is a
rule, that 'whatsoever science is not consonant to presuppositions,
must pray in aid of similitudes'.[12]

Furthermore, what he calls 'allusive or parabolical' poetry has a
special purpose:

Allusive or Parabolical [poesy] is a narration applied only to
express some special purpose or conceit. Which latter kind of
parabolical wisdom was much more in use in the ancient times, as
by the fables of Aesop, and the brief sentences of the Seven and the
use of hieroglyphics may appear.[13]

An example of this in Bacon's own writings is *De sapientia veterum* which purports to be a collection of ancient myths to be interpreted in terms of his own scientific preferences. The *New Atlantis* is hardly a hieroglyph of the new learning, but it can be described as 'parabolical wisdom' that gives us a glimpse of the Baconian scientific method in action. Even in factual reportage, such as writing histories, the poetic has its part to play. When writing histories, 'poesy endueth them [historical events] with more rareness, and more unexpected and alternative variations'.[14]

Bacon was a writer highly conscious of his craft, and careful in the means by which he chose to present his ideas. With its in-built cross-referencing to More and to Plato, the *New Atlantis* claims a pedigree in the best utopian tradition. The text also refers back to his earlier writings in major ways. The most obvious one is the account of the scientific investigations carried out in Salomon's House. The closeness of the relationship between the experiments conducted in the *New Atlantis* and the *desiderata* of Bacon's own programme is mirrored in the language, for, at this point in the tale, the narrative gives way to what can only be described as a catalogue. The programmatic ending that describes the 'Preparations and Instruments', the laboratories and achievements of Salomon's House, is little more than a list. The typography of the first edition separates this section from the rest with a change of type-size. This entire section could be excerpted and appended to the list entitled *Magnalia naturalia* printed in the same volume.

Content aside, the very conceit of a 'new Atlantis' links the tale to Bacon's oeuvre as a whole. The New Atlantis of the story is a new-found land where the whole of society is organised to promote investigations that appear new to the travellers from the old world. The motif of a new world of learning beyond the seas waiting to be discovered is figured in the title page of the volume in which the story was first printed, *Sylva Sylvarum*.[15] Here the Atlantic is signified by the imposing frame of the Pillars of Hercules – the markers of the limits of the old world. Whether this title page represents Bacon's posthumous intentions, or whether it was proposed by his secretary, we cannot be certain. Whatever the case, the aptness of the motif for Bacon's writings is striking: for it deftly recapitulates the title page of *The Advancement of Learning* which uses the same image of the Pillars of Hercules, but has an outward-bound ship in place of the seaborne globe ('mundus Intellectualis') at the centre of the title page of *Sylva Sylvarum*. The motif of the Pillars of Hercules is taken up in the dedication of the second book of *The Advancement of Learning* where Bacon asks:

> For why should a few received authors stand up like Hercules' columns beyond which there should be no sailing or discovering?[16]

As his simile indicates, the Pillars of Hercules are signifiers of intellect, denoting the limits of knowledge. By implication, the Atlantic beyond is the pathway to new learning. A classical precedent for this interpretation may be found in Lucian's satirical dialogue, *A True Relation*, where the narrator, disgusted by the emptiness and charlatanism of the philosophical systems he has encountered in the known world, sets out westwards from the Pillars of Hercules in pursuit of true philosophy.

Bacon's choice of metaphor was never accidental; judicious, even forensic, would be more apt descriptions.[17] His reworking of this particular image has further connotations: as other critics have noted, the Pillars of Hercules are an image of power. They were the centre-piece of an emblem used by the Emperor Charles V, ruler of much of Europe and the Americas.[18] The imperial connotations of this image were clear to sixteenth-century commentators whose 'happie conquest of the West Indies', as Paolo Giovio put it in Samuel Daniel's translation, 'eclipseth the glory of the old Romaines'.[19]

While Bacon's application of the motif is an unmistakable allusion to the imperialism of Charles V, its connotations are not exclusively imperialist. Before concluding that the content of his fable should be read as epitomising the epistemological hegemony of science, we should recall the instrumental function of the work signalled by its utopian format. More's *Utopia* imagines an ideal state, but the narrative of Raphael Hythlodaeus' journey there is presented as the outcome of a discussion on how to influence princes and potentates. In this respect the foundational text of utopian fiction is a version of the Renaissance 'advice to princes' genre. *Utopia* is the product of the centralised and autocratic Renaissance state. As a practical man of affairs, Bacon, like Sir Thomas More before him, was conscious of the difficulties to be encountered when trying to advise rulers and introduce new policies. Bacon's own political advice reminds us that rhetoric in its wider sense is political. Persuasion is part of the business of everyday life. And, as Bacon himself notes in his aptly named Essay, 'Of Negotiating', the business of persuasion requires techniques other than reason and logic:

> If you would work any man, [writes Bacon] you must either know his nature and fashions, and so lead him; or his ends, and so persuade him; or his weakness and disadvantages, and so awe him; or those that have interest in him, and so govern him.[20]

Successful persuasion is contingent upon knowledge of 'ends'. The man whose 'ends' Bacon 'knew' and whom he hoped to enlist as patron for his project for achieving new, practical knowledge through the reform of learning was the king himself.

The rhetoric of the *New Atlantis* bespeaks the political circumstances of its creation. It is a fiction adapted to the aspirations of those whom Bacon would persuade. The story presents a vision of Bacon's programme put into effect and allied to a vision of empire. The trope of new horizons links the new world of learning with a new world to be conquered. The trope of Atlantic voyages takes us back to the dedicatee of *The Advancement of Learning*, to British Solomon himself, James I. Indeed, the verbal use of the trope in the dedication to the king specifically connects him with the theme of *plus ultra*, sailing beyond the pillars of Hercules. To complete the quotation cited earlier:

> For why should a few received authors stand up like Hercules' Columns, beyond which there should be no sailing *or discovering, since we have so bright and benign a star as your Majesty to conduct and prosper us*? (my italics)[21]

Bacon's choice of tropes, therefore, must be put into the context of the type of political power with which their author had to reckon. As we know, the political ambience to which the *New Atlantis* refers is hardly a revolutionary one. We might, however, speculate that, had Bacon been writing in the 1650s, he would have adjusted his tale to the political circumstances of the English Republic. At a later date his text might also have addressed educational reformers of the Comenian or Hartlibian stamp.[22] In the 1620s, when Bacon was writing the *New Atlantis*, political reality and the patronage that it commanded were very different. If Bacon's best hope of seeing his proposals for the reform of systems of enquiry put into effect was monarchical patronage, he had to write in terms that would appeal to the king. As he himself observes: where the logician does not need to adapt to his audience, the rhetorician does, 'for the proofs and demonstrations of Logic are toward all men indifferent and the same; but the proofs and persuasions of Rhetoric ought to differ according to the auditors'.[23] It is, therefore, important to draw a distinction between the content of the *New Atlantis* and the readers whom Bacon was addressing.

The audience Bacon had in mind for the *New Atlantis* was, of course, not the single audience of kingly patronage. That the effecting of his programme required the involvement of others is implicit in the trope of Hercules and his labours. As the Lucianic example cited earlier shows, the Pillars of Hercules was not an exclusively imperialist motif in the Renaissance, while the Labours of Hercules commonly had other import. One of the best-known expositions of the significance of the Labours of Hercules in the Renaissance was that contained in Erasmus' *Adagia*. Erasmus construes it as applying to works of great design, altruistic in application and requiring much toil. Hercules' labours denote 'something great and manifold which needs the strength of Hercules' but also 'of a kind to bring the greatest advantage to others, and little or no profit to the doer except a little fame and a lot envy'.[24] Such was Bacon's programme for the advancement of learning. Bacon draws on Erasmus to represent seekers after truth as 'Hercules' followers in learning, that is, the more severe and laborious sort of inquirers into truth'.[25]

The special relevance of the Erasmian explanation of the trope to *Sylva Sylvarum* reinforces the rhetorical link between that book and the *New Atlantis*. For, of all Bacon's writings, *Sylva Sylvarum* is the one that best exemplifies his foundational aspirations and the laboriousness, not to say tedium, of the process of putting them into effect. It was compiled with the practical goal of laying the foundations of a new natural philosophy, and therefore of producing concrete advances in knowledge. Rawley tells us:

> the Scope which his Lordship intendeth, is to write such a *Natural History*, as may be Fundamentall to the Erecting and Building of a

true *Philosophy*: For the Illumination of the Vnderstanding; the
Extracting of Axiomes; and the producing of many Noble *Works*,
and *Effects*.[26]

This work of compilation of data is a prerequisite also for the
exercise of the art of rhetoric. The Latin term *silva*, used by Bacon
in the title of the work, is taken from Cicero's *De inventione* where
it signifies the assembled data on which the rhetor must work. In
*The Advancement of Learning* Bacon himself notes the importance
of amassing 'stuff and variety', or 'that which Cicero calleth *sylva*
and *supellex*', which logic and rhetoric will 'set forth and dispose'.[27]
Because Bacon's projected new philosophy has not yet been
achieved, the work of *Sylva Sylvarum* is incomplete. But the intention of the book being to lay foundations of that new science, it
contains, nonetheless, a completable project. Moreover, according
to Rawley, the connection between an unmethodical way of
writing and the expectation that others would contribute to the
project of new discovery, and hence completion of the project, is
not accidental. On the authority of the author himself he tells us:

> I have heard his Lordship say also, that one great Reason, why he
> would not put these Particulars into any exact Method ... was,
> because he conceived that other men would now think that they
> could do the like; And so goe on with a further Collection: which if
> the *Method* had been Exact, many would have despaired to attaine
> by Imitation.[28]

Bacon's preferred medium for recording and communicating
his natural history was the aphorism. Because of the brevity of
the form, the writer of aphorisms escapes the perils of *copia*, 'for
discourse of illustration is cut off; recitals of examples are cut off;
discourse of connection and order is cut off; descriptions of practice are cut off; so there remaineth nothing to fill the Aphorisms
but some good quantity of observation'.[29] But aphorisms are also
to be recommended because of their potential for continuity.
Aphorisms, as Bacon reminds us, represent 'a knowledge broken'.
Their incompleteness is their virtue, for by it they 'invite men to
inquire further'.[30] Arguably, therefore, the rough-hewn effect of
*Sylva Sylvarum* is deliberate design, intended to differentiate the
book from those 'Naturall Histories' whose aim is to entertain
('gathered for Delight and Use, are full of pleasant Descriptions
and Pictures; and affect and seek after Admiration, Rarities, and

Secrets'). Juxtaposed with *Sylva Sylvarum*, the *New Atlantis* invites
the reader to do just that: enquire further. In its published format
as the sister text *Sylva Sylvarum*, the *New Atlantis* appears less an
unfinished account of a fixed scientific ideal than as an open-
ended fiction designed to engage the involvement of others in
the grand project for which *Sylva Sylvarum* lays the ground.
Such an enterprise requires the involvement of others. It bespeaks
co-operation, openness and inclusiveness, a very different political
model from the imperialist aspirations of Bacon's patron.[31]

It is, perhaps, testimony to the persuasiveness of the *New
Atlantis* that among its earliest readers, it did indeed become a
model. Well before the Royal Society declared its Baconianism,
the utopian writings of the English revolution indicate cognis-
ance of Bacon's Bensalem and propound Baconian scientific
ideas,[32] for example, Gabriel Plattes' *A Description of the Famous
Kingdome of Macaria* (1641), Peter Chamberlen's *Poor Man's
Advocate* (1649), Peter Cornelius Plockhoy's *A Way Propounded
to Make the Poor Happy* (1659), and even Gerard Winstanley's
*Law of Freedom* (1652). The work by which Bacon's project was
best known in the seventeenth century was *Sylva Sylvarum*. It was
the most widely read of Bacon's writings in that century, with
more editions than of any other of his works.[33] These editions
also included the *New Atlantis*. It is impossible to explain the
popularity of *Sylva Sylvarum* either in partisan political terms
(since it was admired by republicans and royalists alike) or in
terms of a universalist scientific ideal that had not, at that time,
yet emerged.[34] The imaginative appeal of the *New Atlantis* to
other scientific utopians suggests that this, the sister text of *Sylva
Sylvarum*, contributed not a little to the success of the latter –
testimony to the 'eloquence of persuasions' of the *New Atlantis*.

## Notes

1  See, especially, L. Jardine, *Discovery and the Art of Discourse* (Cambridge,
   Cambridge University Press, 1974); B. Vickers, 'Bacon and rhetoric', in M.
   Peltonen (ed.), *The Cambridge Companion to Francis Bacon* (Cambridge,
   Cambridge University Press, 1996), pp. 200–31; K. R. Wallace, *Francis
   Bacon on Communication and Rhetoric* (Chapel Hill, NC, University of North
   Carolina Press, 1943); M. Cogan, 'Rhetoric and action in Francis Bacon',
   *Philosophy and Rhetoric* 14 (1981), 212–33.

2  Francis Bacon, *The Advancement of Learning*, in Brian Vickers (ed.), *Francis Bacon: A Critical Edition of the Major Works* (Oxford, Oxford University Press, 1996), p. 139. All further references to *The Advancement of Learning* are to this edition.

3  Famously, Benjamin Farrington regarded the *New Atlantis* as a prototype of modern industrialism, *Francis Bacon, Philosopher of Industrial Science* (London, Lawrence and Wishart, 1951).

4  The incompleteness of Bacon's sole venture into utopian fiction might also seem fitting to those mid-twentieth-century critics who regarded Bacon as antipathetic to fiction, not to say the enemy of the imagination, e.g. L. C. Knights, 'Bacon and the dissociation of sensibility', *Explorations* (Harmondsworth, Peregrine Books, 1964; first published 1946).

5  *The Advancement of Learning*, p. 237.

6  *Ibid.*, p. 238.

7  See Graham Rees, 'An unpublished manuscript by Francis Bacon, *Sylva Sylvarum* drafts and other working notes', *Annals of Science*, 28 (1981), 377–412.

8  *The Advancement of Learning*, p. 237.

9  *Ibid.*, p. 121.

10  *Ibid.*, p. 186.

11  *Ibid.*, pp. 235–6.

12  *Ibid.*, p. 236.

13  *Ibid.*, p. 187.

14  *Ibid.*, p. 186.

15  J. E. Steadman, 'Beyond Hercules: Bacon and the scientist as hero', *Studies in the Literary Imagination*, 4 (1971), 3–48; A. D. Burnett, 'The engraved title page of Bacon's *Instauratio Magna*: an icon and paradigm of science and its wider implication', *Durham Thomas Harriot Seminar Occasional Papers*, 27 (1998).

16  *Ibid.*, p. 169.

17  On Bacon's use of metaphor, see Brian Vickers, *Francis Bacon and Renaissance Prose* (Cambridge, Cambridge University Press, 1968).

18  E. Rosenthal, 'Plus Ultra, non plus ultra and the columnar device of the Emperor Charles V at the Court of Burgundy in Flanders in 1510', *Journal of the Warburg and Courtauld Institutes*, 36 (1971), 204–8.

19  Paulo Giovio, *The Worthy Tracte of Paulus Iouius* (London, 1585), trans. Samuel Daniel, sig. Biii[9].

20  Bacon, *Essays*, 47, 'Of Negotiating', in Vickers (ed.), *Francis Bacon*, p. 436.

21  *Ibid.*, p. 169.

22  On the take-up of Bacon's ideas during the English revolution, see Charles Webster, *The Great Instauration: Science, Medicine and Reform, 1620–1675* (London, Duckworth, 1975).

23  *The Advancement of Learning*, p. 239. Cf. *De augmentis*, VI. 3.

24  Margaret Mann Phillips, *The Adages of Erasmus. A Study with Translations* (Cambridge, Cambridge University Press, 1994), pp. 190–2.

25  *The Advancement of Learning*, p. 140. Bacon invokes these Herculean labourers when discussing stylistic excess, 'the first distemper of learning, when men study words and not matter' (*ibid.*, p. 139). Hercules' followers exemplify those who shun stylistic affectation.

26  *Sylva Sylvarum* (London, 1627), sig. A1v.

27  Cicero, *De inventione*, l. 34; Bacon, *The Advancement of Learning*, p. 173.

28  *Ibid.*, Preface.

29  *Ibid.*, p. 234.

30  *Ibid.*, p. 235. On Bacon's use of aphorisms, see Vickers, *Francis Bacon* (1968), Chapter 3.

31  It has latterly become customary to interpret Bacon as a political conservative, if not a proponent of monarchical absolutism. See especially, Julian Martin, *Francis Bacon, the State and the Reform of Natural Philosophy* (Cambridge, Cambridge University Press, 1992). Also, J. E. Leary, *Francis Bacon and the Politics of Science* (Iowa, Iowa State University Press, 1994). Others argue against reading the *New Atlantis* as pro-monarchical. See Markku Peltonen, 'Bacon's political philosophy', in *Cambridge Companion*, pp. 283–310, and the studies cited therein.

32  According to Charles Webster, 'Winstanley exhibited a kind of intuitive Baconianism, championing the "actor" against the "contemplator", as a contributor to fruitful learning. His designation of the various spheres of knowledge ... closely paralleled the Baconian programme for histories of trade. Thus the inhabitants of Winstanley's communes were expected to share in the benefits of experimental philosophy in the same manner as the citizens of the *New Atlantis* or *Macaria*' (*Great Instauration*, pp. 367–8).

33  Aside from European translations, there were seventeen English printings of the combined volume. See Graham Rees, 'An unpublished manuscript by Francis Bacon'. The claims of title pages are not reliable. The 1651 edition calls itself the sixth, and the 1664 edition the eighth. Two Latin editions, Amsterdam, Elsevir, 1648 and 1661; French, Paris, 1631.

34  Of course, the role of Isaac Gruter and his brother, Jacob, in securing a European readership for Bacon should not be underestimated. See Graham Rees, 'The transmission of Bacon's texts: some unanswered questions', in W. A. Sessions (ed.), *Francis Bacon's Legacy of Texts* (New York, AMS Press, 1990), pp. 291–310. See also Paul Dibon, 'Sur la réception de l'oeuvre de Francis Bacon en Hollande dans la première moitié du XVIIe siècle', in Martha Fattori (ed.), *Francesco Bacone. Terminologiae fortuna nel XVIII secolo* (Rome, Ateneo, 1984), pp. 91–115.

# 4

# Ethics and politics in the *New Atlantis*

## DAVID COLCLOUGH

God forbid that we should give out a dream of our own imagination for a pattern of the world; rather may he graciously grant to us to write an apocalypse or true vision of the footsteps of the Creator imprinted on his creatures.[1]

I

The *New Atlantis* is a text about natural philosophy which seems to offer connections at almost every point with moral and political philosophy. The celebrated description of Salomon's House raises the question of the place of the scientist in society and the allusion to Plato's *Critias* and *Timaeus* in the work's title suggests an engagement with that philosopher's description of the ideal state.[2] Furthermore, a reference to More's *Utopia*, together with the recognisably 'utopian' framework of the narrative, promises responses to other 'best state' exercises, perhaps including Andreae's *Christianopolis* (1619) and Campanella's *Civitas Solis* (1623).[3] Bacon's own political activities are well known, and in successive editions of the *Essays*, as well as in his speeches and pieces of advice, he had shown himself willing and able to treat what he considered the most pressing issues of political and ethical theory and practical negotiation. Nor was this engagement halted by Bacon's disgrace in 1621: in the years after his fall from office, he wrote a series of works which could be read as attempts to regain favour and political influence; the *New Atlantis* could well be read as an unfinished contribution to this project. Finally, the *New Atlantis* was drawn upon by Gabriel Plattes in his starkly utilitarian *Macaria* of 1641 in apparent testimony to the political applicability of Bacon's text,[4] while Salomon's House was imitated by both the mid-century republicans and the monarchist founders of the Royal Society.[5]

However, when one turns to the text itself, the ethical and the political are above all striking by their absence. Even the prefatory note attached to the work by Bacon's chaplain, William Rawley, draws attention to its failure to provide a fully fledged utopian vision, asserting (however unreliably) that 'his Lordship thought also in this present fable to have composed a frame of Laws, or the best state or mould of a commonwealth; but foreseeing that it would be a long work, his desire of collecting the Natural History diverted him.'[6] Natural history is privileged above political theory, just as the *New Atlantis* itself, 'A Worke unfinished', is placed at the end of the volume containing the *Sylva Sylvarum*, natural history collected from a mixture of observation and reading. In the *New Atlantis*, the practice of science appears to be kept institutionally and geographically separate from politics, with considerable autonomy being given to the scientific community.[7] While in More's work Hythloday offers a detailed description of Utopia's geography, government and laws, the moral philosophy of the inhabitants and their domestic or oeconomic arrangements, and while the island narrative of Book II is used as an example of a specific moral and political argument (that private property should be abolished), readers of the *New Atlantis* remain ignorant of most of these aspects of Bensalem.[8] There is a remarkable lack of detail about the nature of the island, other than that it is 'five thousand six hundred miles in circuit, and of rare fertility of soil in the greatest part' (469–70). As far as its constitution and administration are concerned, we know of Solamona's laws concerning strangers, and that he established other 'fundamental laws' (470), but we are not told what they are; 'the king' is mentioned at page 474, but we know nothing of his rule or his government. The only insight we gain into the oeconomical governance of the island is the curious Feast of the Family (472–5); no ethical system is outlined and most of the disturbing questions posed to moral philosophy at the time of the text's composition are glossed over, if not ignored. The islanders exist in a vaguely outlined but allegedly desirable state of peace, political contentment, and Christian–Hebraic virtue, which fosters or is fostered by the natural philosophical researches of Salomon's House. The 'Fathers' of this research institution are venerated and appear in magnificent procession, but their specific place in the social hierarchy and the precise extent of their authority remains unclear.

If we consider the ground rules for a best-state exercise laid down in Book VII of Aristotle's *Politics*, the problems become even clearer. Aristotle writes that 'he who would duly inquire about the best form of a state ought first to determine which is the most eligible life.'[9] At a pinch, the *New Atlantis* could be regarded as an attempt to describe this life as it might be lived, rather than to list the component virtues of which it should consist. But this begs the further question of how to decide whether such a hazily described life as that of the people of Bensalem can properly be assessed as conducive or otherwise to *eudaimonia*, which Aristotle has deemed in the *Ethics* to be the aim of life.[10]

I would suggest, in contrast, that to attempt to read the *New Atlantis* as a utopia in the Morean mould and to search the text for a system of, or even a series of *sententiae* about, ethics or politics, is misguided. Bacon's response to the textual tradition of Aristotle, Plato and More consists here in a manipulation of certain formal features to very different ends from theirs. Expectations are raised in the reader, and deliberately, I would argue, disappointed. Bacon seems to be aware of the kinds of questions readers might ask about this imaginary society and to half-answer each of them. The end result might be – although this has singularly failed to happen in many scholarly interpretations of the text – that the reader becomes aware that they are asking the *wrong* questions of the work. Ian Box, who is also puzzled by the absence from the *New Atlantis* of the kind of political and ethical thought which makes up the *Essays*, ascribes this gap to a fundamental contradiction between Bacon's identities as a 'scientist' and a 'statesman'.[11] It is certainly clear from several of his works that Bacon found a degree of incommensurability between ethical (specifically Christian) and civic values,[12] and that many of the conditions praised in his natural philosophy are condemned elsewhere in his writings. Markku Peltonen stresses that the repeated identification of Bacon's philosophical with his political thought relies upon a 'rhetorical similarity' which can obscure the distinction Bacon makes between those qualities and values that are required for the advancement of sciences and those needed for political success.[13] While in his works on the pursuit of greatness Bacon stresses the importance of a large armed populace engaged in regular warfare, he frequently emphasises that the advancement of learning demands peace, international co-operation and the absence of religious controversy.[14] Rather than reading Bacon's wide-ranging writings into an unhappily homogeneous unity, it is better to think of each work as making a different and specific intervention into a particular debate.[15]

## II

Bensalem, the island whose name means 'son of peace', conforms, as it soon becomes clear in the *New Atlantis*, to virtually all of Bacon's social and political criteria for the reform of knowledge.[16] Its peacefulness is unrivalled, the only military encounter mentioned being the ancient attack by the Coyans (Peruvians), which was foiled by the Bensalemite King Altabin. Even his victory was a peaceful one: 'after they were at his mercy, contenting himself only with their oath that they should no more bear arms against him, [he] dismissed them all in safety' (468). The conditions of the sailors' landing similarly suggest the peacefulness of the society: they are asked to swear that they 'are no pirates' and that they have not 'shed blood lawfully or unlawfully within forty days past' (459). The island itself is Christian (the sailors' first question to the Governor of the Strangers' House is how the conversion took place), but free of the confessional division that rent contemporary Europe. Moreover, freedom of worship is extended to the Jews, who were expelled from England in 1290 (though the narrator is careful to point out that the Jews of Bensalem 'are of a far differing disposition from the Jews in other parts' (475–6)).[17] In the first part of the text there is a striking preponderance of Biblical references, from the providential arrival of the sailors at Bensalem to their frequent invocation of Scriptural passages, specifically the psalms. For example, in a reference to Psalm

137:6 which suggests an equivalence between Bensalem and Jerusalem, the sailors swear to the Governor of the Strangers' House that 'our tongues should first cleave to the roofs of our mouths, ere we should forget either his reverent person or this whole nation in our prayers' (463).[18] References to Solomon, who both is and is not the lawgiver Solamona, abound, while Salomon's House, which *is* named after the Biblical king, is also known as the College of the Six Days' Works, a typical example of Bacon's insistence that the new philosophy should proceed through faith in God's creation, and of his fascination with hexaemeral schemes (*The Great Instauration* was conceived in six parts).[19] It is Salomon's House, the 'noblest foundation [...] that ever was upon the earth' (471), which above all demonstrates that the island of Bensalem is the ideal scientific polity. As has been pointed out many times in the past, this is just the sort of research institution whose establishment Bacon dreamt of for Jacobean England.[20] Established by a monarch and a central part of the state (indeed, the 'very eye' and the 'lanthorn of this kingdom' (464, 471)), it both provides the long-anticipated 'fruits' of the new philosophy and proceeds according to rigorously Baconian methods.

Despite conforming almost perfectly to Bacon's prescriptions of the ideal conditions for the advancement of knowledge, Bensalem diverges from them in one crucial matter, namely the international co-operation whose importance Bacon increasingly stressed and sought through the translation of several of his works into Latin and European vernaculars.[21] The Bensalemites clearly require assistance from overseas: we are twice told of the twelve-yearly expeditions of the 'Merchants of Light', who venture abroad 'under the names of other nations' and investigate 'the sciences, arts, manufactures, and inventions of all the world', bringing back 'books, instruments, and patterns' (471; cf. 486). This process has been much remarked upon, partly no doubt because it is one apparently explicitly political aspect of the *New Atlantis*. Critics have tended to regard the secret expeditions as highly exploitative, and as an example of ruthless political control allegedly concealed beneath Bensalem's apparent perfection.[22] Thus Charles Whitney contends that while 'on the literal level [...] Bensalem, seems to be sustained by a covert form of colonization', 'allegorically' it offers 'an ideal colonialist solution to the challenge of empire facing Britain in the early seventeenth century' and 'an apt analogy for the ideally exploitative class relationship between scientists and the artisans and mechanics whose inventive skills and useful devices Bacon would harness'.[23]

So is this the real political import of the text? Is the ideal Baconian state 'linked inseparably to external and even internal colonization', as Whitney would have us believe?[24] The activities engaged in by the Merchants of Light are not immediately recognisable as those of colonists: they do not attempt to establish settlements in the countries they visit, nor to subdue local cultures or peoples, nor to impose themselves or their Bensalemite customs. Rather, they attempt to assimilate themselves within their host community as successfully as possible in order to keep their origins secret. Far from attempting to 'buy' or simply claim parts of land so that local produce can be exported, they instead behave in strikingly merchant-like fashion, buying whatever provisions or objects they need and rewarding those who have been of service to them. It is, of course, the very secrecy and the supposed inequality of these transactions that has exercised critics. They argue that money is handed over by the Merchants of Light in return for information and equipment which is of much greater use to the members of Salomon's House than it is to those who sell it. Beads are exchanged for gold, in an encounter typical of imperialist enterprise through the ages.[25]

This interpretation of the Merchants of Light, however, is rather simplistic. Certainly, these knowledge-gathering voyages of the merchants resemble small military or mercantile sorties, but given their striking difference from most colonial endeavours, their most interesting aspect is surely their commodification of knowledge. Knowledge is like, and yet unlike, other mercantile commodities; 'thus,' says the Governor of the Strangers' House, 'you see we maintain a trade, not for gold, silver, or jewels; nor for silks; nor any commodity of matter; but only for God's first creature, which was *Light*: to have *light* (I say) of the growth of all parts of the world' (472). This is not a colonial relationship to the knowledge the Merchants find on their travels, even if it is possibly an exploitative one.

Exploitative or not, Bensalem's trade and foreign policies are indisputably isolationist, and the divergence from Bacon's praise of co-operation thus remains unresolved. The reason, I would argue, is that once again we may be approaching Bacon's 'fable' (as Rawley described it) in the wrong way. This is, after all, a fable, a fiction. For the remainder of this chapter I will argue that it is a fable about knowledge and about reading, about the past and the future, far more than it is a description of an ideal 'feigned commonwealth'. We have noted that in his description of the mercantile acquisition of knowledge from other societies, Bacon implies that those societies are less 'developed' or sophisticated in natural philosophy than Bensalem. Nonetheless, their 'light' is still valuable. This relationship is strikingly similar to Bacon's frequently articulated attitude towards – and use of – the texts of the ancients and other philosophers, which he regards as flawed. Bacon attached a great deal of importance to the kind of naming and shaming exercise undertaken in the *Temporis partus masculus* of c. 1602–03, where he attacks, one by one, the 'sham philosophers' of the past, and he is often concerned to dismiss out of hand the works and methods of Aristotle in particular and the 'ancients' in general. But he also repeatedly draws upon their works in the process of representing himself as an uncommonly privileged reader, able to winnow the wheat of wisdom from the chaff of false methodology. His allegorical reinterpretation of classical myths and fables in *De sapientia veterum* (1609) is characteristic of this strategy, as is his juxtaposition in the *Sylva Sylvarum* and natural histories (e.g. *Historia Ventorum, Historia Vitae et Mortis*, published 1622–23) of the results of experiments with 'facts' drawn from Pliny, della Porta and others.[26] Just as the 'light' bought by Bensalem's merchants is valuable despite being under-used or not even recognised for what it is by its vendors, so the fact that the methods and even the conclusions of the ancients may be inadequate or inaccurate does nothing to prevent us from seeing that much can still be gleaned from their works through an eclectic approach such as that displayed by Bacon throughout his writings.

Bensalem's use of the Merchants of Light thus represents the proper Baconian relationship of the present to the past, and of the natural philosopher to his 'ancient' forebears. This reading relationship is one of re-use and re-appropriation; it is an active, pragmatic and purposeful form of interpretation that Bacon regularly elevated over the passive reception of a text's accepted meaning. In the *New Atlantis*, as elsewhere, Bacon points to the generative possibilities of reading the past as it is figured by the present. This process comprises the active appropriation of texts through an act of incorporation whereby the texts of the past come to make up the body of the writer, but are themselves transformed by being deployed to new ends.[27] The task of the seventeenth-century natural philosopher, he declares, is to enter into trade with, rather than to seek conquest over, the books and knowledge-systems of the past, just as the Bensalemites do with their Merchants of Light. If we pursue this allegory, the *New Atlantis* thus offers in Bensalem a picture of how the future could be if only Bacon's readers take his lesson and recognise both the central importance of natural philosophy to the best life and the vital importance of the Baconian method as expressed in his other writings.

## III

It is not only the description of the Merchants of Light that may be read as a model of reading and of the proper use of knowledge. The text as a whole is susceptible to such an interpretation, and, I would hazard, makes much more sense if read in this way than if we treat it as a transparent description of a model society. There is a distinct lack of individuals through whom ethical questions may be pursued because the text is concerned with problems of thought and of knowledge rather than with the description of the individuals who might do the thinking. As Michèle Le Doeuff has written, both personal identity and the knowing subject are absent from the text.[28] In this way, it goes beyond that eradication of the private sphere, which J. C. Davis has described as a crucial component of utopian texts in this period.[29]

Bensalem, as I have suggested, may be interpreted as a representation of the Baconian future, in a fruitful 'trading' relationship with the textual past. This makes even more sense if we consider Bensalem as at least in part the model of the ideal Baconian mind, and as exemplifying certain precepts expressed in other Baconian texts concerning the encounter with the new philosophy. The reformation of the subject necessary for the pursuit of this new philosophy consists, for Bacon, in the eradication of mental impediments – the smashing of various 'idols', or habits of thought.[30] In *Temporis partus masculus*, Bacon attempts to find a means for the promulgation of the new philosophy and to work out how it could be accepted by his contemporaries, writing that: 'when all the entrances and approaches to men's minds are beset and blocked by the most obscure idols [...] A new method must be found for quiet entry into minds so choked and overgrown.'[31] Throughout his discussions of this insinuative pedagogy, however, Bacon is beset by a paradox: in order to clear the mind of its 'idols', one must understand the new philosophy; but in order to understand the new philosophy, one's mind must have been cleared. As the speaker puts it at the end of *Temporis partus masculus*,

> if I should ask you to grapple immediately with the bewildering complexities of experimental science [*Experientiae*] before your mind has been purged of its idols, beyond a peradventure you would promptly desert your leader. Nor, even if you wished to do so, could you rid yourself of idols by simply taking my advice without familiarising yourself with nature.[32]

One of Bacon's strategies for describing the entry of new knowledge into the mind is to contrast it with the image of a wax tablet. In the same text he explains that 'On tablets, unless you have wiped out the earlier things, you will not write other things. In the mind it is otherwise: unless you write other things, you will not have wiped out earlier things.'[33] The passage is echoed closely in *Redargutio philosophiarum*, in a typical instance of Baconian self-quotation: 'certainly, on wax tablets you will not write other things unless you will have wiped out the earlier things; in the mind you will scarcely have wiped out the earlier things unless you write in other things.'[34] Once again, Bacon describes a rather more sophisticated conception of the *pars destruens* of his philosophy than is usually acknowledged by his critics: the old certainly must be surpassed, he states, but this can only be done by letting in the new. The old is thus required as a foundation. The mind cannot be transformed into a clean slate with which the whole process of learning can begin again; those authorities and traditions which are to be rejected are entirely necessary, and it is better that they should be rejected than that they should never have been known at all. The minds of those who would follow Bacon thus need neither to be solely reliant upon accepted traditions and modes of thought nor upon the desire for new knowledge, but rather should be open and exploratory as well as aware of the foundations of their knowledge, however jerry-built they might be.[35] It seems clear that Bacon saw his reformation of knowledge, his 'instauration', as divided into, on the one hand, developing a method or logic whereby nature might best be perceived *as it is* and, on the other, discovering a means by which this new method and new knowledge could be accepted by the corrupt minds of his contemporaries. At the beginning of the *Novum Organum* (1620) he writes:

> such then are the provisions I make for finding the genuine light of nature and kindling and bringing it to bear. And they would be sufficient of themselves, if the human intellect were even, and like a fair sheet of paper with no writing on it. But since the minds of men are strangely possessed and beset, so that there is no true and even surface left to reflect the genuine rays of things, it is necessary to seek a remedy for this also.[36]

It is this remedy that the *New Atlantis* is meant, at least in part, to provide. Bacon makes the text into a fable with a philosophical imperative by describing the Bensalemites not simply as a variety of perfect human beings with minds 'like a fair sheet of paper,' or like a wax tablet, but as representatives of the Baconian mind in action. Unlike the inhabitants of Aldous Huxley's *Island*, left to work out perfection entirely in isolation through the efforts of their own reason in a latter-day Rousseau-esque fable, the Bensalemites use their island state as a basis for exploration and exploitation of other forms of knowledge. They require the past and its errors or half-truths, and, being in an ideal natural-philosophical state, they are able to take them a step (or several leagues) further towards 'finding the genuine light of nature'.[37]

The sailors, by contrast, are at an earlier stage: they are voyagers into the future, somewhat like Bacon himself, at first dazzled and almost struck dumb by what they see and hear – they are, after all, as the narrator states in terms that extravagantly exceed the geographical, 'beyond both the old world and the new' (461). The narrator describes their reaction to the account of the Merchants of Light in precisely these terms: 'when [the Governor of the Strangers' House] had said this, he was silent;

and so were we all. For indeed we were all astonished to hear so
strange things so probably told' (472). This state of confused
awakening is also described at the conclusion of the *Redargutio
philosophiarum*, where the audience of the lecture reported in the
text discuss what they have heard: 'they talked to one another
saying that they were like men who had come suddenly out of
thick shade into the open light and were for the moment dazzled,
but carried with them a sure and happy augury of better sight to
come'.[38] In the *Novum Organum*, moreover, Bacon compares the
entrance into the 'kingdom of man' via the new natural philosophy to that into the kingdom of heaven, 'whereinto none may
enter except as a little child': the sailors are those innocents,
denied even names or nationality.[39]

Bensalem is thus the future of natural philosophy in both its
methodological and its instrumental form (the latter being described in detail through Salomon's House).[40] As I have suggested
above, in describing this future Bacon is concerned to stress its
attainability, abiding by Aristotle's dictum that 'in framing an
ideal we may assume what we wish, but should avoid impossibi-
lities'.[41] In attempting to demonstrate the shape of natural philosophy to come, though, Bacon goes further than this, as is evident
from my epigraph: there he explicitly rejects the utopian project,
associating it implicitly with those ways of thinking which
derive from the passions and preoccupations of the individual
rather than from the facts of nature. A little later in the *Novum
Organum* he writes that 'the human mind is no dry light, but
receives an infusion from the will and affections; whence proceed
sciences which may be called "sciences as one would".'[42] The
*New Atlantis* is not to be read as 'science (or society) as Bacon
would' so much as 'thought as it might be practised'.

The ethical and political, both in terms of the detailed description of an ideal commonwealth and of recommended codes of
conduct, are thus absent partly because Bacon is offering a model
of the use of knowledge and reading for any society (even if most
specifically seventeenth-century England), rather than a model
of a new, perfect society. A more perfect society may well result
from this, it is implied, but it is the better society which is consequent on the reform of knowledge rather than new knowledge
which results from a reformed or transformed society. In the

epigraph to this chapter Bacon expresses his concern that instead of an imaginative utopia, 'the best state or mould of a commonwealth', the natural philosopher should be committed to writing an apocalypse, or revelation of divine secrets in nature: the speech of the Father of Salomon's House is just such a discourse, but so is the rest of the text, *in extenso*.[43] The politics of the *New Atlantis* are above all those of conservative reform; but conservative, it would appear from the paucity of material support given to Bacon's plans, and of vocal support to his methodological treatises, only in the mind of the writer.[44] It is difficult to over-emphasise Bacon's determination that his mental and institutional reforms were within reach: for all the exoticism of Bensalem as another New World 'discovery', critics have perhaps thought too much in terms of the wonder of the new colonies and not enough about the implications of the analogy for Bacon's argument about the advancement of learning. The point is surely not that Bensalem is so distant as to be necessarily imaginary, but that it is, in the context of recent voyages, eminently probable.[45] Bacon's ship on the title page of the *Novum Organum*, we can hardly forget, sails proudly through the Pillars of Hercules, extending the bounds of the known world: his oft-repeated (mis)quotation of Daniel 12:4 prophesies that 'many shall go about and knowledge will be increased.'[46] That this image of the future should be more or less universally applicable to almost any readership Bacon may have envisaged for his text is shown by the confessional and national anonymity of the sailors. That it is intended to appeal to those readers as singling out their culture in particular (whatever it may be) is illustrated by the direct address of the narrator and his frequent reference to things which are almost, *but not quite*, like those to be encountered in Europe: a medicinal fruit is 'like an orange, but of colour between orange-tawny and scarlet', and so on.[47] In this way, the *New Atlantis* is a notably more didactic and monologic work than More's *Utopia*, where Hythloday's insistence that the abolition of private property is the key to happiness is questioned, undermined, and ironised just as much as are More's insistence to the contrary and arguments about the importance of becoming a counsellor. Many writers have seen in the description of the Father of Salomon's House a wistful self-portrait of the author, and there is some truth in this; but to me the force of the description is in Bacon's conviction that such a role could be filled by one such as himself, not in the pathos of the self-delusion that it is purported to represent. The narrator of the *New Atlantis* writes of Bensalem that 'if there be a mirror in the world worthy to hold men's eyes, it is that country' (472): the mirror is intended, as in the literature of the *speculum principis* tradition, to serve a dual function of both reflecting back the faults of the beholder and offering him or her an ideal image to which he or she can aspire.

## IV

The politics and the ethics to be found in the *New Atlantis* thus return, as do many of Bacon's heuristic and propaedeutic writings, to a basic set of propositions concerning the necessity of a reform of attitudes towards and practices of thinking and reading about natural philosophy. As Brian Vickers has pointed out, one of Bacon's main achievements was to 'take the *vita activa* tradition, with its goals of open communication, exchange, knowledge to be used for the benefit of man, and to appropriate it for science'; the *New Atlantis* is a prime example of this appropriation in action.[48] In its gesturing towards a possible but highly uncertain future, however, the text goes beyond the general reflections on the ethics of reading which I have sketched here. It offers a reflection on the possible reception of Bacon's own texts and their future fortunes, a subject by which he was considerably exercised. The proleptic gesture is present almost everywhere in his writings. For example, in the *Novum Organum* he writes: '[I] hold it enough if in the intermediate business [before the sixth part of the *Instauratio*] I bear myself soberly and profitably, sowing in the meantime for future ages the seeds of a purer truth, and performing my part towards the commencement of the great undertaking', while in his will he (rather more bitterly) bequeathed his 'name and memory' to 'men's charitable speeches, and to foreign nations, and the next ages'.[49]

Though Bacon's status as a thinker 'ahead of his time' has often been asserted,[50] it is important to recognise his conviction that in fact the time was ripe for his ideas and the reforms they necessitated: he did not always think of sowing as a solitary occupation. He did, however, make a distinction between the preparation and the fruition of his ideas, and also the different textual forms that would be required for each. In the *De interpretatione Naturae Proemium*, an undated piece first published by Gruter in 1653, he writes that:

> those parts of the work which have it for their object to find out and bring into correspondence such minds as are prepared and disposed for the argument, and to purge the floors of men's understandings, I wish to be published to the world and circulate from mouth to mouth: the rest I would have passed from hand to hand, with selection and judgement.[51]

The *New Atlantis* can easily be seen as an allegory for this relationship between secrecy and publicity that Bacon imagined for his works. First, he argued, ideas and methods would be developed among a select group and brought to perfection, and then they would be widely disseminated. Bensalem has kept itself concealed from the rest of the world for thousands of years, but at the conclusion of his discourse the Father of Salomon's House signals the end of this isolation: 'I give thee leave,' he tells the narrator, 'to publish [this relation] for the good of other nations; for we are here in God's bosom, a land unknown' (488) – and, of course, the narrator complies, for we are holding in our hands the published narrative.[52] This suggests, first, that the scientific knowledge of Bensalem is sufficiently perfected to allow its dissemination throughout other lands and, second, that this is a propitious time for scientific reform or revolution in Bacon's Europe.

In its self-reflexiveness and its concern with textual dissemination, the *New Atlantis* echoes the *Redargutio philosophiarum*; and other illuminating correspondences between the two works can be identified: the Father of Salomon's House has 'an aspect as if he pitied men' (478), while the face of the lecturer in the *Redargutio* has become 'habituated to the expression of pity';[53] the narrator of the *New Atlantis* is invited to sit beside the Father as he delivers his 'relation', while the lecturer of the earlier work speaks 'not on a platform or pulpit, but on level with the rest'.[54] Just as in the *Redargutio*, an illuminating discourse is entrusted to its hearer for further dissemination, and the reader of the text itself is co-opted into this chain of transmission. The

*Redargutio* consists, as I have indicated, of a 'lecture' framed by an introductory and concluding narrative: the introduction explains how the main text came into the hands of the writer, while the conclusion ensures the publication of that text: the writer's friend requests that if the narration has found favour, '"will you, when you write on these matters, find room to include my report and not suffer the fruits of my travels to perish." "A fair request,"' replies the writer, '"and I shall not forget."'[55] But there is also the possibility of corruption through this transmission: the friend admits that even his report is 'very inferior' to the original lecture, while further telling may lead to greater corruption and to the discourse losing its force.[56] Bacon is concerned that his texts and ideas are needed now but that they will only be heeded in the future, if at all. He has what could be called a Cassandra complex – and he explains in *De sapientia veterum* the problematic results of 'untimely admonitions'.[57] A similar concern is present in the *New Atlantis*: early in the text, the Governor of the Strangers' House explains that very few of the sailors who happened upon the island have ever returned to their own countries, so entranced were they by Bensalem: 'what those few that returned may have reported', he goes on, 'I know not. But you must think, whatsoever they have said could be taken where they came but for a dream' (470). And yet at the very end of the text the Father of Salomon's House explicitly sanctions the narrator to report his experiences and the description of the House to the rest of the world. This raises the question of how it can be guaranteed that he will be believed while those before him have not. Thus the reader of the *New Atlantis*, coming to the end of this natural-philosophical fable, is placed in the position of an incredulous European meeting the narrator on his return, challenged to believe the account and yet with a space already opened up for disbelief.

This strategy is both a typical Baconian textual joke and, more importantly I would suggest, a challenge to the reader, another mark of the work's pragmatic imperative. If the reader treats the *New Atlantis* simply as an entertaining fable, or as a model, for discussion, of a perfect society, the text will fail and the reader will have missed a vital opportunity. Instead he or she must have some form of faith in the fable and in the attainability of Bacon's natural-philosophical goals: this is why the island is both strange and familiar, and why the list of inventions from Salomon's House mixes things that have already been achieved in Europe with things that appear impossible. The text refuses the prescriptive modes of political writing, but also turns from the dialogic and ironic strategies offered in More's inaugural utopian work. Instead, it both describes and exemplifies in itself a way of reading and an allegory for the new knowledge, suggesting ways of understanding the past and the future, at the same time as describing the kind of society that would result from Bacon's reforms. The projections into the future were, for Bacon, remarkably successful, with members of the Hartlib circle and the Royal Society at various points in the seventeenth century invoking Salomon's House as a model for their own designs of a natural-philosophical College.[58] As well as offering a blueprint for such a College, however, it is by now clear, I hope, that the *New Atlantis* had far-reaching reforming aims. As an extended reflection on the ethics and the politics of the philosopher's relations with past authorities and present and future readers, and on the vital force of the imagination in attaining a 'true vision', it is unrivalled among Bacon's works.

## Notes

I am very grateful to Markku Peltonen, Lucinda Platt and Quentin Skinner for their comments on this chapter.

1 Francis Bacon, 'The Plan of the Work', in *The Works of Francis Bacon*, ed. James Spedding, Robert Leslie Ellis and Douglas Denon Heath, 14 vols (London, Longman, 1857–74), vol. IV, p. 32, trans. Spedding.

2 On the Atlantis myth, see Plato, *Timaeus* and *Critias*, trans. H. D. P. Lee (Harmondsworth, Penguin, 1971); *Timaeus*, 24–5, pp. 37–8; *Critias*, *passim*.

3 The reference to More's *Utopia* (1516) ('a book of one of your men, of a Feigned Commonwealth') is at p. 478. On the possible influence of Andreae and Campanella, see Eleanor Dickinson Blodgett, 'Bacon's *New Atlantis* and Campanella's *Civitas Solis*: A study in relationships', *Publications of the Modern Language Association of America*, 46:3 (September 1931) 763–80; Michèle Le Doeuff, 'Introduction' to Francis Bacon, *La Nouvelle Atlantide*, trans. Michèle Le Doeuff and Margaret Llasera (Paris, GF Flammarion, 1995), pp. 21–2.

4 See Gabriel Plattes, *A Description of the Famous Kingdome of Macaria* (London, 1641), facsimile reproduction in Charles Webster, *Utopian*

*Planning and the Puritan Revolution. Gabriel Plattes, Samuel Hartlib and MACARIA* (Oxford, Wellcome Unit for the History of Medicine, 1979). Plattes seems to have been especially influenced by the *New Atlantis* in his description of a 'College of Experience', which bears a close resemblance to Salomon's House (sig. B). On Bacon's reception by the Hartlib circle, see Stephen Clucas, 'In search of "The True Logick": methodological eclecticism among the "Baconian reformers"', in Mark Greengrass, Michael Leslie and Timothy Raylor (eds), *Samuel Hartlib and Universal Reformation: Studies in Intellectual Communication* (Cambridge, Cambridge University Press, 1994), pp. 51–74.

5  On Bacon's followers in the mid- and late seventeenth century, see Christopher Hill, *Intellectual Origins of the English Revolution* (Oxford, Clarendon Press, 1965), Chapter III, 'Bacon and the Parliamentarians', pp. 85–130; Charles Webster, *The Great Instauration: Science, Medicine and Reform 1626–1660* (London, Duckworth, 1975); Antonio Pérez-Ramos, *Francis Bacon's Idea of Science and the Maker's Knowledge Tradition* (Oxford, Clarendon Press, 1988), p. 16.

6  Quoted in Brian Vickers (ed.), *Francis Bacon: A Critical Edition of the Major Works* (Oxford, Oxford University Press, 1996), p. 785. References to the *New Atlantis* will be to the edition contained in this volume, pp. 457–89, and will be given parenthetically in the text.

7  See Paolo Rossi, 'Bacon's idea of science', in Markku Peltonen (ed.), *The Cambridge Companion to Bacon* (Cambridge, Cambridge University Press, 1996), pp. 25–46 (p. 34). I am grateful to Markku Peltonen for this point.

8  Even the title New *Atlantis* invites comparison with *Utopia*; cf. More's *De optimo reipublicae statu deque nova insula Utopia libellus vere aureus, nec minus salutaris quam festivus* (my emphases).

9  Aristotle, *The Politics*, ed. Stephen Everson (Cambridge, Cambridge University Press, 1988) VII.1 ($1323^a$), p. 156.

10  See *ibid.*, VII.1–2 ($1323^a$–$1323^b$), pp. 156–7; Aristotle, *Ethics*, trans. H. Rackham (London, Heinemann, 1934) I.iv.1–3 ($1095^a$ 14 ff.), pp. 10–11.

11  See Ian Box, 'Politics and philosophy: Bacon on the values of peace and war', *The Seventeenth Century*, VII:2 (Autumn 1992) 113–27; 121, 115.

12  See, for example, the essay 'Of Simulation and Dissimulation', in Vickers (ed.), *Francis Bacon*, pp. 349–51.

13  Specifically the pursuit of greatness, or *grandezza*; see Markku Peltonen, 'Politics and science: Francis Bacon and the true greatness of states', *Historical Journal*, 35:2 (1992) 279–305; Peltonen, *Classical Humanism and Republicanism in English Political Thought 1570–1640* (Cambridge, Cambridge University Press, 1995), Chapter 4, 'Francis Bacon, Thomas Hedley and the true greatness of Britain', pp. 190–228; p. 195.

14  See Peltonen, 'Politics and Science', pp. 279–82; David Colclough, '"Of the alleadging of authors": the construction and reception of textual authority in English prose, c. 1600–1630' (unpublished D.Phil. dissertation, University of Oxford, 1996), pp. 53–4.

15 B. H. G. Wormald sees what he identifies as the project of the Great Instauration and Bacon's 'grand strategy' in policy as 'at the very least organically connected' (*Francis Bacon: History, Politics and Science 1561–1626* (Cambridge, Cambridge University Press, 1993), p. 8 *et passim*); while Julian Martin argues that Bacon's intellectual enterprise is primarily a political one, and that his reformation of the grounds of natural philosophy is part of a wider attempt to render the production of knowledge part of the provenance of the state (*Francis Bacon, the State, and the Reform of Natural Philosophy* (Cambridge, Cambridge University Press, 1992), *passim*). In *The Advancement of Learning*, however, Bacon writes that 'the proofs and persuasions of rhetoric ought to differ according to the auditors' (Francis Bacon, *The Advancement of Learning*, in Vickers (ed.), *Francis Bacon*, Book II, p. 239). See also Lisa Jardine, *Francis Bacon: Discovery and the Art of Discourse* (Cambridge, Cambridge University Press, 1974), p. 173; Peltonen, 'Politics and science', pp. 303–5; Colclough, '"Of the alleadging of authors"', pp. 50 4.

16 See Peltonen, 'Politics and science', pp. 294–6.

17 On the importance of religious toleration to Bacon's natural philosophy in general and to the *New Atlantis* in particular, see Le Doeuff, 'Introduction' to Bacon, *La Nouvelle Atlantide*, pp. 30–5. Le Doeuff notes that '*La Nouvelle Atlantide* est donc strictement oecuménique, et s'écrit sur la base de la plus large concorde judéo-chrétienne qu'on ait imaginée à l'époque' (p. 32).

18 A glance at Vickers' notes conveys the density of Scriptural reference in the text. For further explication of some allusions, see Elizabeth McCutcheon, 'Bacon and the cherubim: an iconographical reading of the *New Atlantis*', *English Literary Renaissance*, 2.3 (Autumn 1972) 334 55.

19 The Governor of the Strangers' House remarks that Solamona found himself 'to symbolize in many things with that king of the Hebrews (which lived many years before him)' (471).

20 In the *Commentarius solutus*, notebooks from 1608, Bacon writes of 'foundac[ion]. of a college for Inventors past and spaces or Bases for Inventors to come And a Library and an Inginary', going on to outline some of the administrative details that would be involved in running such an institution, including 'qu. of the Maner and praescripts touching Secrecy, tradition, and publication'. He also amasses a heterogeneous list of potential participants, including the Earl of Northumberland, Sir Walter Ralegh, Thomas Hariot, Archbishop Bancroft, Lancelot Andrewes and Prince Henry (two of whom were imprisoned in the Tower of London on treason charges at the time that Bacon was writing); another instance of his willingness to cross serious political and religious divides in the cause of natural philosophy (*Works*, vol. XI, p. 66). For examples of later attempts to fulfil Bacon's dream, and of the potency of Salomon's House as a model, see Michael Hunter and Paul B. Wood, 'Towards Solomon's House: rival strategies for reforming the early Royal Society', *History of Science*, 24 (1986) 49–108.

21  See Rose-Mary Sargent, 'Bacon as an advocate for cooperative scientific research', in Peltonen (ed.), *The Cambridge Companion to Bacon*, pp. 146–71. There were eleven Italian translations of the *Essays* between 1617 and 1626, and four in French between 1619 and 1622; *De sapientia veterum*, originally published in Latin in 1609, went through three editions between 1619 and 1622 in English, while a French version appeared in 1619; the expanded Latin *Advancement of Learning*, the *De augmentis scientarium*, was first published in 1623, while a French collection of Bacon's *Oeuvres morales et politiques* was published in 1626. See R. W. Gibson, *Francis Bacon: A Bibliography of his Works and of Baconiana to the Year 1750* (Oxford, Scrivener Press, 1950) and Gibson, *Supplement* (privately issued typescript, 1959). On French translations of Bacon, see Michèle Le Doeuff, 'Bacon chez les Grands au siècle de Louis XIII', in Marta Fattori (ed.), *Francis Bacon. Terminologia e fortuna nel XVII secolo* (Rome, Edizione dell'Ateneo, 1984), pp. 155–78.

22  See, for instance, Amy Boesky, 'Bacon's *New Atlantis* and the laboratory of prose', in Elizabeth Fowler and Roland Greene (eds), *The Project of Prose in Early Modern Europe and the New World* (Cambridge, Cambridge University Press, 1997), pp. 138–53.

23  Charles Whitney, 'Merchants of Light: science as colonization in the *New Atlantis*', in William A. Sessions (ed.), *Francis Bacon's Legacy of Texts: 'The Art of Discovery Grows with Discovery'* (New York, AMS Press, 1990), pp. 255–68; p. 256. So determined is Whitney to read the *New Atlantis* into a transhistorical colonialist narrative that he appears insensitive to anachronisms such as the notion of a seventeenth-century 'British' 'empire'.

24  Whitney, 'Merchants of Light', p. 257. Boesky, 'Bacon's *New Atlantis*', also links the *New Atlantis* with colonialism, suggesting (unconvincingly to my mind) a conjunction between 'scientific and imperial goals [. . .] in the Baconian program' (p. 141).

25  Whitney, 'Merchants of Light', for example, writes, 'secrecy, one infers, must ensure ridiculously low prices for "light," since the sellers do not know the value of their products' (p. 258).

26  See Paolo Rossi, *Francis Bacon: From Magic to Science*, trans. Sacha Rabinovitch (London, Routledge and Kegan Paul, 1968), p. 12. See further David Colclough, '"Non canimus surdis, respondent omnia sylvae": Francis Bacon and the transmission of knowledge', in Philippa Berry and Margaret Tudeau-Clayton (eds), *The Texture of Renaissance Knowledge* (Palgrave, forthcoming).

27  A development of the Horatian bee topos; see Horace, *Odes* IV:4, ll. 27–32, in Horace, *Odes and Epodes*, trans. C. E. Bennett (London, Heinemann, 1927), p. 288. See further Jürgen von Stackelberg, 'Das Bienengleichnis', *Romanische Forschungen*, 68 (1956) 271–93. On other uses of the incorporation topos by early-modern writers, see Terence Cave, *The Cornucopian Text: problems of writing in the French renaissance* (Oxford, Clarendon Press, 1979), p. 37.

28  See Le Doeuff, 'Introduction' to Bacon, *La Nouvelle Atlantide*: 'l'identité personelle [. . .] est absente du texte [. . . .] il n'ya pas de sujet connaissant' (p. 62).

29  See J. C. Davis, 'Utopianism', in J. H. Burns (ed.), with the assistance of Mark Goldie, *The Cambridge History of Political Thought, 1450–1700* (Cambridge, Cambridge University Press, 1991), pp. 329–44; p. 343.

30  The doctrine of the Idols appears for the first time in *Valerius Terminus of the Interpretation of Nature* (Bacon, *Works*, vol. III, p. 242), and in *Temporis Partus Masculus* the term 'idolum' appears sixteen times. See Didier Deleule, introduction to Francis Bacon, *Récusation des doctrines philosophiques et autres opuscules*, trans. Georges Rombi and Didier Deleule, ed. Didier Deleule (Paris, Presses Universitaires de France, 1987), p. 11. The doctrine appears most famously in the *Novum Organum*, in Bacon, *Works*, vol. IV, pp. 53–68.

31  *Temporis partus masculus*, in Benjamin Farrington, *The Philosophy of Francis Bacon: An Essay on its Development from 1603 to 1609 with new translations of fundamental texts* (Liverpool, Liverpool University Press, 1964), p. 62.

32  Farrington, *The Philosophy of Francis Bacon*, p. 72.

33  'In tabulis nisi priora deliveris, non alia inscripseris. In mente contra: nisi alia inscripseris, non priora deliveris' (*Temporis partus masculus*, in Bacon, *Works*, vol. III, p. 539). In this and the following passage I have substituted my own translation for that of Farrington in order to emphasise their very close similarity and to attempt to replicate Bacon's rather complex use of tenses, both of which are obscured by Farrington.

34  'Sane in tabellis non alia inscripseris, nisi priora deliveris; in mente aegre priora deliveris, nisi alia inscripseris' (*Redargutio philosophiarum*, in Bacon, *Works*, vol. III, p. 558).

35  As is displayed by his use of the term 'instauration' (renewal or repetition) for his project.

36  Bacon, *Works*, vol. IV, pp. 26–7.

37  See Aldous Huxley, *Island* (London, Chatto & Windus, 1962), *passim*.

38  Farrington, *The Philosophy of Francis Bacon*, p. 133. Cf. Plato's description of the painful dazzlement of the cave-dwellers if they were exposed to direct light; *Republic* VII.vii, 515d.

39  See Bacon, *Novum Organum*, aphorism LXVIII, in *Works*, vol. IV, p. 69. On Bacon's refusal to give the sailors a nationality, see Le Doeuff, 'Introduction' to Bacon, *La Nouvelle Atlantide*, p. 40. This authorial diffidence has not prevented critics from declaring them to be either English or Spanish. See Blodgett, 'Bacon's *New Atlantis* and Campanella's *Civitas Solis*' 767 (English); Denise Albanese, 'The *New Atlantis* and the uses of utopia', *English Literary History*, 57 (1990) 503–28; 508 (Spanish). With typical sagacity, Michèle Le Doeuff and Margaret Llasera note the implication of the sailors' vulnerability and ignorance, pointing out that they are 'à la fois enfants et lecteurs, au total écoliers' (Michèle Le Doeuff and Margaret Llasera, 'Voyage dans la Pensée Baroque', in Francis Bacon, *La Nouvelle*

*Atlantide*, trans. Michèle Le Doeuff and Margaret Llasera (Paris, Payot, 1983), p. 95).

40 In the *Novum Organum*, Bacon outlines the importance of making the kind of natural-philosophical wish-list that the Father's description includes and with which the *New Atlantis* concludes (in the section headed 'magnalia naturae, praecipue quoad usus humanos'): 'in the work itself of interpretation in each particular subject, I always assign a place to the *Human Chart*, or *Chart of things to be wished for*. For to form judicious wishes is as much a part of knowledge as to ask judicious questions' (aphorism XLIX; *Works*, vol. IV, p. 233).

41 Aristotle, *The Politics*, II.6, p. 30; cf. VII.4, p. 162.

42 Bacon, *Works*, vol. IV, p. 57.

43 On the apocalyptic influence, see Brian Vickers' headnote to the *New Atlantis* in *Francis Bacon*, ed. Vickers, p. 786.

44 On Bacon as a conservative reformer in the *New Atlantis*, see Sharon Achinstein, 'How to be a progressive without looking like one: history and knowledge in Bacon's *New Atlantis*', *CLIO*, 17:3 (Spring 1988) 249–64, which offers an astute analysis only vitiated by its treatment of the text as openly utopian and as a 'summary of Bacon's political teaching' (250).

45 On the topos of the discovery of islands as providing a counter to the notion that all is known, see Le Doeuff, 'Introduction' to Bacon, *La Nouvelle Atlantide*, p. 49.

46 The Vulgate version is 'plurimi pertransibunt et multiplex erit scientia'. See also *Redargutio philosophiarum*, in Farrington, *The Philosophy of Francis Bacon*, p. 132. In a perhaps unintentionally ironic reflection on the mutual dependence of individual research, collective scholarship and extensive financial patronage, this phrase is quoted on the benefactors' plaque in the Bodleian Library, that 'ark of learning' praised by Bacon in letters to his friend. On patronage versus collective action in Bacon, see Le Doeuff, 'Introduction' to Bacon, *La Nouvelle Atlantide*, pp. 19–21.

47 Michèle Le Doeuff notes this important topos, also linking it with Bacon's reformism: 'on remarquera [. . .] que tout y est "comme en Europe" ou "comme chez nous", au degré de perfection près' (Le Doeuff, 'Introduction' to Bacon, *La Nouvelle Atlantide*, p. 54).

48 Brian Vickers, 'Bacon's so-called "utilitarianism": sources and influence', in Fattori (ed.), *Francis Bacon. Terminologia e fortuna*, pp. 281–313; p. 313. For Bacon's praise of the active life, see Peltonen, *Classical Humanism*, pp. 139–45.

49 Aphorism CXVI: Bacon, *Works*, vol. IV, p. 104; *Works*, vol. XIV, p. 539.

50 See, most recently, Perez Zagorin, *Francis Bacon* (Princeton, Princeton University Press, 1998).

51 Bacon, *Works*, vol. X, p. 87.

52 The *New Atlantis* was only printed posthumously, but I assume here that some circulation was intended by Bacon, whether in manuscript or print.

53  Farrington, *The Philosophy of Francis Bacon*, p. 104.

54  *Ibid.*, p. 105.

55  *Ibid.*, p. 133.

56  *Ibid.*, p. 105.

57  See 'Cassandra, siue parrhesia', in Francis Bacon, *De sapientia veterum* (London, 1609), sigs. B-B2; cf. Francis Bacon, *The Wisedome of the Ancients*, trans. Sir Arthur Gorges (London, 1619), sigs. A-A2$^{v}$.

58  Joseph Glanvill, *Scepsis Scientifica* (London, 1665), declares openly that '*Solomon's House*, in the NEW ATLANTIS, was a Prophetick Scheam of the ROYAL SOCIETY' (sig. c); see Vickers' headnote in Vickers (ed.), *Francis Bacon*, pp. 788–9. See also Hunter and Wood, 'Towards Solomon's House', *passim*.

# 5

# Natural knowledge in
the *New Atlantis*

## RICHARD SERJEANTSON

> The End of our Foundation is the knowledge of Causes, and secret
> motions of things; and the enlarging of the bounds of Human
> Empire, to the effecting of all things possible.
>
> And amongst them we have a water which we call Water of Para-
> dise, being, by that we do to it, made very sovereign for health,
> and prolongation of life.[1]

## Francis Bacon and early modern 'science'

At the heart of Francis Bacon's *New Atlantis* there is an institution for the systematic pursuit of something that it is very tempt-
ing to call 'science'. In Salomon's House there are instruments for
generating heat and sound, 'engine-houses' for producing motion,
and 'perspective-houses' for demonstrating the effects of light.
There are also 'shops' for making medicines, 'parks and inclo-
sures' for observing and experimenting upon animals, orchards
and gardens for cultivating crops, and 'bake-houses and kitchens'
for making food and drink 'of special effects' (480–6). And
finally, Salomon's House has a permanent staff of fellows who
carry out various specialised tasks, almost all of which involve
'experiments' in some way (486–7). The purpose of the institution is to produce knowledge (480); the kind of knowledge
sought is, without exception, the knowledge of nature.

If Francis Bacon is famous for anything, it is for a singular concern with natural science. In a series of works, Bacon lambasted

his contemporaries for their ignorance and complacency about the natural world, and proposed a series of increasingly bold plans to remedy the situation. In his grand encyclopaedia of human ignorance, *The Advancement of Learning* (1605), he anatomised the failings in the contemporary human understanding of the natural, human and divine worlds. As part of his vastly ambitious (and largely unfinished) programme of 'Great Renewal' (*Instauratio magna*), he elaborated in the *New Instrument* (*Novum Organum*) of 1620 a general procedure for systematically investigating the natural world. And in the *Sylva Sylvarum* Bacon discussed a thousand different experiments on the natural world that he had either read about or done himself.

These and other works laid the foundation of Bacon's reputation. He was widely celebrated after his death for the power of his message about the importance of studying the natural world. From the middle years of the seventeenth century in England, through the eighteenth-century French *encyclopédistes* and nineteenth-century English Baconians like William Whewell, to twentieth-century scholarship, Bacon has been held up – with good cause – as one of the pre-eminent intellectual patrons of natural science.[2] The *New Atlantis* is an important document in this reception history, for it was often reprinted, was widely read, and indeed was sometimes even continued by other writers keen to exploit its ambitious, optimistic, but ultimately unfinished qualities.

Is 'science' in fact the best word, though, to describe Bacon's interests? It is certainly a convenient label, a useful shorthand that seems to cover in one term the whole range of the activities pursued in Salomon's House in the *New Atlantis*. But it is also an anachronistic word. 'Science', in the modern sense, did not exist when Bacon was writing: the categories of 'science' and the 'scientist' are creations of the nineteenth, not of the seventeenth century.[3] Scholars in the past (even the recent past) have perhaps been a little too quick to see Bacon as a 'modern scientist', and indeed even to see the *New Atlantis* as a key text in 'the emergence of modern scientific practices from within late Renaissance culture'.[4] In order to avoid the problems with thinking of Bacon as someone who was writing about 'science', I prefer to talk in this essay about 'natural knowledge'. This, as it happens, is a fair enough translation of the Renaissance Latin term *scientia naturalis*.

But it is also a good broad historical category for thinking about all the other ways in which the natural world was understood in the early seventeenth century – some of which are rather a long way from modern 'science'.

The reason we should be wary of looking at Bacon through modern conceptual spectacles is this: if we are too quick to call the concerns of the *New Atlantis* 'science', we may miss the significance of what is actually happening in the work. If we concentrate on Bacon in his capacity as a prophet of modern science, we may miss the importance of the medieval and Renaissance traditions of natural knowledge that suffuse his works. Indeed, this issue has produced polarised views about the *New Atlantis*. According to some writers, Bacon actually foresaw the industrial revolution – and all its problems – in his 'prophecy of modern science'.[5] *Per contra* – according to Rosalie Colie – Bacon in fact took all of the 'tricks' in the *New Atlantis* from 'late medieval and Renaissance compendia of the natural sciences'.[6] We do not need to endorse the idea that Bacon had especially prophetic powers about the course of subsequent history. But we can nonetheless see that it might be possible both for him to have derived the ideas in Salomon's House from contemporary forms of natural knowledge, and then to have turned these materials into things quite novel and different. Later on in this essay, I shall show how this is so in the case of two forms of natural knowledge that Bacon takes up and develops in the *New Atlantis*: natural magic, and medicine.

## The works of nature

We should begin, however, by surveying the range of natural knowledge evident in Salomon's House and assessing its significance. In his introduction to the *New Atlantis*, which he published after Bacon's death, Bacon's chaplain William Rawley described the purpose of the *New Atlantis* as 'the producing of great and marvellous works for the benefit of men' (785). The term 'works' holds the key to understanding the natural knowledge of the *New Atlantis*. The pursuits in Salomon's House are practical, not theoretical. Its experiments aim to do things to the natural world: to change it and to use it, not just to observe and understand it. Its fellows pride themselves on finding out about all the 'manufactures, and inventions' of the world, as much as they do about finding out about its 'sciences, [and] arts' (471).

This emphasis on practical knowledge – on making and doing as the best means of understanding the world – was central to Bacon's philosophy of science.[7] It lay behind his scathing critique of the contemporary natural philosophy that he thought he found in the universities of late Renaissance Europe. This natural philosophy was a contemplative science; it sought knowledge of universal causes, rather than particular effects. It emphasised generalised 'experience' over particular 'experiment'.[8] Even worse, to Bacon's mind, was that its preferred form of argument was the syllogism: this, he complained in the *Instauratio magna*, 'lets nature slip out of its hands'.[9] Instead, Bacon advocated understanding nature through its works. In the *Novum Organum* he listed the kinds of people who actually tackled nature in this way: mechanics, mathematical practitioners, medical doctors, alchemists, and magicians. But none of them, according to Bacon, had either tried very hard, or achieved very much.[10]

Nonetheless, ideas from all of these occupations inform the *New Atlantis*. And for the past fifty years or so, scholars have tried to understand some of the ways in which this is so. Rosalie Colie, in particular, showed beautifully how some of the inventions of the *New Atlantis* were well known in early seventeenth-century London. She explains how several of the experiments in the *New Atlantis* are reminiscent of the marvels exhibited to the court of King James I by the Dutch inventor Cornelis Drebbel. Like the experimenters of Salomon's House who use sunken caves for 'coagulations, indurations, refrigerations, and conservations of bodies' (480), Drebbel engaged in demonstrations involving heat and cold. He managed to chill the Great Hall at Westminster so thoroughly that it drove the King and his retinue away. He even built a remarkable submersible vessel in which he descended beneath the Thames for three hours in 1620, in front of an audience that included James I and also the Dutch visitor Constantijn Huygens, who wrote a vivid account of the occasion. Bacon must have heard of this technological triumph – he was perhaps even present on the occasion – by the time he had the Father of Salomon's House state laconically that 'we have ships and boats for going under water' (486).[11]

J. Peter Zetterberg developed Colie's study by discussing some English works that described artificial curiosities and wonders: books like William Bourne's *Inventions and Devises* (1578) and Thomas Tymme's *A Dialogue Philosophicall* (1612), which partially translates Drebbel. Zetterberg emphasises the ways in which Bacon's *New Atlantis* picks up on a large literature – and a substantial body of practice – about ways of making art imitate nature.[12] This is an important insight into the significance of some of the activities of Bacon's contemporaries for the *New Atlantis*. But we should also not forget that the purpose of Salomon's House is 'enlarging the bounds of Human Empire'. Bacon is interested in more than imitating nature: he wants to 'conquer' it as well.[13]

Penelope Gouk, too, has argued that court masques – elaborate one-off dramatic entertainments performed before the King – provided a model for the 'sound-houses' described in the *New Atlantis*. And she goes on to observe that Bacon's claims for what could be achieved in them were not fanciful, but rather 'embodied the achievements of contemporary musicians, artisans and engineers'. These achievements included producing sounds by means of air and water, after the manner of the ancient Greek mathematician Hero of Alexandria or – a more proximate model – Salomon de Caus.[14] In the same way, the fellows of Salomon's House 'represent and imitate all articulate sounds and letters, and the voices and notes of beasts and birds' (485). Other early modern natural philosophers were also interested in the relations between musical instruments, the language of animals, and human speech, and Bacon himself elsewhere discusses the possibility of artificially imitating human voices.[15] The preoccupations of the *New Atlantis* are quite characteristic, in fact, of the widespread Renaissance quest to uncover the 'secrets of nature'. Indeed, one historian of this quest has suggested that a reason for the popularity of the *New Atlantis* in the seventeenth century was that it picks up to such a degree on the practical experimentalism in these 'books of secrets'.[16]

We should not imagine, however, that natural knowledge, for Bacon or his Bensalemites, is merely for human utility.[17] It has at its heart a very much higher purpose: one that is suggested by the Governor of the Strangers' House when he explains that

Salomon's House is dedicated 'to the study of the Works and Creatures of God' (471). By studying nature, Bacon suggests, the inhabitants of the New Atlantis are also honouring the Creator. The Governor explains that 'in ancient records' Salomon's House is sometimes also called 'the College of the Six Days Works' – after the six days of creation described at the beginning of the Book of Genesis. Pre-modern treatises of natural knowledge are sometimes even organised according to a 'hexameral' schema derived from the events of each of the six days.[18] It was common-place in the sixteenth and seventeenth centuries to speak of the two books of God: the Bible as the Book of Revelation, and the world as the Book of Nature. The existence of God could be read from both, and it was the task of natural philosophy to under-stand the second book, as it was that of theology to understand the first.[19] In this way, then, the 'science' of the New Atlantis is also a kind of divine worship and, quite explicitly, a means of human betterment in repairing the damage caused by the Fall from Paradise – a Fall brought about by the same Adam and Eve whose pools are used to establish the physical health of pros-pective marriage partners in Bensalem (478).[20]

## Natural magic

The 'works' of nature, then, were studied in the Renaissance in many different ways and for many different purposes. But there is one tradition of natural knowledge that the New Atlantis perhaps owes more to than any other: natural magic. It is impor-tant to realise that what was called natural magic in the Renais-sance is a long way from what might now be understood as magic. The modern understanding of magic is closer to what in the Renaissance was called spiritual and demonic magic. This kind of magic invoked spirits to perform feats – often nefarious ones – that were 'against nature'.[21] Natural magic was quite different. As its name suggests, it was concerned exclusively with natural, not with supernatural effects. Its proponents often described it as the 'active' part of natural knowledge, because it performed marvellous effects that could not be explained by human reason. They could not be explained because they were hidden or, in early modern terms, 'occult'. Natural magic had some fairly esoteric theoretical justifications involving occult sympathies between disparate objects – which Bacon rejected.[22] In practice, though, natural magic was mostly concerned with producing wonderful, and in the terms of Renaissance natural philosophy, inexplicable, effects. And on account of its practical inclination, writers on natural magic sometimes described it as the 'pinnacle' of the natural sciences.[23]

Bacon was well acquainted with late Renaissance works on natural magic, and in particular with one of the most important of these, the *Natural Magic* (*Magia naturalis*, 1558, 1589) of the Neapolitan magus Giovan Battista della Porta. Scholars have long known that many of the experiments in Bacon's main work of natural history, the *Sylva Sylvarum*, are developed from those in della Porta, although in the final version of the work Bacon never deigns to mention the Italian by name.[24] It is less often pointed out how many of Bacon's preoccupations in the *New Atlantis* are also staples of the natural magic tradition.[25] Thus the fellows busy themselves not only in experimenting upon animals, but also breeding them to 'make them greater or taller' and 'more fruitful and bearing than their kind is' (482); experiments and tips for breeding fill the second book of della Porta's *Natural Magic*. Likewise, della Porta deals (in book eleven) with making perfumes and producing smells – just as they do in Salomon's House (485). Other interests, such as processes of distillation, were shared by Bacon, della Porta (book ten) and numerous other practical writers (484).

In fact, it is Bacon himself who establishes explicitly the association between his own interests and the tradition of natural magic. In the course of an experiment on how to change the colour of bird feathers in the *Sylva Sylvarum*, Bacon makes the remarkable claim that the *Sylva* is, 'to speak properly', not just natural history but 'a high kind of natural magic': 'For it is not a description of nature only, but a breaking of nature into great and strange works'.[26] This description would serve even more appropriately for the *New Atlantis*.

Bacon's interest in the tricks and striking effects of the natural magic tradition brought with it a problem, however. Many of these experiments were specifically intended to baffle and amaze those who saw them. It was this meretricious marvellousness that encouraged both fascination with and hostility to natural magic and wonders of all kinds in the Renaissance.[27] It also meant that the problem of separating true miracles from false ones became a recurrent preoccupation of writers in the period. A common justification for studying natural philosophy and the mathematical sciences was that they helped 'discover impostures, and false miracles'.[28] Bacon felt this problem particularly strongly, as becomes clear from the *New Atlantis*. The very last experiments the Father of Salomon's House mentions are those carried out in the 'houses of deceits of the senses; where we represent all manner of feats of juggling, false apparitions, impostures and illusions'. He observes that they know how to accomplish so many things which 'induce admiration' that they could easily be put to bad uses. 'But we do hate all impostures and lies,' he goes on, which is why the fellows are sworn to exhibit their natural knowledge 'without all affectation of strangeness' (486).

In fact, Bacon has already illustrated this concern with distinguishing true from false miracles earlier on in the *New Atlantis*. We learn from the Governor of the Strangers' House that 'about twenty years after the ascension of our Saviour', the Bensalemites received the Bible in a cedar chest hidden in a great pillar of light out at sea. There was much 'wonder' among the people of the city of Renfusa at this 'marvellous sight'. But the person who decides that it is 'a true Miracle' is one of the fellows of Salomon's House, to whom it has been given 'to know thy [God's] works of creation, ... and to discern ... between divine miracles, works of nature, works of art, and impostures and illusions of all sorts'. After he has 'devoutly viewed and contemplated this pillar', this fellow is able to know that it is indeed a miracle and not a work of magic – or worse (464). The people of Bensalem become Christians because of their excellent understanding of nature; they are, in short, consummate natural theologians.[29]

## Medicine and hygiene

The inhabitants of Bensalem, however, do not belabour their study of the Creator through his works. They are more immediately concerned with merely human means of bettering their lot. In this, they reflect Bacon's preoccupations, and in one respect

especially: their cultivation of the art of medicine. As he grew
older, Bacon became increasingly concerned with ways of
escaping, or at least delaying, the clutches of mortality, and his
interest in medical questions correspondingly grew. The section
on medicine in the later Latin version of *The Advancement of
Learning* (*De augmentis scientiarum*, 1623) is substantially enlarged
from the English version of eighteen years before (1605). Bacon
also wrote at length elsewhere on matters of health, sickness and
nutrition, mostly in his late natural histories: the *Sylva Sylvarum*,
and the *History of Life and Death* (*Historia vitae et mortis*, 1623).
These medical issues are a vital – but rather neglected – aspect of
Bacon's interest in nature.[30] Moreover, his growing preoccupation with medicine emerges strongly in the late *New Atlantis*.
The work as a whole manifests a deep interest in the central
questions of Renaissance medicine: how to cure disease, how to
preserve health, and – in particular – how to prolong life.

The importance of medicine and health for the *New Atlantis*
is indicated throughout the work. The European visitors'
exposure to the food, drink, and medicine of Bensalem is the
most important way in which they appreciate their hosts' power
over the natural world before the Father of Salomon's House
finally begins his discourse. The only reason, in fact, that the
visitors are allowed to land on Bensalem in the first place is that
their sick 'were many, and in very ill case' (458). Despite – or
rather because of – the charity the Bensalemites extend to the
Europeans, they also show an extreme consciousness of the
dangers of disease. The 'great person' who asks whether the
visitors are Christians maintains a safe distance from the ship on
the instructions of the city's Conservator of Health (an office
found in Renaissance Italy, if not perhaps early modern London).[31]
The notary who comes aboard the Europeans' ship uses an orange-
like fruit '(as it seemeth) for a preservative against infection' (459) –
infection theories of disease were a recurrent preoccupation at
the time.[32] We hear about this fruit again later on, when the
Europeans are told that it is 'an assured remedy for sickness
taken at sea'. The Bensalemites have an excellent understanding
of nursing and medicine. The infirmary is well maintained; the
Europeans are dispensed 'small grey or whitish' pills to hasten
their recovery (461). The regime of the Strangers' House is so

successful that in just three days the European visitors express 'joy of the amendment of our sick'. Indeed, so well do they become, and so quickly, that they imagine themselves 'cast into some divine pool of healing' – the sort of pool, in fact, that we subsequently learn the Bensalemites actually have (462, 482).

When we come to hear about Salomon's House proper, medical arts and instruments become even more prominent. In the Chambers of Health, the air is regulated to allow both for the 'cure of divers diseases' and for the 'preservation of health' (481). There are baths which are used 'for the cure of diseases, and the restoring of man's body' (482). Many of the plants cultivated in Bensalem's gardens are not just larger and tastier than their European counterparts, but are also of 'medicinal use' – such as, presumably, the fruitarian antidote to sea-sickness (482). There are foods that can sustain long fasts or endow bodies with a hardness or strength far beyond the normal (483). The medicine shops of Bensalem exploit the full extent of the island's rich flora and fauna to produce a much 'greater variety' of medicines than 'you have in Europe' (483).[33] And Salomon's House even has those 'healing pools' which – if not divine – are certainly efficacious 'for the cure of diseases, and the restoring of man's body from arefaction [i.e. desiccation]: and ... for the confirming of it in strength of sinews, vital parts, and the very juice and substance of the body' (482). Moreover, there are also less therapeutic investigations into physiology: the fellows 'find many strange effects' in living animals, such as keeping them alive even after various parts that European physicians take to be necessary to life have been removed (482).[34]

Many of these instances have their counterpart in Renaissance medical theories and practices. The composition of the air was indeed thought to be vital to both disease and cure.[35] Balneology (bathing) had become an important form of medical research and practice by the late Renaissance, although typically Bacon thought it was not pursued thoroughly enough.[36] The medical use of plants, and their cultivation in 'physic gardens', was practically universal by the later sixteenth century. Moreover, the New World had become an important source of new and powerful medical ingredients (*materia medica*) that had been unknown to the Renaissance's ancient authorities, such as

Dioscorides. Finally, Bacon's interest in moving beyond gross anatomy to more profound physiological enquiry is paralleled by developments in later sixteenth- and earlier seventeenth-century medical research.[37]

But the area of medicine that Bacon develops most thoroughly in the *New Atlantis* is the realm of hygiene. Medicine in the Renaissance was often divided into two broad parts: the cure of disease – therapy – and the prevention of disease – hygiene. Unlike the various forms of therapy, hygiene dealt with ways of preserving health and prolonging life, rather than with dealing with diseases after they had appeared.[38] Hygiene was the part of medicine that Bacon prized above all: he complained more than once in his later writings that modern physicians needlessly restricted themselves to 'humble cures', and so were 'honoured for necessity only'. Instead of this, he said, they should seek a nobler goal: not just curing diseases, but actively preventing them.[39]

In the Renaissance, one of the most important means of preventing disease was held to be diet. Many works were written that discussed the kinds of food useful for maintaining health, from the first book on ageing – Gabriele de Zerbi's *Care of the Old* (*Gerontocomia*, 1489) – to Tobias Venner's treatise on the health value of the different kinds of English food: the *Right Road to a Long Life* (*Via recta ad vitam longam*, 1622).[40] Bacon's Bensalemites, too, are much occupied by questions of diet. As well as orchards and fields, they have 'brewhouses, bake-houses, and kitchens', where they make drinks, breads, and foods that are 'rare and of special effects' (483). And the effects that the Father of Salomon's House describes are indeed remarkable: their drinks last for many years, and even replace solid food. Other drinks, extraordinarily, are so refined they can pass through the hand. They have breads baked with fish and meat that can of themselves provide enough nourishment for life – indeed, for a 'very long' life. And the food in the Strangers' House, as well as being good, is also varied and healthful; the drink, in particular, is 'wonderful pleasing and refreshing' (461) – in sharp contrast to the dirty water and tepid 'small beer' that was the usual fare of most people in early modern England.[41]

## The prolongation of life

The food and drink of Salomon's House are good at preserving health.[42] But they are even better at achieving the other abiding goal of early modern medical hygiene: the prolongation of life. It is not too strong to say that, by the time he came to write the *New Atlantis*, Bacon had become obsessed by the problem of how to extend human life. He read widely in earlier literature on the subject, from Arnold of Villanova in the middle ages to Alvise Cornaro's immensely popular *Treatise on the sober life* (*Trattato de la vita sobria*, 1558).[43] Bacon collected a set of medical recipes with the title 'The Grains of Youth'; one of them is for 'Methusalem water'.[44] Much of the manuscript treatise *De vijs mortis* ('On the Ways of Death', written in the 1610s), and the later *History of Life and Death* are devoted to the question of the prolongation of life.[45] Bacon added a substantial discussion of the failings of previous ideas about increasing human longevity to the Latin version of *The Advancement of Learning*, that has no precursor in the English text.[46] As if to remind us how important it is for the *New Atlantis*, 'The prolongation of life' is the very first of the 'Wonderful works of nature' (*Magnalia naturae*) that are listed at the end of that work (488). So important did Bacon find the question of prolongation, in fact, that he assigned a whole department of medicine to the question, noting that it was 'new, and deficient; and the noblest of all'.[47]

The Bensalemites of the *New Atlantis* are not deficient in ways of extending life. The experiments in Salomon's House return repeatedly to the issue. Among the first things we hear about it is that they use caverns 'for prolongation of life in some hermits that choose to live there', and who 'indeed live very long' (480). There is the bread which, as well as being able to sustain life 'without any other meat', also allows its eaters to 'live very long' (483). The Father of Salomon's House even speaks of 'a water, which we call Water of Paradise, being by that we do to it made very sovereign for health and prolongation of life' (481).

Despite his own claims for it, however, it is hard to see Bacon's preoccupation with the prolongation of life as the 'new science', the terms in which so many commentators like to describe his interests. The Bensalemites' 'Water of Paradise', in fact, tastes

suspiciously like Old World wine in New Atlantan bottles. Far
from being a new pursuit, the quest for prolongation was as old
as medieval alchemy, and several authors in that tradition had
even discussed the possibility of an 'Elixir of Life' that would
allow those who drank it vastly to extend their normal span.[48]
Frequent suggestions were made about ingredients that might
lengthen life, among the most common of which were 'potable
gold' and precious stones. Bacon was not as scornful of these
suggestions as he was about other suggested ingredients –
ambergris, vipers' flesh, stag marrow and 'the fume of youth'
breathed from a young virgin.[49] He was a little more respectful of
other theories based on the existence of a 'radical moisture'
which dried up in the course of life and caused death when it was
exhausted – but not much.[50] During the Renaissance, efforts to
achieve the prolongation of life intensified.[51] One of the best-
known accounts was offered by the Italian neoplatonist Marsilio
Ficino, in the second of his *Three Books on Life* (*De vita triplici*,
1489). Among Ficino's many recommendations was that old men
might restore their strength by sucking blood from the arm of a
'willing, happy, healthy, temperate' youth. Bacon knew this
suggestion well – and rejected it, twice.[52] He also rejected an idea
developed by a follower of the medical radical, Paracelsus (1493–
1541), who proposed that if we could somehow absorb the 'spirit'
of living creatures, we would become immortal.[53]

Thus Bacon's concern in the *New Atlantis* with food and
drink as a means of prolongation is quite consistent with his
comment in the *History of Life and Death* that properly prepared
food and drink is much more important for preserving life than
earlier physicians' 'fables' about ingesting gold or precious
stones. Of the pretensions of astrologers to determine length of
life by the stars, he was frankly scornful. Like Alvise Cornaro,
although not to the same degree as him, Bacon considered diet,
not elixirs or infusions, to be the key to long life. 'The curing of
diseases', he wrote, 'is done by temporary medicines; but the prolongation of life must be sought through diets'.[54]

Despite his acquaintance with earlier writings on prolongation, however, Bacon had little time for their recommendations.
In a typically inflated statement of his own novelty, he claimed to
be the first to discuss the question of the prolongation of life

solely as an aspect of medicine.[55] Of other traditional determin-
ants of longevity – sufficient sleep, or sexual moderation – Bacon
had little to say. But we can find other elements in the *New
Atlantis* that we know he believed conduced to longevity. He
thought a religious life, perhaps like that lived by the hermits,
was good (480). He thought island-dwellers lived longer than
those on continents: Bensalem is an island, albeit a large one
(469). He collected stories showing that cave-dwellers – like the
hermits who live in the caverns of the Lower Regions (480–1) –
regularly reached great ages. And, in good Baconian fashion,
Bacon thought he had proved from the historical examples of
ancient natural philosophers that a life spent contemplating
nature was a powerful way to prolong it; this describes exactly
the fellows of Salomon's House.[56]

If Bacon's interest in the prolongation of life was a very
traditional one, his proposals for achieving it were a little less so.
He elaborated a detailed account of how 'arefaction' was one of
the principal processes of physical decay.[57] He was also fascin-
ated by the prospect of making food and drink that lasted a very
long time – just like the Bensalemites (483). This was a problem
he returned to repeatedly – and which, according to John Aubrey,
eventually killed him: he reputedly caught a chill preserving a
chicken in snow.[58] The reason for this fascination was that Bacon
believed the longer food was kept, the better it would be at
prolonging life. The ideal was to create food and – especially –
drink, that achieved the difficult (to Bacon's mind) task of being
both very refined and losing all its bitterness. In Bacon's terms,
these generated 'roscid' (fatty) juices in the body, which
conduced to longevity. And the best way to make them was to
keep them a long time.[59] This is exactly what the aged drinks in
the *New Atlantis* achieve. They are of such 'thin parts' that they
can pass from one side of the hand to the other. But they are not
bitter: there is no 'biting, sharpness, or fretting' (483). In his
other works, Bacon even suggested the kinds of 'simples' from
which such drinks might be made: elder-flowers, dwarf-pine, or
peony.[60] In Bensalem, no doubt, the ingredients are different
(483). But whatever they are made from, these drinks are
masterpieces of the 'subtlety' that Bacon sought to uncover and
exploit in nature.[61]

Theory and institutions

Many of the experiments in Salomon's House, then, have their origins in different forms of late Renaissance natural knowledge. The mines, optical experiments, furnaces and pools of the *New Atlantis* all have some counterpart in investigations of the natural world contemporary with Bacon. And, as we have seen, the 'works' of the natural magic tradition and the preoccupations of Renaissance medicine also have an important part to play in understanding the natural science of the *New Atlantis*. So far, however, most of this discussion has concentrated on the 'Preparations and Instruments' of Salomon's House (480). We have not said anything about the 'employments and offices' of its fellows – the 'Depredators', 'Mystery-men', 'Compilers', and 'Interpreters of Nature' (486–7). But these offices are no less important in understanding how the *New Atlantis* relates to Bacon's other writings, and to contemporary institutions of natural knowledge, than the experiments they perform. For Bacon's *New Atlantis* shares with other Renaissance utopias a fascination with the educational institutions, as well as the raw knowledge, of society.[62]

The relationship between knowledge and institutions in the *New Atlantis* is very close. There seems little doubt that the 'employments and offices' (486–7) of the fellows of Salomon's House are the institutional embodiment of the 'art of discovery' laid out in Bacon's theoretical works.[63] The three 'Depredators', who 'collect the experiments which are in all books', seem to be engaged in gathering what in the Latin *Advancement* Bacon calls 'learned experience' (*experientia literata*).[64] The 'Pioners or Miners' who 'try new experiments, such as themselves think good', are performing the first stage in the process of discovery laid down in the *Novum Organum*: preparing the 'Natural and Experimental history' that is the foundation of everything that follows. The 'Compilers', who draw experiments 'into titles and tables, to give the better light for the drawing of observations and axioms out of them' are likewise carrying out the next stage of investigation in the *Novum Organum*: forming the 'Tables and Coordinations of Instances' that arrange the information in the natural history.[65] The 'Dowry-men or Benefactors' seem to relate to the task, which

Bacon never fully explained in the unfinished *Novum Organum*, of '*Leading forth to Practice*, or to that which relates to men'.[66] The 'Lamps', who 'direct new experiments' developed from the ones already conducted (487), are 'deducing or deriving new experiments from the axioms' generated by their fellows.[67] Finally, and most importantly, there are the three 'Interpreters of Nature'. The interpretation of nature was one of Bacon's most longstanding preoccupations. It is the ultimate goal of the *Novum Organum*, the process that will finally replace the Aristotelian conception of science.[68] The interpreters of nature are those who arrive at the higher goal of philosophical understanding: they 'raise' the discoveries made by all the other fellows into 'greater observations, axioms, and aphorisms' (487). In a broad sense this was the task of the entire book II of the *Novum Organum* – and of all the previous works Bacon had written on the question.[69] In a narrower sense, the production of axioms that proceeded from sensory particulars to highest metaphysical generality was, according to the *Novum Organum*, the only genuine way to discover truth.[70] Unlike the Renaissance universities, which Bacon stigmatised as slaves to Aristotle and verbal disputation, Salomon's House is an institution for the systematic and fruitful production of natural knowledge in the form of works.

## Technology and magic

The *New Atlantis* recounts an imaginary voyage to an advanced and indeed in some sense ideal civilisation. Bacon wrote the 'fable' conscious that the world was still an imperfectly known and unexplored place. In this sense it is a work, not of colonialism, but of precolonialism.[71] Instead of the historical actuality of Europeans travelling to and defeating, converting, or otherwise overwhelming the indigenous peoples of the New World, the *New Atlantis* presents an account of a much more advanced society. The New Atlantans are superior to their European visitors in terms of material wealth, medicine, technology, and learning generally; they are also chaster and religiously much more peaceable (477). Furthermore, one of the reasons for the success of the Bensalemites in the realm of natural knowledge is that they have successfully remembered their past. They know far more about the world's ancient history – about the first Atlantis, America, and about ancient Europe – than is recorded in European records. For Bacon, who in the *Wisdom of the Ancients* (*De sapientia veterum*, 1609) interpreted the fragmentary knowledge of earliest Greek myth in terms of a lost system of natural knowledge, and who entitled his final programme of natural investigation the 'Great Renewal' (*Instauratio magna*), this is a positive qualification.[72]

We have seen how many of Bacon's preoccupations in the *New Atlantis* derive from earlier traditions of natural knowledge – dietetics, medicine, mechanics, alchemy, natural magic. But we must end by acknowledging that, in comparison with most of these books, the *New Atlantis* is ultimately a powerfully imaginative work. This may not immediately appear from the abrupt lists of inventions and achievements given by the Father of Salomon's House. But if we compare, for instance, the accounts of the food and drink in the *New Atlantis* with their parallel descriptions in a work like Tobias Venner's *Right Road to a Long Life*, it becomes clearer what Bacon has done. He has taken a common preoccupation of his time – such as dietetics; removed all the circumstances that make it familiar – like the names of plants or animals; and let his imagination develop the possibilities of what might be achieved in an appropriately constituted institution working with unlimited resources. Whereas contemporary treatises on health, and even books of secrets, are concerned precisely with things that are known – that can be described and named – Bacon uses the *New Atlantis* to imagine the possibilities of a place, and an institution, where the intellectual and physical materials are both quite new. In the *New Atlantis*, Bacon was unconstrained by the need to remain in the realm of fact, or to offer explanations and causes – imperatives that govern all his other writings on nature. William Rawley claimed that Bacon said of the *Sylva Sylvarum* that there was 'nothing of imagination' in it.[73] The *New Atlantis* was published with the *Sylva* and has much in common with it, but in this respect they differ: the *New Atlantis* has much of imagination in it. Bacon's 'fable' does not merely select striking 'tricks' from various earlier traditions of natural knowledge. Rather, from a starting point in these traditions, Bacon takes the opportunity to trump them at every turn.

A well-known science-fiction writer of the twentieth century has written that 'any sufficiently advanced technology is indistinguishable from magic.'[74] If any early-modern work can legitimately be called science fiction, then perhaps Bacon's *New Atlantis* can, with its voyage into a technically advanced society that is futuristic partly by virtue of being very old. But Bacon's *New Atlantis* looks back to sixteenth-century traditions like natural magic as much as it looks forward to the control over nature achieved in later centuries.

## Notes

I am most grateful to Kristine Haugen, Heikki Mikkeli, Graham Rees, Nancy Siraisi, Andrew Sparling, the participants of the 25. Internationaler Wolfenbütteler Sommerkursus on 'Learned Medicine in the Late Renaissance' for their various helpful contributions to this essay.

1  Francis Bacon, *New Atlantis*, in Brian Vickers (ed.), *Francis Bacon: A Critical Edition of the Major Works* (Oxford, Oxford University Press, 1996), pp. 457–89 (pp. 480, 481). All subsequent references to the *New Atlantis* are to this edition and are given in parentheses in the text.

2  On Bacon's posthumous reception, see Antonio Pérez-Ramos, 'Bacon's legacy', in Markku Peltonen (ed.), *The Cambridge Companion to Bacon* (Cambridge, Cambridge University Press, 1996), pp. 311–34.

3  Andrew Cunningham and Perry Williams, 'De-centring the "big picture": *The Origins of Modern Science* and the modern origins of science', *British Journal for the History of Science*, 26 (1993), 407–32.

4  Denise Albanese, 'The *New Atlantis* and the uses of utopia', *English Literary History*, 57 (1990), 503–28 (p. 506).

5  David Renaker, 'A miracle of engineering: the conversion of Bensalem in Francis Bacon's *New Atlantis*', *Studies in Philology*, 87 (1990), 181–93 (p. 182). See also Anthony F. C. Wallace, *The Social Context of Innovation: Bureaucrats, Families and Heroes in the Early Industrial Revolution, as Foreseen in Bacon's 'New Atlantis'* (Princeton, Princeton University Press, 1982); Robert K. Faulkner, *Francis Bacon and the Project of Progress* (Lanham, MD: Rowman & Littlefield, 1993).

6  Rosalie L. Colie, 'Some paradoxes in the language of things', in J. A. Mazzeo (ed.), *Reason and the Imagination: Studies in the History of Ideas 1600–1800* (New York, Columbia University Press, 1962), pp. 93–128 (pp. 94–5).

7  Antonio Pérez-Ramos, *Francis Bacon's Idea of Science and the Maker's Knowledge Tradition* (Oxford, Clarendon Press, 1988).

8  See further Nicholas Jardine, 'Epistemology of the sciences', in Charles B. Schmitt, Quentin Skinner, Eckhard Kessler, Jill Kraye (eds), *The Cambridge*

*History of Renaissance Philosophy* (Cambridge, Cambridge University Press, 1988), pp. 685–711; Peter Dear, 'Jesuit mathematical science and the reconstitution of experience in the early seventeenth century', *Studies in History and Philosophy of Science*, 18 (1987), 133–75.

9  Bacon, *Distributio operis*, in *The Works of Francis Bacon*, ed. James Spedding, Robert Leslie Ellis, and Douglas Denon Heath, 7 vols (London, Longman, 1857), vol. I, 136: 'At nos demonstrationem per syllogismum rejicimus, quod confusius agat, et naturam emittat e manibus' (But we reject demonstration by syllogism, which hunts too erratically, and lets nature slip out of its hands).

10  Bacon, *Novum Organum*, in *Works*, I, 157 (1. 5).

11  Rosalie L. Colie, 'Cornelis Drebbel and Salomon de Caus: two Jacobean models for Salomon's House', *Huntington Library Quarterly*, 18 (1954–55), 245–69. On Bacon's relations to Drebbel see further Graham Rees, 'Introduction', to Francis Bacon, *Philosophical Studies c.1611–c.1619*, ed. Rees, *The Oxford Francis Bacon VI* (Oxford, Clarendon Press, 1996), pp. xvii–cx (p. xxvii) and Rees, 'Commentary on *Historia densi & rari*', in Bacon, *The Instauratio Magna: Last writings*, ed. Rees, *The Oxford Francis Bacon XIII* (Oxford, Clarendon Press, 2000), pp. 269–304 (pp. 301, 303–4). The English mathematician John Napier had also proposed building 'devices of sailing under the water' in 1596 (*New Atlantis*, ed. Vickers, p. 800; note to p. 486).

12  J. Peter Zetterberg, 'Echoes of nature in Salomon's House', *Journal of the History of Ideas*, 43 (1982), 179–93 (p. 189).

13  Bacon, *Novum Organum*, in *Works*, I, 157 (1. 3): 'Natura enim non nisi parendo vincitur' (for nature is not conquered unless it is obeyed).

14  Penelope Gouk, *Music, Science and Natural Magic in Seventeenth-Century England* (New Haven, Yale University Press, 1999), pp. 32, 159; Zetterberg, 'Echoes', p. 190; Salomon de Caus, *Les Raisons des forces mouvantes* (Frankfurt, Jan Norton, 1615).

15  Hieronymus Fabricius ab Aquapendente, *De brutorum loquela* (Padua, Laurentius Pasquatius, 1603). Francis Bacon, *Sylva Sylvarum: or a Natural History* [1627], in *Works*, II, 413 (§200). See further Zetterberg, 'Echoes', p. 190.

16  William Eamon, *Science and the Secrets of Nature: Books of Secrets in Medieval and Early Modern Culture* (Princeton, Princeton University Press, 1996), pp. 290–1.

17  For further discussion of this question, see Brian Vickers, 'Bacon's so-called "Utilitarianism": sources and influence', in M. Fattori (ed.), *Francis Bacon: Terminologia e Fortuna nel XVII Secolo* (Rome, Edizioni dell'Ateneo, 1984), pp. 281–314.

18  Virgil K. Whitaker, 'Francis Bacon's intellectual milieu', in Brian Vickers (ed.), *Essential Articles for the Study of Francis Bacon* (Hamden, CT, Archon, 1968), pp. 28–50 (pp. 30–1).

19  Andrew Cunningham, 'Getting the game right: some plain words on the identity and invention of science', *Studies in History and Philosophy of Science*, 19 (1988), 365–89.

20  For Bacon's views on this point, see *Novum Organum*, in *Works*, I, 365 (2. 52).

21  For the distinction between demonic and natural magic, see Giovan Battista della Porta, *Magiae naturalis libri viginti* (Frankfurt, Apud Andreae Wecheli heredes, 1591), p. 2 (1. 2), and further D. P. Walker, *Spiritual and Demonic Magic from Ficino to Campanella* (London, Warburg Insitute, 1958).

22  Francis Bacon, *The Advancement of Learning* [1605], Michael Kiernan (ed.), *The Oxford Francis Bacon IV* (Oxford, Clarendon Press, 2000), p. 89.

23  See Heinrich Cornelius Agrippa, *De incertitudine & vanitate scientiarum & artium atque excellentia verbi Dei declamatio* (Antwerp, Joannes Grapheus, 1530), sig. N4$^r$; della Porta, *Magia naturalis*, pp. 2–3 (1. 2). See further Wayne Shumaker, *Natural Magic and Modern Science: Four treatises 1590–1657* (Binghamton, NY, Medieval & Renaissance Texts & Studies, 1989), p. 17; Brian P. Copenhaver, 'Natural magic, hermeticism, and occultism in early modern science', in David C. Lindburg and Robert S. Westman (eds), *Reappraisals of the Scientific Revolution* (Cambridge, Cambridge University Press, 1990), pp. 261–302 (pp. 280–1).

24  On the importance of della Porta for the *Sylva*, see Robert Leslie Ellis, 'Preface to the *Sylva Sylvarum*', in Bacon, *Works*, II, 326, 328; Rees, 'An unpublished manuscript', pp. 389, 408, who notes that sixty-two experiments in the *Sylva* are taken from the *Magia naturalis*, which Bacon read the Frankfurt edition of 1591; Rees, 'Bacon's *Sylva Sylvarum*: prelude to remarks on the influence of the *Magia naturalis*', in E. Garin (ed.), *Giovan Battista della Porta nell'Europa del suo tempo* (Naples, Guida, 1991), pp. 261–72.

25  An exception is the excellent study by Paolo Rossi, *Francis Bacon: From Magic to Science*, trans. Sacha Rabinovitch (London, Routledge and Kegan Paul, 1968), Chapter 1, although Rossi ultimately separates Bacon sharply from the Renaissance magical tradition.

26  Bacon, *Sylva*, in *Works*, II, 378 (§93), and compare *ibid.* II, 663 (§969). See further Rees, 'Bacon's *Sylva Sylvarum*', p. 270.

27  Lorraine Daston and Katherine Park, *Wonders and the Order of Nature 1150–1750* (New York, Zone, 1998).

28  Meric Casaubon, *Generall Learning: A Seventeenth-Century Treatise on the Formation of the General Scholar*, ed. Richard Serjeantson (Cambridge, RTM, 1999), p. 181. See also Zetterberg, 'Echoes', p. 191.

29  On this point see also Renaker, 'A miracle', p. 191.

30  But see Ian Box, 'Medicine and medical imagery in Bacon's *Great Instauration*', *Historical Reflections/Réflexions historiques*, 16 (1989), 351–65.

31  On this and further suggestive parallels between Bensalem and Venice, see Michèle Le Doeuff, 'Introduction', to Francis Bacon, *La Nouvelle Atlantide*,

trans. Michèle Le Doeuff and Margaret Llasera (Paris, GF-Flammarion, 1995), pp. 7–75 (pp. 46–7); also Wallace, *Social Context of Innovation*, pp. 28–31.

32  On the ancient and Renaissance background to theories of infectious disease, see Nancy Siraisi, *Medieval and Early Renaissance Medicine: An Introduction to Knowledge and Practice* (Chicago, University of Chicago Press, 1990), pp. 128–30; Vivian Nutton, 'The seeds of disease: an explanation of contagion and infection from the Greeks to the Renaissance', *Medical History*, 27 (1983), 1–34; Nutton, 'The reception of Fracastoro's theory of contagion: the seed that fell among thorns?', *Osiris*, 6 (1990), 196–234.

33  Although Bacon elsewhere argues that many medicines mean few cures: *Historia vitae*, in *Works*, II, 192 (trans. V, 300).

34  Bacon elsewhere manifests an interest in discovering what parts of animals are essential for life: *Sylva*, in *Works*, II, 474 (§400); *Historia vitae*, in *Works*, II, 208–9 (trans. V, 316); 'Historia & inquisitio de animato & inanimato', in *Instauratio Magna: Last Writings*, pp. 227–35; see also *De augmentis*, in *Works*, I, 593–4 (trans. IV, 386).

35  Richard Palmer, 'Health, hygiene and longevity in medieval and Renaissance Europe', in Y. Kawakita, S. Sakai and Y. Otsuka (eds), *History of Hygiene* (Tokyo, Ishiyaku EuroAmerica, 1991), pp. 75–98 (p. 80).

36  Richard Palmer, '"In this our lightye and learned tyme": Italian baths in the era of the Renaissance', in R. S. Porter (ed.), *The Medical History of Waters and Spas* (London, Wellcome Institute for the History of Medicine, 1990), pp. 14–22; Bacon, *Advancement*, pp. 101–2.

37  Andrew Cunningham, 'Fabricius and the "Aristotle project" in anatomical teaching and research at Padua', in A. Wear, R. K. French and I. M. Lonie (eds), *The Medical Renaissance of the Sixteenth Century* (Cambridge, Cambridge University Press, 1985), pp. 195–222; see also Bacon, *Advancement*, pp. 99–100.

38  See further Heikki Mikkeli, *Hygiene in the Early Modern Tradition* (Helsinki, Academia Scientiarum Fennica, 1999), esp. pp. 32–40.

39  Bacon, *De augmentis*, in *Works*, I, 598 (4. 2) (trans. IV, 290); Bacon, *Historia vitae*, in *Works*, II, 103, 155 (trans. V, 215, 263). Bacon was in fact repeating a common accusation that learned physicians made against 'empirics' at the time: see Harold J. Cook, 'The new philosophy and medicine in seventeenth-century England', in David Lindberg and Robert S. Westman (eds), *Reappraisals of the Scientific Revolution* (Cambridge, Cambridge University Press, 1990) pp. 397–436 (pp. 409–10).

40  On Zerbi, see Mikkeli, *Hygiene*, p. 77; on Venner, Andrew Wear, 'Epistemology and learned medicine in early modern England', in *Knowledge and the Scholarly Medical Traditions* (Cambridge, Cambridge University Press, 1995), pp. 151–73 (pp. 156–9). Despite its title, Venner's book is in English.

41  Keith Thomas, *Religion and the Decline of Magic: Studies in Popular Beliefs in Sixteenth and Seventeenth Century England* (London, Weidenfeld and Nicolson, 1971), pp. 21–2.

42 Their food and drink are not, then, just tokens of Bensalemite 'consumerism', as is argued by Robert P. Adams, 'The social responsibilities of science in the *Utopia, New Atlantis* and after', *Journal of the History of Ideas*, 10 (1949), 374–98 (p. 387).

43 See *Historia vitae*, especially at *Works*, II, 157–8 (trans. V, 265–6).

44 Bacon, 'The Grains of Youth', in *Works*, III, 827–9. Methusalah, the oldest person in the Bible, lived to 969.

45 Francis Bacon, 'De vijs mortis', in *Philosophical Studies c.1611–c.1619*, pp. 269–359.

46 Bacon, *Advancement*, pp. 99–102; Bacon *De augmentis*, in *Works*, I, 586–602 (trans. IV, 379–94).

47 Bacon, *De augmentis scientiarum*, in *Works*, I, 598–602 (4. 2): 'nova est, et desideratur; estque omnium nobilissima' (p. 598). On this passage see Mikkeli, *Hygiene*, p. 79, and further on Bacon's theories of prolongation, Rees, 'Introduction', to Bacon, *Philosophical Studies c.1611–c.1619*, pp. lxv–lxix.

48 Nancy G. Siraisi, *The Clock and the Mirror: Girolamo Cardano and Renaissance Medicine* (Princeton, Princeton University Press, 1997), p. 78; Michela Pereira, 'Un tesoro inestimabile: elixir e "prolongatio vitae" nel l'alchimia del '300', *Micrologus*, 1 (1993), 161–87.

49 Palmer, 'Health', p. 88. Bacon, *Historia vitae*, in *Works*, II, 157; Bacon, *De augmentis*, in *Works*, I, 599 (trans. IV, 391).

50 Laurent Joubert, *Popular Errors* [1578], trans. Gregory David de Rocher (Tuscaloosa, University of Alabama Press, 1989), p. 41. Thomas S. Hall, 'Life, death and the radical moisture', *Clio medica*, 6 (1971), 3–23 (esp. p. 15). Bacon, *Historia vitae*, in *Works*, II, 105–6, 158. Later commentators took issue with Bacon on this: see Bacon, *Historia vitae et mortis cum annotationibus Barthol[omei] Moseri* (Dillingen, Typis academiae, 1645), pp. 7–9.

51 Palmer, 'Health', pp. 87–91; Mikkeli, *Hygiene*, pp. 73–9.

52 Marsilio Ficino, *Three Books on Life*, ed. and trans. Carol V. Kaske and John R. Clark (Tempe, AZ, Medieval & Renaissance Texts & Studies, 1998), pp. 196–9 (2. 11): 'volentis, inquam, adolescentis, sani, laeti, temperati, cui sanguis quidem sit optimus, sed forte nimius' (a youth, I say, who is willing, healthy, happy, and temperate, whose blood is of the best but perhaps too abundant). Bacon, *Sylva*, in *Works*, II, 625 (§859); *Historia vitae*, in *Works*, II, 199 (trans. V, 307).

53 Bacon, *Sylva*, in *Works*, II, 555 (§692).

54 Bacon, *Historia vitae*, in *Works*, II, 195 (trans. V, 302); *ibid.*, II, 109, 153 (trans. V, 221, 261); *ibid.* II, 224: 'Curatio morborum temporariis eget medicinis; at longaevitas vitae expectanda est a diaetis'; *ibid.*, II, 159 (qualifies Cornaro). On Cornaro, see Palmer, 'Health', pp. 90–5; Mikkeli, *Hygiene*, pp. 86–92.

55 Bacon, *De augmentis*, in *Works*, I, 602 (trans. IV, 394).

56  Bacon, *Historia vitae*, in *Works*, II, 154 (trans. V, 262); *ibid.*, II, 149 (trans. V, 257); *ibid.*, II, 135, 142, 159, 175 (trans. V, 246, 251, 266, 283); *ibid.*, II, 154, 172 (trans. V, 263, 280).

57  Bacon, *Historia vitae*, in *Works*, II, 109, 115–16 (trans. V, 222, 227–8).

58  Rees, 'An unpublished manuscript', p. 402: ('preseruat. of Herbs' and 'Trialls for the Conseruatory of Snowe'); Bacon, *Sylva*, in *Works*, II, 445–50 (§§312–26); Bacon, *Historia vitae*, in *Works*, II, 116–18 (trans. V, 228–9). Lisa Jardine and Alan Stewart, *Hostage to Fortune: The Troubled Life of Francis Bacon* (London, Gollancz, 1998), pp. 502–3.

59  Bacon, *Historia vitae*, in *Works*, II, 221 (trans. V, 330); *ibid.*, II, 185 (trans. V, 292–3). See further Bacon, *Sylva*, in *Works*, II, 555 (§692).

60  Bacon, *Sylva*, in *Works*, II, 555 (§692). Compare Bacon, *Historia vitae*, in *Works*, II, 186 (trans. V, 293).

61  Graham Rees, 'Atomism and "subtlety" in Francis Bacon's philosophy', *Annals of Science*, 37 (1980), 549–71.

62  Compare Tommaso Campanella, *La Città del sole: dialogo poetico / The City of the Sun: A poetical dialogue* [1623], trans. Daniel J. Donno (Berkeley, University of California Press, 1981), esp. pp. 92–7; Johann Valentin Andreae, *Christianopolis*, trans. Edward H. Thompson (Dordrecht, Kluwer, 1999), esp. pp. 186–257; and see further Michèle Le Doeuff, 'Utopias: scholarly', *Social Research*, 49 (1982), 441–66.

63  As Brian Vickers' note on the 'Compilers' suggests (800). Compare with Julian Martin, *Francis Bacon, the State and the Reform of Natural Philosophy* (Cambridge, Cambridge University Press, 1992), pp. 168–9; Wallace, *Social Context of Innovation*, pp. 16–18.

64  Bacon, *De augmentis*, in *Works*, I, 622–33 (5. 2) (trans. IV, 413–21).

65  Bacon, *Novum Organum*, in *Works*, I, 236 (2. 10): 'Historia … Naturalis et Experimentalis', 'Tabulae et Coordinationes Instantiarum'.

66  Bacon, *Novum Organum*, in *Works*, I, 268 (2. 21): 'Dicemus itaque … de Deductione ad Praxin, sive de eo quod est in ordine ad Hominem'.

67  Bacon, *Novum Organum*, in *Works*, I, 235 (2. 10): 'deducendis aut derivandis experimentis novis ab axiomatibus'.

68  See further Lisa Jardine, *Francis Bacon: Discovery and the Art of Discourse* (Cambridge, Cambridge University Press, 1974); Jean Marie Pousseur, 'De l'interpretation: une logique pour l'invention', *La revue internationale de philosophie*, 40 (1986), 378–98.

69  Bacon, *Valerius Terminus of the Interpretation of Nature*, in *Works*, III, 199–252; *De interpretatione naturae prœmium*, in *Works*, III, 518–20; *Delineatio et argumentum*, in *Works*, III, 547–57; *De interpretatione naturae sententiae xii*, in *Works*, III, 783–8; *Novum Organum, sive indicia vera de interpretatione naturae*, in *Works*, I, 70–365.

70  Bacon, *Novum Organum*, in *Works*, I, 159 (1. 10); cf. the final stage of interpretation in *ibid.*, I, 268 (2. 21).

71  On the *New Atlantis* as a 'colonialist' document, see Charles C. Whitney, 'Merchants of light: science as colonization in *New Atlantis*', in William A. Sessions (ed.), *Francis Bacon's Legacy of Texts: 'The Art of Discovery Grows with Discovery'* (New York, AMS, 1990), pp. 255–68; Amy Boesky, 'Bacon's *New Atlantis* and the laboratory of prose', in Elizabeth Fowler and Roland Greene (eds), *The Project of Prose in Early Modern Europe and the New World* (Cambridge, Cambridge University Press, 1997), pp. 138–53 (p. 141); and Albanese, '*New Atlantis*'.

72  Francis Bacon, *De sapientia veterum* (London, 1609). See further Robert Ginsberg, 'Francis Bacon's *De sapientia veterum*: interpretation and insight', in *Acta Conventus Neo-Latini Turonensis*, 2 vols, ed. Jean-Claude Margolin (Paris, Vrin, 1980), pp. 229–35. On 'Renewal' as the best translation of *Instauratio*, see Lisa Jardine, 'Introduction', to Bacon, *The New Organon*, Jardine (ed.), trans. Michael Silverthorne (Cambridge, Cambridge University Press, 2000), pp. vii–xxviii (p. xiii).

73  William Rawley, 'To the reader', in Bacon, *Sylva*, in *Works*, II, 337. See further Michèle Le Doeuff, 'Un rationaliste chez Augias: de la force de l'imagination dans la *Sylva Sylvarum*', *Les Études philosophiques*, 3 (1985), 325–34.

74  Arthur C. Clarke, 'Hazards of prophecy: the failure of imagination' [1962], in *Profiles of the Future* (New York, Holt, Rinehart, and Winston, 1984), p. 26 ('Clarke's Third Law').

# 6

## On the miracles in Bacon's *New Atlantis*

### JERRY WEINBERGER

Bacon's *New Atlantis* depicts the world to be produced by his famous project for modern science and technology and the consequent mastery of nature and 'relief of man's estate'. The sailors who come upon the island leave a world where they are buffeted by the destructive forces of nature – wind, calm, famine, and disease – and enter one where the weather is controlled, needs met, and sickness cured. The key element of Bensalemite history is the founding by King Solamona, nineteen hundred years prior to the sailors' visit, of Salomon's House. This institution, a technological-scientific think tank, is described as the 'noblest foundation' ever on earth. It is the light of Bensalem and 'dedicated to the study of the works and creatures of God', and source of 'the knowledge of causes, and secret motions of things; and the enlarging of the bounds of human empire [and] ... effecting of all things possible'. It is, in other words, the engine of otherwise unheard material progress and human self-reliance.[1]

Even so, the story opens with the intimation that the sailors' rescue from dire straits at sea – their coming upon Bensalem – is a miracle, God's answer to their prayer that he 'discover' land to them just as he had 'discovered the face of the deep' in 'the beginning'. At least as far as the sailors are concerned, human self-reliance is not itself self-starting or a bootstrap phenomenon, but rather depends on divine intervention. Moreover, the society founded on science and technology has not forgotten the power and presence of God. While at first the sailors are suspicious and afraid of their extraordinary hosts, and not without apparent reasons, they soon come to see their hosts as benevolent and humane. They do so in large part because of the overt displays of religion, in particular Christianity, in their hosts' initial behaviour and in so many aspects of Bensalemite life and society. The Bensalemites' first communication with the sailors is in the form of a document, presented by an officer, warning them not to land but festooned with a cross and cherubim's wings. While finding the warning disturbing, the sailors were comforted by the sign of the cross, which they found 'a certain presage of good'. When approached soon after by a high-ranking Bensalemite, the first question asked by him of the sailors is whether they were Christians, after which they are asked to swear, by the Saviour Jesus and his merits, that they are not pirates. In Bensalem, Christian priests serve as officers of the state (38–9, 44).

There are some apparently good reasons for thinking that Bacon believed human beings could not live by technology alone and, rather, need religion as much as they need the conquest of nature. The first is a matter of general impression: there is just something unsettling and even creepy about the Bensalemites. They refuse well-meaning tips. They show gushing, teary-eyed hospitality and tenderness toward strangers. Their military history involves no killing. The people are always standing in orderly rows. The name of the one Bensalemite city mentioned, Renfusa, means 'sheep natured'. The chief festival, the Feast of the Family, honours primarily the father of the family called the Tirsan, a name derived from the Persian word for 'timid'. At this festival they declare in unison 'happy are the people of Bensalem'. Everything has its complicated ritual. Indeed, the sailors say that they have come to a 'land of angels' (39–41, 42–3, 45–7, 60–4). In short, the Bensalemites appear to have been denatured. Their happiness seems that of contented cows (or, to speak more accurately, sheep), their orderliness lobotomised. On the one hand, we wonder how much more like zombies they would be without the spiritualising effects of their religiosity. On the other hand, perhaps these super-flat souls need even more softening, by Christianity, for them safely to possess the extraordinary powers of technology.

Other reasons are more concrete and reveal much that is fishy about the Bensalemites' exceeding niceness and humanity. Two examples will suffice. Since the Bensalemites secretly spy on the rest of the world but are themselves undiscovered, and since they can control the weather, it is entirely possible that the sailors' happening on the island was no accident. It is possible, in other words, that the Bensalemites, for their own ends, forced the sailors to the island. The narrator of the story reports that the sailors were first unnerved by their confinement by the Bensalemites. Not convinced of their hosts' declarations of hospitality, the sailors feared unwelcome surveillance and worried that they should mind their behaviour lest some harm befall them. Later, the sailors are told that they may anticipate a long and enjoyable stay because their quarters – called the Strangers' House – is well stocked since it has been thirty-seven years since anyone has visited the island. When still later the Bensalemite 'laws of secrecy', restricting travel in and out of the island, are explained, the sailors are told that no strangers have been detained against their will, that no visiting ship has ever chosen to leave, that but thirteen individuals have left in Bensalemite ships, and the sailors 'must think' that whatever those few who returned reported would have been 'taken where they came from but for a dream'. That the sailors 'must think' this latter fact does not make it true. Moreover, according to the account of the laws of secrecy, King Solamona, who promulgated these laws, ordained the kindly treatment of visitors because it was 'against policy' that strangers should return and 'discover their knowledge' of Bensalem. Contrary to what the sailors are told they must think, the fact is that the laws of secrecy, intended to protect the island from foreign moral corruption, presume the credulousness of non-Bensalemites. If Bensalemite laws and policy were consistent, strangers unwilling to stay – or judged unfit to stay – would have to be restrained by force or killed. The sailors' initial trepidation was not without warrant (42–6, 51–9, 72).

Towards the end of the story the sailor–narrator converses with a Bensalemite Jew, described as a wise man and 'learned and of great policy and excellently seen in the laws and customs' of Bensalem. The narrator asks for clarification of an extraordinary Bensalemite ceremony – the Feast of the Tirsan – that honours especially fecund Bensalemites. The narrator comments that population increase seems to be valued by the Bensalemites and, given that fact, wonders if the Bensalemites practise polygamy. To these questions, the wise Jew describes Bensalem as the 'virgin of the world' and launches a tirade against European sexual morality, where red light districts and brothels have 'put marriage out of office'. The Jew then reports on the Bensalemites' marriage laws, which include a prohibition against polygamy, a one-month waiting period, a penalty for marrying without parental permission, and the strange institution called Adam and Eve's Pools. These pools, located near every town, are for solving the problem of post-nuptial disappointment caused by 'many hidden defects in men and women's bodies'. The Jew remarks that the Bensalemite arrangement is superior to that described by 'one of your men' in a 'feigned commonwealth, where the married couple are permitted, before they contract, to see one another naked'. Thinking the practice a good idea in principle, but that 'it is a scorn to give refusal after so familiar knowledge', the Bensalemites allow a friend of the man and a friend of the woman 'to see them severally bathe naked' (64–8).

The feigned commonwealth referred to by the Jew is probably More's Utopia, although it could also be, less probably, Plato's Magnesia.[2] In either case, however, it is hard to see how Bensalem's practice of pre-nuptial review is an improvement over either one. In Utopia, a responsible and respectable woman presents the naked woman – whether a virgin or a widow – to the man, and some respectable man presents the naked male suitor to the prospective bride. In Magnesia, boys and girls will see each other frequently and in common in naked play, although only within limits set by a moderate sense of shame. In Utopia, Magnesia, and Bensalem the purpose of pre-nuptial review is to ensure informed and mistake-free matches. And in Utopia and Bensalem the ultimate purpose is to prevent adultery and promiscuity and, by clear implication, the conflict and social disruption that ensue from these vices. We surely have to wonder how, in Bensalem, this end is served by having friends – not even identified as to gender – act as the agents of the naked review. In stark contrast to both Plato and More, no mention is made here of the character of the agent or the conditions of the viewing.

Surely accuracy calls for the male to be judged from the woman's point of view, and vice versa, and what is to prevent the agent, moved by inflamed desire, from falsely reporting and pursuing for himself or herself the object of desire? And what is to prevent the coveting of one's friend's spouse after such familiar knowledge? As described, the Bensalemite practice of pre-nuptial review appears so poorly contrived as to produce the opposite of its intended effect.

Moreover, only a blockhead could miss the following: the character who describes the bizarre institution is named Joabin – after the vicious Joab who, among other perfidies, helped King David murder Uriah the Hittite. As every schoolboy knows, David saw Uriah's wife Bathsheeba bathing naked. David was moved by the sight to kill Uriah and marry Bathsheeba, a sin that evoked the momentous prophecy of Nathan. The Bensalemite institution of the Adam and Eve's pools is modelled on the circumstances of David's temptation and related by the namesake of the agent of David's sin. Are we to conclude that Bensalem, with its science and technology, has turned Joab into an angel and solved the problem of unruly human desire? Or does Bacon wish rather to say that the human soul is always crooked wood that cannot be straightened by technology?

The Bensalemites' general creepiness, the ominous threat suggested by Bensalem's laws of secrecy, and the moral ambiguity of Joabin's account of the Adam and Eve's pools, all suggest a decidedly mixed Baconian message about the technological future: that the conquest of nature may just as likely be for ill as for good. Bensalem seems haunted by the problems of the soul debased by materialism, bad means used for good ends, and the lawless use of technological power. The *New Atlantis* suggests the problem, as much as the promise, of technology and the story raises questions about the ways and means of the scientific project, the ends and the limits of the conquest of nature, and the implications of science and technology for human life and values. Nothing in the *New Atlantis* tells us where the guiding principles of the technological project come from, with the exception of the Christianity that so pervades Bensalem.

Moreover, modern science needs Christianity for more than just its moral compass. We learn in the story that while natural

science, as represented by Salomon's House, was founded well
before the arrival of Christianity to Bensalem, the House of
Salomon was named after the King of the Hebrews by King
Solamona, who, having 'learned from the Hebrews that God had
created the world and all that therein is in six days', also called it
'the College of the Six Days' Works' (58). These facts and the
chronology they imply are not merely historical. That science is
preceded at least by the teaching of the Hebrews – if not by
Christianity – comports with Bacon's argument, spelled out in
*The Advancement of Learning*, that genuine science required the
mind's liberation from the tyranny of ancient thought, especially
that of Plato and Aristotle. The basic problem of ancient thought
was its *pagan* confusion of the natural and the divine, its belief
that 'the world is an image of God and that man is an extract or
compendious image of the world'.[3] According to Bacon, this confusion led to circular, empty, and fruitless teleological thinking,
as well as to a misplaced reverence for nature. Ancient thought
thus prevented our fathoming the true and often invisible causes
at work in nature, and it inhibited the development of technological power: if nature is divine, we should not presume to
transform it or see it as the source of limits to be overcome.
Without the 'sacred truth' that the world, with the exception of
man, is but a created thing and neither itself divine nor an image
of the divine, genuine science and technology have no air to
breathe. That science and technology should arise and flourish
depends importantly on the genuine truth of the Biblical
revelation.

Thus, as depicted in the *New Atlantis*, the modern project is
crucially dependent on two fundamental miracles: the miracle of
creation and the miracle of divine revelation. No wonder, then,
that a central feature of the *New Atlantis* is a story about a
miracle, told to the narrator to explain how the Bensalemites
became Christians (47–9). According to the story, twenty years
after the ascension of Christ, the Bensalemites saw a huge pillar of
light, on top of which was a cross of more brilliant light, about a
mile out to sea. The people gathered on the beach to wonder at
the 'strange spectacle' and then approached it in boats. The boats
were stopped, by some unseen force, some yards from the pillar,
so that the Bensalemites were arrayed around it as if in a theatre

and beheld the light 'as an heavenly sign'. A wise man of Salomon's House – presumably a natural scientist – was in one of the boats and, after having contemplated the pillar and cross 'attentively and devoutly', delivered a prayer to the 'Lord God of heaven and earth'. In the prayer, the wise man said that God has enabled the scientific establishment to know God's 'works of creation and the secrets of them, and to discern (as far as pertains to the generations of men) between divine miracles, works of nature, works of art, and impostures and illusions of all sorts'. The wise man then acknowledged and testified that the pillar was the finger of God and a 'true miracle' and said that 'forasmuch as we learn in our books that thou never workest miracles but to a divine and excellent end, (for the laws of nature are thine own laws, and thou exceedest them not but upon great cause,) we most humbly beseech thee to prosper this great sign, and to give us interpretation and use of it in mercy; which thou dost in some part secretly promise by sending it to us.'

At this point, and as if God answered the prayer immediately, the wise man's boat became free to approach the pillar. But before he reached it the pillar broke up, leaving but an ark floating in the water. In the ark was a book containing all the canonical books of the Old and New Testaments, the Apocalypse, and some other books of the New Testament that were not at that time written. The book was accompanied by a letter from St Bartholomew in which the Apostle testified that whoever found the ark received peace and salvation from Jesus and the Father. A final 'great miracle' then took place when some Hebrews, Persians, and Indians, who at that time lived in Bensalem, were able to read the book and the letter as if they had been written in their own languages.

Now, one of Bacon's concerns in telling this story is to establish the veracity of miracles. The Bensalemites, although they approach the pillar as a heavenly sign, must have been sensitive to a significant problem for believers, which is the sceptics' claim that miracles can be faked or explained away as misunderstood natural phenomena. The Bensalemites' answer is to rely not just on the internal evidence of the experience of faith, but also on the power of science to determine that an apparent miracle is not a natural, artificial, or illusory or deceitful event. This reliance explains why the miracle of the pillar of light is, in addition to its other features, a miracle of original revelation (it disclosed books of the New Testament *that had not yet been written*) and the gift of tongues. It is possible that Bensalemite scientists were present when Jesus performed his miracles and was resurrected. But so far as we know, or the Bensalemites admit, there were none present. There certainly were none present when Moses received the tablets of the law from God at Sinai. But in Bensalem, the narration of these at-the-time unverified events is supplied by a scientifically verified miracle, which is enough to establish their bona fides. Assume that Moses and Jesus were both frauds and that the parting of the Red Sea was but a timely, if rare, natural occurrence. If the *representation* of them as genuine miracles is itself a genuine miracle, that fact is by itself enough to establish that we should live as if they were genuine and that they *could* have been genuine miracles. The miracle that transpires in Bensalem is not just an adjunct to the miracles it discloses. It is, ultimately, the epistemic foundation of those prior miracles.

The problem is that it is impossible for science demonstrably to establish the reality of miracles. That there is no scientifically known cause for an apparent miracle does not establish that it is in fact a miracle, rather than just something we cannot *yet* explain by recourse to nature (including psychology). In order to prove scientifically and demonstrably that an event is supernatural, it would be necessary to have disclosed every single law and phenomenon of nature, every hidden cause and possibility. The Bensalemite scientist themselves, it seems, do not think such complete knowledge possible. For in his prayer the wise man of Salomon's House declares that God has given the scientists the power to know the works of divine creation and to discern between miracles and works of nature, art, and imposture and illusion 'as far as it appertaineth to the generations of men'. To this it could be objected that Bacon himself disagrees with this Bensalemite modesty. In *The Advancement of Learning*, Bacon says that Solomon's comment that man 'cannot … find out the work which God worketh from the beginning to the end' refers not to the mind's capacity to grasp nature, but only to 'the impediments, as of shortness of life, ill conjunction of labours, ill tradition of knowledge over from hand to hand, and many other inconveniences

whereunto the condition of man is subject'.[4] These inconveniences can be overcome with the right method and organisation of
knowledge so that not just in principle, but also in practice, it is
possible, within Bacon's scheme, to grasp the entirety of nature
and hence to determine that an event is supernatural.

However, the attainment of such complete Baconian knowledge exacerbates a different impediment to discerning the reality
of miracles. According to Bacon, 'human knowledge and human
power meet in one.'[5] The courses of nature reveal themselves
through the things that can be done by 'vexing' nature, and, in
principle, nothing, short of creation *ex nihilo*, is beyond the power
of human knowledge – including the 'restitution and renovation
of things corruptible', i.e., the resurrection of the dead.[6] The
scientists of Bensalem themselves make this point in spades. The
scientists of Salomon's House 'have so many things truly natural
that induce admiration' that they 'could in a world of particulars
deceive the senses, if [they] would disguise those things and
labour to make them seem more miraculous' (80). Such fakery is
forbidden and punished with ignominy and fines. But the fact is
that the very knowledge that supposedly enables the scientists to
determine the genuineness of miracles empowers them to commit
successful religious fraud. Even a complete grasp of nature
would still leave miracles with essentially the same status as the
pre-scientific miracles of the Bible: dependent on the uncertain
veracity of those who report or judge them. In fact the situation
is worse. If one could imagine oneself transported to Sinai or
Jerusalem at the times of Moses and Jesus, and one were, however otherwise hard-headed and sceptical, an *actual* witness to
God's speaking to Moses or Jesus' rising up from the dead, one
would be hard pressed not to believe the evidence of one's own
eyes. Not so in Bensalem, where such things could actually happen
by means of technology or be faked by means of technology.

As regards reason and miracles, Bacon reverses the usual order
of things. Rather than claim reason and miracles to be at odds, he
argues, quite dubiously, that reason can validate miracles. His
reason for this move is not difficult to fathom. As he says in *Of
Atheism*,[7] one cause of atheism is 'learned times, specially with
peace and prosperity, for troubles and adversities do more bow
men's minds to religion'. In a similar vein, 'a little philosophy

inclineth man's mind to atheism'. In an enlightened and techno-
logically enriched society, the people will be inclined to atheism,
which, Bacon says, deprives man of his nobility and magnanimity:
'for certainly man is of kin to the beasts by his body; and, if he be
not of kin to God by his spirit, he is a base and ignoble creature'.
As we have seen, such atheism would also prevent our finding
guidance for wielding the awesome power of technology. According to the essay, however, atheism is actually rare, because
the mere sight of nature is enough to cause men to believe in God.
As Bacon says, 'God never wrought miracle to convince atheism,
because his ordinary works convince it.' To say that the people
will be inclined to atheism, then, is not to say that atheism will
necessarily become common. Much more likely is a certain
weakening of faith, along with the spread of superstition, one
cause of which is 'the taking aim at divine matters by human,
which cannot but breed mixture of imaginations'.[8] The project of
science surely takes aim at many matters thought to be divine –
not the least of which is death and resurrection – and so, by this
argument, a technological society should be given to superstition. Moreover, while atheism would be dangerous for depriving
technological power of guidance and for debasing human
character, according to *Of Superstition,* atheism is otherwise not
really dangerous and 'did never perturb states'. Superstition, on
the other hand, 'hath been the confusion of many states' and has
ravished 'all the spheres of government'. Since 'the master of
superstition is the people; and in all superstition wise men follow
fools', it is well for the people to adhere to an orthodoxy supported by miracles verified by those whose power (other than
God's) they revere and need the most – the natural scientists.
Another cause of superstition is 'the stratagems of prelates for
their own ambition and lucre'. In Bensalem, both the art and the
authority of the scientists guarantee that the people believe, and
that they do so in a way that puts the priests in their place.

   In Bensalem, what could well be a noble lie told by scientists
lends scientific credence to a miracle that could have been
fabricated by the scientists themselves. Had the miracle never
really happened, policy would have dictated its fabrication for at
least the following reasons: it prevents the Bensalemites from
descending into an utterly degraded materialism (they seem

quite flat-headed enough), it allows for a general and tolerant
orthodoxy and the consequent subordination and political integration of priests, and it provides the regulative principles for
the enormous power unleashed by Bensalemite science and
technology.

But a serious puzzle remains. First, there seems a tension
between the ultimate goal of Bensalemite science (the restitution
and renovation of corruptible things) and the basic teaching of
Bensalemite religion: that death is the wages of sin. If there is a
God, then Bensalemite science seems determined to put him out
of business. Second, if it is true, as Bacon says, that human beings
are base and ignoble without the kinship of the spirit to God,
then a lot rides on the reality of miracles: if God and miracles
exist, then human nature is characterised by the possibility of
nobility and dignity. But if God and miracles do not exist, then
such nobility and dignity rest on an illusion which, in principle,
can be dispelled. Were it so, it would then be possible at least to
contemplate a world based entirely on reason, in which there is
nothing transcendent and noble to serve as a model for human
behaviour and to which obeisance and sacrifice should be made.
In such a rational world, the only principle of human action
would be self-interest and only such self-interest as is material
and can be satisfied by science and technology. This would be a
world in which all interests could be harmonised, because they
all can be indulged at the technological trough. Without miracles
there can be nothing divine, and without the divine as a model
there is nothing to us beyond those needs that can be satisfied by
technology. As attractive as such a world is to us who suffer from
unconquered nature, even Bacon indicates that, on reflection, we
shudder at its prospect.[9] So whether the miracle at the centre of
the *New Atlantis* is or could be real, *really* matters. The answer
tells us whether or not the possibilities of technology exhaust
what human beings really are.

While the *New Atlantis* points to the impossibility of miracles,
or at least to the impossibility of ever proving that they are real,
nothing in the story allows us to say with certainty that miracles
do not exist. Despite what the Bensalemites seem to think, science
simply cannot settle the matter: while it cannot prove the existence of miracles, neither can it demonstrate their impossibility. It

cannot establish, for example, that an explainable event might not, in fact and in a particular instance, be the product of a miraculous cause. So long as such uncertainty remains, the complete rationalisation and flattening of life need not be inevitable. It would still be possible to experience faith and heed the call of God and thus avoid the advent of a world devoid of human nobility and dignity. We would not be left dependent upon but a temporary and flimsy stopgap, such as a noble religious lie propagated by science.

There is a fly in this saving, agnostic ointment, however. As Bacon presents the miracle, natural science is not the only criterion for establishing its reality. When the wise man of Salomon's House pronounces the pillar to be a true miracle and the finger of God, he says that 'forasmuch as we learn in our books that thou never workest miracles but to a divine and excellent end (for the laws of nature are thine own laws and thou exceedest them not but upon great cause), we most humbly beseech thee to prosper this great sign, and to give us the interpretation and use of it in mercy; which thou dost in some part secretly promise by sending it unto us' (48). A miracle must not only be other than a work of nature, a work of art, an imposture, and an illusion. It must also be for a divine and excellent end. It must be for the good.

Now Bacon stresses over and over again that great damage to both reason and religion results from confusing the realms of the natural and the divine. This was, he says, the great defect of ancient (pagan) thought and as well of post-Christian thought to the extent that it was balefully influenced by the major ancient thinkers, Plato and Aristotle. Bacon argues accordingly that there is little we can learn about God from the study of nature. In *The Advancement of Learning*, Bacon says that natural theology is the 'knowledge of God that can be had by contemplating God's creatures'. But this knowledge is very limited: no light of nature, says Bacon, can declare the will and thus the worship of God. Just as any work of art shows the power and skill of the artisan, but not his image (who he is and why he made the artefact), so the natural works of God show his power and wisdom but not his image – not his will and purpose. All this said, however, Bacon then changes his mind, even in the immediate context. A few lines later, Bacon says that 'by the contemplation of nature to induce and enforce acknowledgement of God, and to demonstrate his power, providence, and goodness, is an excellent argument, and hath been excellently handled by diverse.'[10]

One has to say that providence and goodness are no minor aspects of divine will – they are surely very important aspects of who God is and why he created the world and human beings. In the *De augmentis*, Bacon goes even further. There he says that the contemplation of nature discloses that God exists, that he is supremely powerful, that he is good, that he is a rewarder, that he is an avenger, and that he is an object of veneration.[11] In other words, divine goodness and providence entail divine rewards and punishments. However, in *The Advancement of Learning*'s later discussion of theology, Bacon says that with the light of nature we cannot understand the creation and the redemption and likewise the 'moral law truly interpreted' – the law that enjoins us to love our enemies, to do good to those who hate us, and to be like our heavenly Father who lets the rain fall on the just and the unjust.[12] So it seems, after all, that nature by itself does not disclose God to be a rewarder and avenger: the rain falls on good and bad alike, the good die young and the wicked live to ripe old age.

Bacon's obvious and deliberate self-contradiction underscores a simple fact: people naïvely want nature to make moral sense and to exhibit divine care (even the Bensalemites think science can prove miracles). But nature – at least as regards our hopes and desires and prior to its conquest by technology – is a jungle where the strong eat the weak or, worse still, is a casino, where winners and losers are decided by sheer luck. The obvious lesson of the *New Atlantis* is that nature is inhospitable and indifferent to our needs, the object of conquest and not reverence. Miracles and miracles alone can disclose divine will, purpose, and care.

However, there is a connection between the naïve, erroneous interpretation of nature and our experience of divine miracles: the assumption of providence, of divine care, which must be good and, therefore, must reward the good and punish the bad. According to Bacon *we do not learn this principle from miracles.* We rather *bring* it to our faith and thereby to our experience of miracles, just as we bring it to our hopeful but erroneous experience of nature. According to Bacon, God never works miracles to convert atheists, but only to convert idolaters and the superstitious. In other words, the experience of miracles presupposes faith, which is one reason why reason and science, which reject faith out of hand, cannot disprove them. But again, our assumption about providence is neither itself miraculous nor revealed by a miracle, nor is it a matter of faith. It is rather an opinion about morality and what any god, if such were to exist, must be in this regard. And unlike faith, this opinion can be examined by reason.

Now about morality, Bacon has much to say. One such discussion is especially important for our purpose and occurs – quite appropriately – in Bacon's consideration and refutation of the 'evil arts' of negotiation. These arts are represented by Machiavelli's infamous advice that one should possess the appearance of virtue rather than virtue itself, because having the reputation for virtue is a help but actually practising virtue is a hindrance, and that men can be ruled only by fear; by the Triumvirs' willingness to sacrifice their friends to gain the deaths of their enemies; by L. Catalina's willingness to use trouble of the states for pursuing his own fortune; or, finally, by the 'principle of Lysander' that children are to be deceived with candy and men by oaths.[13]

To refute these immoral maxims, Bacon says that if men 'be in their own power and do bear and sustain themselves' and are not 'carried away with a whirlwind or tempest of ambition', they should, in pursuing their fortunes, and in addition to keeping in mind the general principle about the world that 'all things are vanity and vexation of spirit', heed six 'particular cards and directions'. First, that virtue is most rewarded by itself, and vice most punished by itself. Second, that eternal providence and divine judgement often foil evil plots. Third, that even if one refrains from evil the ceaseless pursuit of fortune leaves no time for making tribute to God. Fourth, that we should not 'purpose' to use ill means for great ends, even though we might benefit from these ends. Fifth, that we should remember that fortune is like a woman in that 'if she be too much wooed she is the further off'. And finally, that such advice about fortune's woman-like character is for those already corrupted and that it is wise for men to build upon the corner stones of divinity and philosophy 'wherein they joint close'. The corner stone of divinity is that we should seek first the kingdom of God and the other things (that we seek in pursuing our fortunes) will follow. The corner stone of philosophy is that we should seek first the good of the mind and these same things will follow or not be wanted.[14]

There is much going on in this rich and compact discussion. But the important thing for us to note is that some of it is very fishy and surprisingly revealing. In his remarks introducing the six 'cards and directions', Bacon comments that we should follow them if we are in control of ourselves and not already in the grip of and carried away by ambition. The six good maxims are thus presented as if they are conditional and do not apply to those already in thrall to ambition. While it makes sense to proffer moral advice to those whom it can most benefit, it seems odd, then, not also to exhort those who, it would seem, most need that advice. Bacon argues as if nothing can be done for those already 'carried away' by ambition. Moreover, he says of them not that they are wicked, but rather that they are not 'in their own power' and do not 'bear and sustain themselves'. If so, however, it is hard to see how those who practise the evil arts can themselves be *blamed* for doing so. We do not blame those not in control of themselves – i.e., those who are not free to choose their maxims. If the sequel presents a lesson about virtue and vice, then it is preceded by at least the suggestion that while men may do things we call evil, they do so involuntarily and so cannot be responsible and thus morally blameworthy for their actions. So much for the first fish.

Even more fragrant are Bacon's comments regarding the first principle – that virtue is its own reward and wickedness its own punishment. Now this principle is at the heart of morality and is especially important for any refutation of Machiavelli. As homely and decent as it sounds, 'honesty is the best policy' is a maxim lethal to morality. It is a contingent statement of fact, which may or may not be true. At the very least, one could say that honesty is the best policy only on the debatable assumption that one's dishonesty will always be discovered and punished. Or it may be that honesty is in general and under normal conditions the best policy, but not good policy in extraordinary circumstances, such as when telling the truth would result in one's death or the death of loved ones or the death of innocent third parties (i.e., hostages on a hijacked plane). Such reasonable exceptions, however, give Machiavelli his basic point: that virtue is a useful means to some extrinsic end rather than an end in itself. This is of course why moralists admonish us to be good and virtuous for its own sake and not for some other end, such as happiness or things such as pleasure, money, fame, good reputation, the interest of one's nation or community, and so on. It is likewise why we tend to think that virtue at its peak, and when it really matters, requires self-sacrifice, and why virtue is diminished if performed for some payoff, even if that payoff is self-satisfaction. Moreover, it simply isn't obvious that virtue is, merely in general, the best policy. Those who strive for virtue often lose out in life and the vicious often win ('nice guys finish last'). In politics, for instance, it is common for success to make scoundrels and even murderers into saints. And so if virtue is not good in itself and its own reward, then Machiavelli is right and virtue is but a useful tool and, ultimately, it is better to seem to be virtuous than actually to be so, especially in extreme circumstances.

It's no surprise, then, that Bacon's first move in refuting the evil arts of negotiation – and in particular Machiavelli – is to distinguish between the kinds of rewards and punishments associated with virtue. Rather than say that virtue is simply and only its own reward, he says that virtue is most rewarded in itself and vice most punished in itself. There are other, additional rewards and punishments (call them the add-ons). This distinction seems perfectly reasonable, since while we think that virtue is diminished when practised for some extrinsic end, we do think it would be a terrible world where the virtuous are miserable and simply food for the wicked. To emphasise his point, Bacon quotes lines from Virgil,[15] in which, Bacon says, the poet 'excellently' makes this distinction between extrinsic rewards for virtue and virtue as its own, and higher and more essential, reward. *However, the Virgilian lines make no such distinction.*

In the context of the quote, the aged Aletes praises the Trojan warriors by saying that the first and best rewards will be paid to them by the gods and by their own worth and the rest will be paid by Aeneas and Ascanius. There are three kinds of rewards: divine, virtue's being its own reward, and rewards provided by men. According to Virgil, the divine rewards and virtue's being its own reward are the same — both are first and best. Now if virtue is *good in itself and therefore its own reward*, then divine rewards, whatever they may be, cannot be the same. They are add-ons. But what does it mean if virtue as its own reward and the divine add-ons are the same or, at least, are commensurable? In this world, it would mean that some sum of add-ons could surpass some sum of virtue-as-good-in-itself. Assuming the add-ons to be such things as happiness, pleasure, good reputation, all the good things in life, then it is entirely possible that virtue as its own reward could be outweighed by some combination of these add-on rewards, achieved by any means, and especially so if virtue required the sacrifice of life itself. In this case, then, Machiavelli wins: it is better to seem to be virtuous than actually to be so. Moreover, the only difference between the afterlife and this life — between worldly add-ons and add-ons as divine reward — is that in the afterlife the rewards are supposedly guaranteed to those who have been virtuous in life, and presumably are eternal and, perhaps, more intensely experienced in some way. However, even as divine rewards they would still be add-ons, and virtue would be a means to them. Machiavelli would win in principle, in that virtue would be a means rather than an end and good in itself, except that he would have erred in not taking divine providence into account.

Perhaps we could say that in heaven the add-ons are mere extras and that just being in heaven is utterly different from them and consists of the eternal experience of being virtuous as good in itself and thus of having it as its own reward. Here, I think, we reach the heart of the matter. How, we ask, does heavenly virtue differ from a perfect virtue in this world? In this world, the quintessence of virtue as good in itself is the sacrifice of *one's all* for another or for some noble end. In heaven, such virtue would consist in the eternal awareness of having sacrificed *one's all* in the world of mortal life. But if so, then the virtue in question cannot consist of pure self-sacrifice, either on earth or in heaven. It cannot be so on earth because of what awaits in heaven. And it cannot be so in heaven, because it consists not in the sacrifice of all, but in the experience (consciousness of, satisfaction at, pleasure in, etc.) of being virtuous. This experience obviously cannot be the sacrifice of all. It is, presumably, the greatest good that can come to human life and is thus no sacrifice at all. Even in heaven, the notion of virtue as good in itself and its own reward really makes no sense.

Now, what has the foregoing to do with the question of miracles and the *New Atlantis*? It reveals, I submit, the heart of the matter as Bacon understands it. As the second piece of advice or direction for refuting the evil arts, Bacon warns their practitioners that eternal providence and divine judgement often foil evil plots. It is not the most heartening advice, however, since God does not *always* thwart the bad guys. Indeed, as Bacon surely knows, it more often happens that the evil prosper and the innocent suffer. All the more reason, then, for the last piece of advice, which is that men should first seek the kingdom of God and remember that while human foundations have some sand mixed in, the 'divine foundation is upon the rock'.[16] While we cannot understand God's specific purpose in the particular and mixed course of worldly events – God moves in mysterious ways, and for all we know has allowed the Bensalemites to use bad means for good secular ends – In the end *et ista omnia adjicientur vobis* ('and all these things shall be added unto you').[17] Even though the evil may prosper in this world, and while the ways and means of divine providence are often mysterious, there is no mystery at the end of days: the ultimate divine purpose is good, not bad. Nobody really thinks that God is an all-powerful monster who, for sport, plays with human beings as a boy plays with flies or ants.

That God is good, as the Bensalemites declare, is *the* opinion that grounds our faith and our experience of divine miracles. Fair enough. But Bacon seems to suggest that our very understanding of that goodness, especially as it bears on divine providence, is utterly confused. Our fundamental conception of what it means to be good is that goodness (or, to be more precise, moral goodness or virtue) is not a means for some other end and must be 'good in itself' – that it must be its 'own reward', to use Bacon's and the still common phrases. That we use these phrases interchangeably suggests that we cannot think of virtue as being good in itself without, in fact, also thinking of virtue in terms of *reward*. But reward and genuine virtue are incompatible. This probable confusion becomes a necessary contradiction when we think of divine providence. As regards divine providence, the very notion of virtue as good in itself is incoherent. We cling to this notion, quite rightly, as a bedrock *moral* intuition, and yet we cannot think of divine providence without betraying that somehow, barely consciously, we do not really believe, because we cannot believe, in such goodness-in-itself. We cannot conceive of divine providence without thinking of moral virtue as a means to other ends – to extrinsic rewards. When we think of divine goodness we cannot but mean that God is *just*, or, as Bacon says, that God rewards the virtuous and punishes the vicious. But if so, then God himself is a Machiavellian. Divine providence assumes that the good for man is a selfish good and that even self-sacrifice is ultimately selfish. Were this fact clear and not hidden in the mists of our moral confusions, it is not obvious that we could believe in such a God, especially if we take divine justice into account. For why would God punish those Machiavellians who, after all, agree with the divine notion that virtue is for the sake of rewards, who believe that virtue is not always the best means to those rewards, and who just happen not to believe that a God exists who ensures that, as a matter of ultimate fact, virtue is the best means to those rewards?

No sane person would *choose* to miss out on the ultimate rewards, and so it cannot be that unbelief is wilful. It's therefore not the unbeliever's fault that he does not believe, any more than one who is 'carried away with a whirlwind or tempest of ambition' is at fault for pursuing Machiavelli's selfish evil arts.[18] Not only does divine providence reveal God to be a Machiavellian; it also reveals God to be one who punishes the innocent and rewards the lucky – and for no discernable good reason. Not even Machiavelli recommends that. Again, could anyone really believe in such a God? Could anyone believe in a God if they realised that his character is an affront to our deepest intuition about morality? Could anyone believe in a God after discovering that the moral horizon necessary for that god's miraculous revelation is incoherent? Bacon certainly sows some seeds of doubt.

   In the fifth and sixth pieces of advice for refuting the evil
arts, Bacon warns the ambitious that fortune is like a woman and,
for that reason, that we should seek the kingdom of God before
and as a means to all other good things. These principles are surely
not the first maxims of the Bensalemites, for whom the conquest
of nature is the project of their kingdom. Moreover, the reference
to Machiavelli, in the context of a refutation of the Machiavellian
evil arts, is impossible to miss. Bacon obviously means for us to
recall that, for Machiavelli, if fortune is a woman then 'it is
necessary, if one wants to hold her down, to beat her and strike
her down. And one sees that she lets herself be won more by the
impetuous than by those who proceed coldly. And so always,
like a woman, she is the friend of the young, because they are less
cautious, more ferocious, and command her with more audacity.'[19]
   This praise of youthful impetuosity and manly violence does
not well suit the Bensalemites, who revere the old and seem
overly sedate and orderly. For the Bensalemites, fortune is not
the changeable political world and the mercurial ebb and flow of
individual and group ambition. It is, rather, the hostile opposition of material nature to the basic human desire for long and
commodious living. When the enemy is material nature rather
than other human beings, the proper response is still something
like the rape Machiavelli describes. For Bacon, the key to understanding and controlling nature is to put it on the rack. But for
those who actually engage in it, the Bensalemite scientists, the
assault on nature proceeds by an organised, methodical, dis-
passionate, and relatively anonymous process. Likewise for the
non-scientific Bensalemites. While they probably do not understand or know much about natural science, they are not for that
reason unaffected by it. As consumers of technological bounty,
they are happy and contented. Bensalemite science – indeed the
Baconian project for the conquest of nature – apparently over-
comes the two main sources of political conflict: the material
difference between haves and have-nots, and the psychological
conflict between the strong and the weak. Thus, at least in
principle, Bensalemite science and technology put an end to all
questions of justice. What the strong want – the freedom and the
means to understand and conquer nature – and what the weak
want – the satisfaction of their material needs – go hand in hand.

Now from what we know (or at least have conjectured) so far, as the concern for justice wanes in Bensalem, the importance and intensity of religion should wane as well. Indeed, the Bensalem-ites' religiosity already seems a tame and laid-back mish-mash: the Christians tolerate the Jews and the Jews believe in the divinity of Jesus, and officials dress like Turks and Persians. The Bensalemites are not yet atheists, probably because death has not yet been conquered. But given their technological conquest of scarcity and suffering, it is doubtful that they still have much truck with miracles. Why? Because they could have little or no concern for the issue at the heart of all credence in miracles: divine providence. Where there is no need to reward virtue and punish vice – since there is no need for the sacrifice of one's interests for another – there is no need for divine guidance, divine reminders, and divine rewards and punishments.

At this point one might well object that if the Bensalemites do not heed providence and, eventually, even become degraded and flat-headed atheists, so much the worse for them. That they cannot heed the divine call proves only that they cannot hear, not that there is no sound. True enough. Indeed, it seems doubt-ful that Bacon thought the denizens of the technological world to come would be the least bit self-reflective or profound. Their lack of religion would spring from satisfied indifference, not from genuine and deepening intellectual struggle or conviction. Their problem, if it were one, would concern the lack of motivation to be open to belief. However, Bacon's argument about the *opinion* necessary for belief is quite another matter. If Bacon is correct that our most basic intuitions about moral virtue are probably incoherent, and are certainly so when they serve as the necessary epistemic foundation of faith, then it cannot be said that a world of technological zombies can be redeemed by new gods – at least not by any gods that we could believe really exist.[20]

Why do we feel unease at the spectre of nature completely conquered? Because the resulting world would be so unrelent-ingly boring. What would its people do? They would *shop*. No god could intervene in and change this world, because life would afford no experience of virtue and vice, justice and injustice. The only alternative would be to break the scientific machine and, wilfully and artificially, to create new 'gods' by reintroducing the conditions of belief – an unlikely and scary possibility. Perhaps we should just be grateful that we are not yet at such a point, and that it is still a long way off.

## Notes

1  *New Atlantis and The Great Instauration*, ed. Jerry Weinberger (Wheeling, Illinois, Harlan Davidson, Inc., 1980, revised edn 1989), pp. 37–9, 56–8, 71. All further references to *New Atlantis* come from this edition and will be cited in parentheses in the main body of my essay.

2  Thomas More, *Utopia*, eds George M. Logan and Robert M. Adams (Cambridge, Cambridge University Press, 1989), pp. 81–4; Plato *Laws* 771e, trans. Thomas L. Pangle (New York, Basic Books, Inc., 1980), p. 159.

3  *The Advancement of Learning*, in *The Works of Francis Bacon*, ed. James Spedding, Robert Leslie Ellis, and Douglas Denon Heath, 14 vols. (London, Longman, 1857–74) vol. III, pp. 349–50, 352–9.

4  *The Advancement of Learning*, p. 265.

5  *Novum Organum* 1: 3, Bacon, *Works*, vol. IV, p. 47.

6  *De sapientia veterum* ('Of the Wisdom of the Ancients') XI, Bacon, *Works*, vol. VI, pp. 646, 721.

7  Bacon, *Works*, vol. VI, pp. 413–15.

8  *Of Superstition*, in Bacon, *Works*, vol. VI, pp. 415–16. Contemporary America comes to mind. In America full-bore materialism consists with widespread but mild religiosity and an abundance of religious novelty and other forms of spiritualism, including pantheism.

9  Nietzsche's chilling description of the Last Man and Heidegger's account of nihilism and technology come to mind. See, for example Nietzsche, *Thus Spoke Zarathustra*, *The Portable Nietzsche*, trans. Walter Kaufmann (New York, Vintage, 1954), pp. 128–31; and Martin Heidegger, *The Question Concerning Technology* in *The Question Concerning Technology and Other Essays*, trans. William Lovitt (New York, Harper and Row, 1971), pp. 3–35.

10  *The Advancement of Learning*, pp. 349–51.

11  *De augmentis*, 3:2, Bacon, *Works*, vol. IV, p. 341.

12  *The Advancement of Learning*, pp. 478–9.

13  *Ibid.*, pp. 471–2.

14  *Ibid.*, pp. 472–3.

15  *Aeneid* 9: 252. Quae vobis, quae digna, viri, pro laudibus istis/praemia posse rear solvi? pulcherrima primum/di moresque dabunt vestri. 'What's worthy, you men, what prize for such laudable deeds? How can we pay you? Gods must give you the finest reward first – and your own character.' Slightly altered from Virgil, *Aeneid*, trans. Edward McCrorie (Ann Arbor, University of Michigan Press, 1995), p. 196.

16  *The Advancement of Learning*, p. 473.

17  *Ibid*, p. 473. Bacon's reference is to Matt 6:33.

18  *The Advancement of Learning*, p. 472.

19  *The Prince*, XXV, trans. Harvey C. Mansfield (Chicago, University of Chicago Press, 1985), p. 101.

20  See *Nur noch ein Gott kann uns retten* ('Only a God Can Save Us Now'), *Der Spiegel* (May 31, 1976), trans. Maria P. Alter and John D. Caputo in *The Heidegger Controversy*, ed. Richard Wolin (Cambridge, The MIT Press, 1993), pp. 91–116.

# 7

## 'Books will speak plain'?
## Colonialism, Jewishness and politics
## in Bacon's *New Atlantis*

### CLAIRE JOWITT

Francis Bacon's *Of Counsel* (1625) asserts that 'Books will speak plain when counsellors blanch.'[1] In other words, a counsellor – even one like Bacon, languishing on the margins of political favour – will find it easier to offer advice to his prince through the medium of the written word. A counsellor can give better advice away from the intimidating presence of his monarch.

Bacon's statement in *Of Counsel* provides a useful way of reading some of the complexities of the *New Atlantis*. It suggests that this scientific utopia might be seen as advice literature directed towards the Stuart monarchy. Bacon's earlier works promoting England's scientific future, such as *The Advancement of Learning* (1605) and *Novum Organum* (1620), had, superficially at least, been approved by James I. For example, while Bacon's dedication to James in *The Advancement of Learning* modestly states 'that though I cannot positively or affirmatively advise your Majesty', it nevertheless asserts that 'I may excite your princely cogitations ... to extract particulars for this purpose [the advancement of learning] agreeable to your magnanimity and wisdom'.[2] Even though James may have ignored Bacon's scientific schemes, he certainly promoted him within governmental hierarchies. Consequently, it appears that the *New Atlantis* could 'speak plain' since it was merely an imaginative continuation of the scientific programme Bacon had previously outlined in theory.

However, given Bacon's precarious position after his impeachment, his ability to 'speak plain' should be seen as more equivocal and complex than reading the *New Atlantis* simply as advice
to princes would imply. Bacon's praise of New Atlantis's system
– particularly King Solamona's role within it – is read here as
covertly criticising James and his rule. On one level, then, the
*New Atlantis* is an advice book that criticises James I in a deliberate, if coded, way. In other words, the *New Atlantis* does offer
advice that might make a counsellor 'blanch', but it certainly
does not 'speak plain'.

Such an analysis suggests that Bacon's fictional world can be
read as a means of discussing England's policies. This interpretation will be tested in this essay by focusing on two contentious
contemporary issues. Specifically, I explore whether Bacon argues
in the *New Atlantis* for England's continued imperial growth and
whether he advocates a policy of Christian toleration of Jews. In
*Of Plantations* Bacon describes colonies as 'heroical works'.[3]
Bacon's attitude to colonial expansion in the *New Atlantis* is
rather more complex. In this utopian world colonial endeavour is
redundant. The scientocracy described in the *New Atlantis* is
able to care for all the population's needs without territorial
expansion or foreign trade. However, for the Spanish sailors in
particular, and for Europe in general, colonial endeavour remains
important. The *New Atlantis*, then, displays different attitudes to
colonialism according to the relative civilisation and scientific
sophistication of the home nation. The *New Atlantis* shows both
the present inadequacies of James' England and offers a model
for the nation's future.

The *New Atlantis*'s figurative representation of England is also
explored by focusing on Bacon's representation of Jewishness.
Early modern culture represented Jewishness in contradictory
ways. Bacon's intervention in this discourse can be seen as similarly ambivalent. This essay shows that Bacon reproduces ideolo-
gically mediated inconsistencies endemic to English culture of
the period. My reading of the *New Atlantis* shows the difficulties
of 'speak[ing] plain' in two ways: first, Bacon's hostility to James
could not be explicitly articulated as 'plain speaking' was a
luxury that politically he could not afford; second, the fact that
the *New Atlantis* reproduces the social contradictions and tensions

of the time means that Bacon was unable to formulate unequivocal policies concerning Christian toleration of Jews and colonial
endeavour. In these discourses, 'plain speech' was a cultural
impossibility.

## Colonialism and travel in the early seventeenth century

By 1627, when Francis Bacon's *New Atlantis* was published, England had established overseas colonies and trade networks in
both the Old and New Worlds.[4] Since the publication of Hakluyt's
ambitious *Principal Navigations, Voyages, Traffiques and Discoveries of the English Nation* in 1589 – when England's empire
was only embryonic – significant increases in both territory and
trade had occurred.[5] East Indies trade started to generate large
profits; until 1615 the Russia Company was successful in its
whaling voyages; in 1618 trade to Africa, controlled by the Africa
Company, was re-established; while in 1606, James I issued the
First Virginia Charters.[6] In the years preceding the *New Atlantis*'s
appearance, then, various attempts were made to expand England's territory in the New World.[7] Promoters of English settle-
ment in North America argued that these activities would either
yield precious metals or establish new routes to the East, via the
West. Finally, and most potently, since precious metals had not
been found strewn lavishly around colonial landscapes, promoters
argued for the benefits of permanent self-supporting colonies
comprising a population that was, for one reason or another,
superfluous in England. There was also a vast body of writings
concerning the New World, offering a bewildering array of
interpretations of the life there. Some commentators argued that
America was an ideal world, others represented it as dissolute.[8] It
could either regenerate or contaminate the Old World. What was
needed was a strategy to manage this dangerous ambivalence.
The formulation of such a strategy was, I argue, Francis Bacon's
chief goal in the *New Atlantis*.

As previous commentators have noted, Bacon's ideal society
was similar to the civilisations described in Thomas More's
*Utopia* (1516), Johann Valentin Andreae's *Christianopolis* (1619),
and Tommaso Campanella's *Civitas Solis* (1625).[9] All of these
imagined societies were organised around particular structuring

principles – religion, state control, or science. The parallels between More's text and the *New Atlantis* are particularly striking since both take the discovery of America as the imaginative opening from which to generate a fantasy society.[10] For Thomas More, writing at the beginning of the sixteenth century, the recognition of America as a New World rather than part of the Old World, the Indies, was a highly topical issue. More's American setting provided both the text *Utopia* and imaginary place Utopia with a context against which Hythlodaeus' discovery narrative appeared authentic, since it anticipated detailed geographic and chorographic information concerning regions whose status was still in dispute. Though writing over one hundred years later, Bacon also connected his imaginary civilisation with the new continent. In the text itself, Bacon refers to 'Atlantis', the island – named after Atlas and, supposedly, inhabited by his descendants – described by Plato in *Timaeus* and *Critias*.[11] In 1552, Francisco Lopez de Gomara in *Historia de la conquista de Mexico* had equated Plato's Atlantis with the continent of America. More correctly, the existing American landmass and people were all that remained of Atlantis because, after an earthquake, the sea had inundated the original continent.[12] Bacon refers to this legend since Great Atlantis (America) had been depopulated by flood in the past.

Bacon's location of New Atlantis in the little-known regions beyond the New World, between Great Atlantis and the Orient, increased both the authenticity and credibility of his narrative. In the 1620s Europeans still did not know the scope of America. French and English colonial outposts were dotted in a piecemeal fashion along North America's eastern coastline, and the Portuguese and Spanish in particular had established sizeable settlements in South America.[13] Indeed, the occasion for the *New Atlantis* is its accidental discovery by Spanish tars attempting to sail from Peru to China and Japan. However, America's Western coastline and, in particular, the continent's interior, had only been sketchily mapped.[14] Most of what we now know as North and South America still had to be surveyed and it was thought highly possible that further discoveries of new lands would be made specifically in these areas. Furthermore, this geographical position had an ideological significance. The East had long been associated with fantastic and marvellous peoples, landscapes, and civilisations.[15] The people imagined to be living in these regions were regularly described as, for example, two-headed, hermaphroditic, prodigious, or monstrous.[16] Consequently, even though in the 1620s America had become incorporated into Western perceptions of the known world since several European states had settlements and subjects there, its nethermost regions could still yield fantastic peoples and civilisations. America and the regions potentially beyond it were simultaneously part of the known world, since reports of the life to be experienced there were in circulation, but could also be represented imaginatively on maps and in literature since their scope was not yet known. By placing New Atlantis in the interstice between America and the Orient, Bacon's text focuses on continuing European assimilative problems (conceptual and practical) with regard to geographically remote regions.

But what was Bacon's attitude to colonialism by the mid–1620s? In his earlier works, such as *The Advancement of Learning* and *The Great Instauration*, he had appeared concerned that England should rival Spanish imperium. On the frontispiece of the latter text, for example, Bacon placed an image of the Pillars of Hercules – the traditional limits of knowledge – with a galleon sailing beyond them.[17] Furthermore, he appropriated the Holy Roman Emperor Charles V's expansionist and heroic motto *plus ultra* (further yet) and applied it to his scientific schemes.[18] Such images were used to argue that future English discoveries – including navigational voyages – would restore Man's lost dominion over Nature. But to discover whether Bacon's confident representation of the benefits of scientific colonialism continues in his later work we need to look at the ways in which Bacon represented science, travel, and colonialism in the *New Atlantis*.

The society described in the *New Atlantis* is an authoritarian one: the state of Bensalem is controlled by an autonomous scientocracy that focuses on the institution of Salomon's House, the centre for empirical research. Contact between the scientists and the larger society is limited; one of the Fathers of Salomon's House visits the capitol in the course of the narrator's stay but this is the only contact in twelve years. Indeed, though this society clearly privileges science, the narrator and reader only

hear about the achievements and advances made by Salomon's
House through the Father's descriptions. Apart from antiseptic
oranges and 'small grey or whitish pills' – which cure the
illnesses of the narrator's compatriots on arrival – no descriptions
of scientific achievements and inventions are provided (461). In
this text, then, both narrator and reader wait to be allowed to see
the social and political benefits of scientocratic rule first-hand.
From the very beginning the narrator is aware that Salomon's
House is the politically dominant institution in the state. The
Governor of the Strangers' House – the place where the narrator
and his compatriots are accommodated on arrival – calls Salomon's House 'the very eye of this kingdom' (464). This metaphor
– with its empirical, ocular resonance – emphasises the all-
powerful nature of the institution. The accolade is given during
the description of New Atlantis' conversion to Christianity.
Indeed, out of all that saw the 'great pillar of light … rising from
the sea a great way up towards heaven', only the scientist from
Salomon's House understood its significance as a message from
God (464). Because of the New Atlantans' concern about identifying the religion of the strangers on arrival, and the importance
that the culture accords to the conversion of New Atlantis to
Christianity, scientific perception, as well as that of the individual scientist, is applauded. However, since Salomon's House and
the larger society of Bensalem are kept apart, the *New Atlantis*
repeatedly digresses from its ostensible aim of making explicit
the benefits of co-operation between science and society. Indeed,
as J. C. Davis argues, the *New Atlantis* can be seen as a quest
narrative since the text never delivers a full account of the
benefits of a society governed by science.[19] Similar to other quest
stories, strangers – mariners and readers alike – have a series of
tests they must pass before being allowed to see the epicentre of
the *New Atlantis*. The close association between the reader and
the narrator is designed to coerce the reader into supporting the
ideology of the world s/he is entering. Just as the mariners must
assert their Christianity before being allowed to land, the text
also attempts to persuade its readers to embrace the normative
values of this society. Furthermore, the mariners' position as
strangers or outsiders to this society also forces readers to support New Atlantan doctrine. Since Bacon appropriates travel

literature's standard narrative technique – an explorer arrives in a strange world and, in the course of his or her stay, observes, with increasing familiarity, the workings of the alien society – the progress of the narrative charts the strangers' gradual assimilation into this foreign environment. Such strategies attempt to disarm opposition to alien cultures. To serve this end, the trial of strangers continues throughout the story. For example, strangers have to show they are prepared to obey the smaller rules of the society, such as agreeing not to go further than a 'karan ... from the walls of the city, without especial leave,' before they are allowed to proceed to the next stage of their quest (462).

Though it mimics the formal characteristics and style of the kind of voyage narrative to be found in Hakluyt's collection, the *New Atlantis* is – paradoxically – distinctly uneasy in its representation of the benefits of travel. This unease is revealed in other contemporary texts, where travel is represented as a potentially subversive activity that needs strict controls placed upon it. For example, Jerome Turler's *The Traveiller* (1575) was sceptical of travel when seeking to define the 'preceptes of traveyling'.[20] Turler argues that a traveller must always remember his homeland and not assume the manners of the people among whom he is living. Thomas More's *Utopia* anticipated these beliefs. More appeared wary of the potential of travel and the contact with strangers which might, he believed, result in social and political discontent in the traveller's home society. The inhabitants of Utopia who wished to travel were allowed to do so by the state only under strict passport controls that defined the limit of their journey.[21] In Bacon's later text, there was a small but vital change to this cautious attitude towards travel. King Solamona also feared the negative consequences of contact with strangers and other cultures. Yet, though he forbade all citizens to travel outside the boundaries of their national waters, he nonetheless authorised two ships to be sent forth every twelve years. Manned by a staff of three 'research fellows', their mission was to acquire knowledge of 'the sciences, arts, manufacturers and inventions of all the world' (471). The blanket ban imposed upon travel outside the state boundaries in More's ideal society is transformed into a selective and controlled policy of reconnaissance in Bacon's text. In the *New Atlantis* independent travel is not permitted, but the scientocracy authorises travel missions that support the aims of the state. Useful discoveries made on these government-defined voyages are, the narrator is informed (though we see scant direct evidence), then disseminated by the state. Contact with other cultures and the potential exchange of values are thus strictly limited. Indeed, New Atlantan policy insists that contact with other cultures be a one-way process. In the host country the visiting scientists remain incognito, 'colour[ing] themselves under the names of other nations' (472). This disguise, or camouflage, of their true identity, and the secrecy which characterises the Governor's tantalising but sketchy description of the practicalities of these missions, illustrates Bacon's desire to control the power of travel to effect change. The whole of the central part of the text deals with the reasons behind Europe's ignorance of the existence of New Atlantis but, since Bacon describes the peaceful, utopian lifestyle such isolation has caused, it is clear that he supports the policy. The scientocracy created a system of espionage that has enabled New Atlantis to learn about other countries without becoming subject to haphazard cultural exchange.

Even more significantly, the state in the *New Atlantis* precludes the possibility of telling travellers' tales. Since the scientists live in isolation and the narrator/reader is given no concrete examples of the results of the scientists' foreign espionage activities, the traveller's tales – which simultaneously describe experiences beyond the traveller's home society and demonstrate a desire to be re-included by the home society – cannot be told.[22] Travellers' tales serve no purpose for a scientocracy: with their ambiguous anti-establishment resonances that hint at the benefits of subversive individual experience, travellers' tales have no place in a society governed and censored by an autocratic institution.

How, then, is this cautious and authoritarian attitude to travel accommodated by a text that so explicitly imitates the rhetorical strategies of a voyage narrative? There are two different attitudes towards travel within this text, depending on whether the narrator's society or New Atlantis's society is described. New Atlantis is represented to the narrator as self-sufficient since it no longer needs to forge economic links with other countries. For example, the Governor of the Strangers' House claims that they 'maintain a trade, not for gold, silver, or jewels; nor for silks; nor for spices; nor any other commodity of matter; but only for God's first creature, which was *Light*: to have *light* (I say) of the growth of all parts of the world' (472). However, he goes on to recount a past history of commercial links. Previously, New Atlantans traded with all the great civilisations including the Phoenicians, the Tyrians, the Carthaginians, the Egyptians, the Palestinians, the Chinese, and the Great Atlantans. These earlier trade networks are no longer valued. The fertility of the land and Salomon's House, which seeks 'the true nature of things' in order to give 'the more fruit in the use of them', provide all the materials necessary for the population to enjoy a life of comfort 'without any aid at all of the foreigner' (472). Furthermore, this history of past contacts is figured as a time of national rivalry and war:

> The said country of Atlantis, as well as that of Peru, then called Coya, as that of Mexico, then named Tyrambel, were mighty and proud kingdoms in arms, shipping, and riches: so mighty; as at one time (or at least within the space of ten years) they both made two great expeditions; they of Tyramble through the Atlantic to the Mediterranean Sea; and they of Coya through the South Sea upon this our island. (467–8)

The Governor is tantalisingly vague about the outcome of this first expedition into Europe. All he is certain about is that 'there never came back either ship nor man from that voyage' (468). He also describes the way a subsequent hostile expedition by these nations against New Atlantis was speedily and peacefully dealt with. This history has important implications for understanding Bacon's views of colonialism. First, Europe was conquered by the warlike and proud states of Tyrambel and Coya; second, 'Great Atlantis' was punished by 'Divine Revenge' for its ambition with a 'particular deluge or inundation' (468). Consequently, inhabitants of Europe are constructed as descendants of these warlike peoples, and native Americans – who were dispersed and isolated afterwards so that they are effectively a thousand years younger than other peoples – are represented as simple and child-like.[23] Only New Atlantis escaped the negative consequences of these colonial expeditions as the country was strong enough to repulse hostile marauders and restrained enough not to trounce them unmercifully. It is in the wake of this history that King Solamona, 'doubting novelties, and commixture of manners', establishes an isolationist policy for his country (470). This would seem to mean that New Atlantis was putting forward an anti-colonial argument in attempting to foster a policy against aggressive empire-building.[24]

However, the text's attitude towards expansion and exploration by European countries is strikingly different from its support of the New Atlantan isolationist policy. The narrator's/reader's contact with this utopian society is designed to be didactic. Though the narrator and his fellows speak Spanish, they function as representatives of Europe as a whole. Neither their Catholicism nor their particular national identity appears important. Rather, these characters are the products of a history of past aggressive colonisation that has affected Europe as a whole. Such a history makes them inferior to their hosts, whose former judiciousness has resulted in a peaceful and advanced civilisation. The appropriation of the rhetorical strategies of a voyage narrative clearly signals that this text was designed to be a learning tool for the reader/narrator. Contact with New Atlantan culture and value systems would enable the voyagers from Europe to observe the workings of a society that would inspire them to implement changes in their homelands on their return to Europe. Indeed, the Father from Salomon's House, at the very end of this fragmentary text, after blessing the narrator (thus showing their shared Christianity), explicitly gives the narrator permission to 'publish it for the good of other nations' (488). The successes of New Atlantis (signalled by its description here as 'God's bosom') need to be promulgated throughout Europe in order to effect the reorganisation of society according to scientific principles.

Bacon's text, then, simultaneously exhibits contrasting attitudes concerning the benefits of colonialism and empire-building. The benefits of government by scientocracy are such that further contact with the outside world is neither necessary nor desirable. New Atlantis is self-sufficient, no longer needing to forge trading links with other areas in the world. Furthermore, the scientocracy is concerned that interaction with less-advanced societies would prove culturally destabilising. However, for the European visitors in New Atlantis, contact with such a sophisticated society can only be beneficial. Until scientocracies dominate Europe, trade, colonialism and empire-building are not only inevitable, but to be encouraged. If Europe – personified by the Spanish-speaking sailors in this text – had not started to expand its horizons by voyages of exploration and the attendant empire-building, then the valuable association with New Atlantis Bacon describes here could not have been established.

## The wisdom of Solomon: the *New Atlantis* and monarchy

Thus far, I have argued that the *New Atlantis* is not a text that explicitly or obviously attacks the Spanish imperium. Rather, Bacon's text refigures the established European hierarchical theory of social development from barbarism to civility.[25] Acosta's *Naturall and Morall Historie of the East and West Indies*, translated into English in 1604, was one of Bacon's sources.[26] Acosta's text shows a progression in human civilisation from pre-Inca barbarity to natural law and civilisation under the Incas, and, ultimately, to the achievement of Christian culture under Spanish colonialism. In Bacon's text, though, New Atlantans have replaced Europeans as the most civilised nation and, importantly, Europe in general is castigated. However, there are some aspects of the *New Atlantis* that are specifically aimed at English domestic and foreign policies. In particular, Bacon uses the *New Atlantis* as a vehicle to address some of the inadequacies of James I's rule.

Indeed, in the *New Atlantis* King Solamona can be seen as the personification and encapsulation of all the values and policies that Bacon wished James I had followed. Similar to King Solomon of the Hebrews, King Solamona was wise and revered. Bacon explicitly appropriates Scriptural quotation associated with Solomon (1 Kings 4:29) when he describes Solamona's 'large heart' (469). But the New Atlantan monarch's lasting achievement in the *New Atlantis* was his policy to institutionalise science. This strategy has, according to the text, brought about prosperity and stability. By 1623–24 James I, the monarch whom Bacon so hopefully praised in the opening pages of *The Advancement of Learning*, had failed to make any significant financial commitment to projects for the institutionalisation of science in England.

Similar to James I, King Solamona supported a pacific foreign policy; but there were crucial differences between the relative situations of the two kings. The New Atlantan monarch's strategy was based on the essential strength of his nation. As Bacon makes clear, Solamona's kingdom is capable of self-sufficiency and, therefore, he instituted a policy of isolation to protect New Atlantis from foreign interference. James's foreign policy was based on the essential weakness of England's position as he sought to construct England as a diplomatic buffer between warring Catholic and Protestant nations in Europe. By maintaining cordial relations with each of these states or monarchies, whose interests were opposed to each other, England could, James believed, fashion a decisive role for itself.[27]

One effect of King Solamona's isolationist policy was New Atlantis's concentration upon the organisation of its own internal workings at an optimum level as the society promoted and institutionalised science. James' policies produced no such utopia: rather, the monarch Bacon served experienced a turbulent reign domestically and did not increase England's influence in Europe. Since James had failed to support Bacon's empirical project, little progress had been achieved in the 'arts or manufactures' that could make England self-sufficient. Furthermore, between 1621 and 1624, England suffered an economic crisis during which the balance of payments was extremely unfavourable.[28] One of the root causes of this economic crisis had been Alderman Cockaygne's project for English cloth merchants to start finishing their cloth products as well as exporting 'in the white' cloth, a policy which received royal support and sponsorship in 1614.[29] Though designed to provide employment for English workers, increase profits, and create revenue for the Crown, Cockaygne's project was a financial disaster. By 1617 the policy was revoked, but the wool industry had entered recession. As markets shrank, wool prices fell and bankruptcies and unemployment were widespread. The blame for this economic crisis was persistently levelled at James' support of Cockaygne's project.[30]

The failure of James' economic and foreign policies for England is contrasted with the success of those favoured by King Solamona in the *New Atlantis*. Facing financial ruin and banished from the court following his impeachment – for James had failed to protect his Chancellor against charges of corruption – Bacon signalled his criticisms of James I by identifying similarities between King Solomon of the Hebrews and King Solamona in the *New Atlantis*, which now pointedly excluded his own monarch.[31] In *The Advancement of Learning* Bacon praised the personal qualities of James I in glowing terms referring to 'the propriety and excellence of your individual person' (120). He also linked him with Solomon by appropriating the Scriptural description about the Hebrew king 'That his heart was as the sands of the sea' (1 Kings: 4: 29) and complimented James' perspicacity (120). In other texts written and published prior to his impeachment Bacon clearly associated Solomon's wisdom with James. For example, when addressing the House of Lords immediately after the king opened the 1618 parliamentary session, Bacon used Solomon's saying, 'The words of the wise are as nails and pins driven in and fastened by the masters of assemblies.' Bacon then advised parliament to heed the King's wishes, 'The King is the master of this assembly, and though his words in regards of the sweetness of them do not prick, yet in regard of the weight and wisdom of them, I know they pierce through and through.'[32] However, by the time Bacon wrote the *New Atlantis*, James – previously represented as the 'English Solomon' by Bacon – was no longer mentioned. Indeed, in the *History of the Reign of King Henry VII* (1622) – the first text he published after his impeachment – Bacon explicitly identified the first Tudor monarch as the 'English Solomon'. Furthermore, he dedicated this text to Prince Charles rather than King James.[33]

In the *New Atlantis* the representation of a model king, who possessed all the positive resemblances of the Hebrew Solomon, served to highlight James's failure to execute the policies Bacon favoured. James was no longer associated with the king whose wisdom Bacon revered. However, even after his impeachment and the king's failure to sign his pardon despite repeated requests, Bacon still did not directly attack his monarch. His critique of James was necessarily subtle: as long as there was even a slim chance of pardon, and with his financial affairs in disarray, an explicit attack would have been foolhardy. Consequently, in the *New Atlantis* Bacon's disillusion with James I – a monarch from whom he had in 1605 confidently expected so much – was translated into an idealised depiction of King Solamona who had, in the fantasy society of Bensalem, enacted all of Bacon's favoured policies. By 1623–24, Bacon's hopes for England's domestic and foreign expansion and growth were directed towards Prince Charles. In the *New Atlantis* Bacon implied that King James I, by refusing to support the furtherance of empirical knowledge, had failed to shape a decisive role for England against foreign competitors.

The *New Atlantis* does not, therefore, criticise the institution of monarchy since the example of Solamona shows the benefits a good king can bring to a nation. The strategy Bacon employs here – criticising his own monarch through the praise of another – is one which is also used in the text's discussion of the relative merits of the Spanish and English empires. Ostensibly, this text does not appear to attack the Spanish imperium since the civilisation of New Atlantis is used to castigate Europe as a whole. However, in the same way that King Solamona both served to highlight the inadequacies of King James and shape the behaviour of future English monarchs, in the *New Atlantis* the Spanish-speaking sailors' presence is designed to act as a spur to English colonial endeavour even as it shows that James's lacklustre policies have allowed foreign rivals to seize the initiative. The fact that the benefit of first contact with Bacon's utopia falls to Spanish speakers does not signal support for the Iberians. Rather, it shows James' failure to invest in the kind of scientific, navigational and colonial enterprises that might have allowed the English to enjoy such spoils. In the *New Atlantis* Columbus, the man who 'discovered the West Indies' for Spain, is venerated by the Fathers of Salomon's House with a 'statua' (487). Yet, importantly, the Portuguese explorer is just one among a long list of inventors who are all either legendary or cannot be identified. Columbus's inclusion within such an uncertain list and the fact that his discovery was only new knowledge to Europe, not to New Atlantan civilisation, casts a shadow over his achievement. Such circumspection about the rights of Spain to sole dominion in certain New World territories is also revealed in other texts. In *The History of King Henry VII*, Bacon caustically comments that Columbus's sponsor, but for a mishap at sea, would have been England's king.[34] The Spanish-speaking sailors' discovery of

New Atlantis works in a similar way: they were fortuitously blown off course from their intended destination of China or Japan. More importantly, though, their discovery of New Atlantis implies that the English are badly governed since James I had not learnt from Henry VII's mistakes. Significant monarchic investment in discovery and new knowledge would have allowed the English to get there first. Not only, then, does Bacon praise Solamona in order to criticise James I, he implies that the Spanish have discovered New Atlantis in order to reveal the lack of emphasis England's monarch places on his country's future international prosperity. The direct expression of such sentiments would indeed make a 'counsellor blanch'.

## Joabin, Jewishness and social contradiction in the *New Atlantis*

We have seen the carefully coded manner in which Bacon attacks James I in the *New Atlantis* as he observes the disparity between England's monarch and the New Atlantan king. Bacon's criticisms of James are also signalled by the fact that it is Spanish speakers, not English speakers, who enjoy first contact with New Atlantis. Given the implied criticism of these remarks, it is not surprising that the *New Atlantis* deliberately chooses not to 'speak plain' concerning such matters. It is a text that debates the merits and success of English colonial and monarchic policies camouflaged as a discussion about the government of a foreign and remote civilisation. The last section of this essay also focuses on the ways the *New Atlantis* refuses to 'speak plain' through an examination of Bacon's contradictory representations of Jewishness. The portrayal of Jewishness in the *New Atlantis* has received little scholarly attention yet, since so much of the narrator's understanding of New Atlantan society (particularly non-scientific aspects) is derived from the Jewish character Joabin, it is an area that calls for further exploration.[35] Furthermore, because Bacon's text invites readers to see New Atlantis as a metaphor for England, we need to examine the representation of Jewishness in the *New Atlantis* in the light of this identification.

Early seventeenth-century English representations of Jewishness are complex. Officially at least, there was no native Jewish population – though some Jewish families were present under licence others were disguised as Conversos, or New Christians.[36] In addition, there was a strong tradition of anti-Semitic depictions of Jews in circulation that imagined them as treasonous, sexually monstrous, foul smelling, and guilty of the ritual murder of Christians.[37] In contrast to these antipathetic depictions, many theologians highlighted the role Christians believed Jews would play in ushering in the millennium. These latter representations were less explicitly hostile, but nevertheless still rendered Jewishness through the filter of Christianity since Jews were only seen positively because they were imminently expected to convert.[38]

Bacon's representation of the character of Joabin appears to be a conflation of these divergent depictions of Jewishness. Superficially Joabin is described in positive ways: he is depicted as 'a wise man, and learned, and of great policy, and excellently seen in the laws and customs of that nation' (476). Furthermore, and more importantly, the Father of Salomon's House appears to be staying with Joabin whilst he is visiting the city. Such an honour would at first sight suggest that Bacon supports the toleration of Jews which Bensalem encourages and wishes to foster it in Europe, and indeed England. Yet, though the character and status of Joabin seem to show the possibility of Jewish–Christian harmony, this interpretation cannot be sustained. Joabin appears to be named after the Old Testament Joab (which means 'Yahweh is father' in Hebrew). Joab was the untrustworthy nephew of King David who treasonably tried to prevent Solomon from becoming king after David had named him as his successor. Furthermore, Joab was a violent and cruel murderer whose 'house' and 'seed' were cursed by both King David and King Solomon.[39] Indeed, Joab is represented in the Bible as a particularly wily individual who is capable of appearing loyal while in fact pursuing his own agenda. Given Bacon's familiarity with Old Testament Scripture and his reverence of Solomon, the choice of 'Joabin', a name resonant with treason, signals unease at the very least.

Bacon's distrust of Jewishness is revealed in other texts. In his 1594 account of the attempt on Elizabeth I's life, *A True Account of the Detestable Treason, Intended by Dr Roderigo Lopez*, the Queen's physician is described as 'a person wholly of a corrupt and mercenary nature'.[40] Indeed Bacon writes, though 'here he [Lopez] conformed himself to the rites of the Christian religion,' nevertheless he was 'suspected to be in sect secretly a Jew'.[41] Bacon's version of the Lopez affair is interesting because the Portuguese Jew's treason is represented as part of Phillip II's plot to oust Elizabeth. Thus Lopez's case is used to maintain English hostility to Spain in the wake of the Armada crisis.[42] Lopez, according to Bacon, is doubly perfidious since for financial gain he treasonously acts against his adoptive homeland, England, and his native land, Portugal. Because of 'pleasing and appliable behaviour' Lopez was 'favoured in court' since his real political allegiances, just like his true religion, were practised secretly.[43] Consequently, Lopez, similar to Joabin in the *New Atlantis*, who is allowed privileged access to the Father of Salomon's House, was not suspected of harbouring malicious intent and was permitted frequent and privy contact with Queen Elizabeth.[44] Lopez' treason and his Jewishness are thus yoked together by Bacon since they both remained a secret and were not discovered until it was almost too late ('by God's marvellous goodness her Majesty hath been preserved').[45]

The difficulty Christians experienced in distinguishing a Jew from a Christian is also revealed in Bacon's *History of the Reign of King Henry VII*. As previously described, Henry VII, not James, is represented as the 'English Solomon' and this text is dedicated to the heir to the throne, not the reigning monarch. Furthermore, Bacon describes Perkin Warbeck, the man who pretended to be Richard Duke of York, as Jewish in origin since he is the son of 'John Osbeck (a converted Jew)' and, 'being known in court, the King either out of religious nobleness, because he was a convert, or upon some private acquaintance, did him the honour as to be godfather to his child.'[46] Bacon's account confuses John Osbeck, Perkin Warbeck's father, with Sir Edward Brompton, alias Duarte Brandão, an Anglo-Portuguese Jewish merchant, who was the godson of Edward IV. Bacon's misidentification is perhaps understandable since Warbeck did have a connection with the Bromptons, having travelled to Portugal with Lady Brompton in 1487.[47] Since King Edward stood as godfather for the young Perkin – a position monarchs often accepted to give some sort of status to their illegitimate offspring – Bacon hints that Warbeck's family might have intimate connections with the Plantagenet king 'upon some private acquaintance'.[48]

Perkin, like Joabin in the *New Atlantis*, who is prone to 'Jewish dreams' concerning Judaism's role in the state of Bensalem, fantasises about his origins (476). However, Warbeck was not Edward's son '(though that were not)'; he was the son of a converted Jew.[49] Yet there remains the problem of his appearance and manner so closely resembling those of a Plantagenet, 'insomuch as it was generally believed, as well amongst great persons, as amongst the vulgar, that he was indeed Duke Richard'.[50] It seems, then, that the son of a converted Jew can imitate an English king so well, both in appearance and deportment, that nobody – noble and vulgar alike – can tell the difference. Bacon's *History of the Reign of King Henry VII* shows the consequences of this inability to distinguish converted Jew – a 'wanderer' and a 'landloper' (a vagabond) – from rightful monarch since Henry VII was forced, over a period of several years, to defend his right to rule against Warbeck and his English and foreign supporters.[51] In this text Bacon highlights the difficulties of telling Jew from Christian, or loyal subject from traitor.

Bacon's representations of Jewishness in his account of the Lopez case and in his *History of the Reign of King Henry VII* signal unease about Christian policies of Jewish toleration. Both Lopez, a Converso, and Warbeck, the son of a Jewish convert, were either allowed to become close to English monarchs, or benefited from connections with them, and yet they were treasonable. The presence and status of Joabin, who is not merely tolerated in Bensalem but is also allowed privileged access to the elusive Father of Salomon's House, appears, in the light of Bacon's other hostile portrayals of Jewishness, to represent a potential threat to the continued peacefulness of the New Atlantan state.

In Bacon's *History of the Reign of King Henry VII* Warbeck's influence on those around him is described in supernatural, even quasi-messianic, terms. Similar to Christ, there are portents of Warbeck's 'birth'; he is referred to as a 'blazing star' and 'a meteor' who is to appear upon 'the horizon of Ireland'.[52] Furthermore, he is so persuasive 'both to move pity, and to induce belief' that he exerts 'a kind of fascination and enchantment to those that saw him or heard him' and converts them to his cause.[53]

Finally, his nativity is miraculous, but unnatural, since he made the post-menopausal Margaret, Duchess of Burgundy, fertile and, 'whereas other natural mothers bring forth children weak ... she bringeth forth tall striplings, able soon after their coming into the world to bid battle to mighty kings'.[54] Such descriptions signal that Warbeck is a false messiah. He is embraced by all those who are either gullible or treasonable in the same way that Christians represent Jews who, since they refuse to acknowledge Jesus, still wait for the true Messiah.

Joabin's 'Jewish dreams' in the *New Atlantis* work in the same way. Joabin believed 'by tradition among the Jews ... that the people thereof were of the generations of Abraham, by another son, whom they call Nachoran' (476). Abraham's brother Nahor (or Nachor) was, similar to their father Terah, known for idolatry (Gn. 31:53 and Jos. 24:2). In other words, though Abraham became the father of Israel and was revered by both Jews and Christians, Nahor enjoyed no such exalted status. Consequently, since Joabin venerates an idolatrous figure within Judaism, Bacon shows the weaknesses of the Bensalem Jews' beliefs. Furthermore, though Joabin 'would ever acknowledge that Christ was born of a Virgin, and that he was more than a man', he was still waiting for the time 'when the Messiah should come' (476). It seems, then, that the Christian narrator's initial assertion that Joabin 'was of a far differing disposition from the Jews in other parts' who 'hate the name of Christ, and have a secret rancour against the people amongst whom they live', is over-optimistic (476). Joabin may not be, in fact, as Christianised as this description implies. He is circumcised and he does not recognise Christ as the Messiah. Such marks of difference signal that, like Joab and like Dr Lopez, Joabin, too, may have a 'secret rancour' against Christians which has not yet been revealed.

What Bacon attempts to represent in his depiction of Joabin's Jewishness in the *New Atlantis* is a strategy that controls difference. The differences signalled by his Jewishness are, at one level, reduced, since Joabin ostensibly reveres Bensalem and is loyal to the state. Indeed, Bacon's depiction of Joabin is similar to his representation of travel in this text. As long as a strategy was in place to manage the changes that travel brought in outlook and experience, then it was something to be encouraged. Joabin is a merchant. Consequently, since Bacon claims in the 1625 edition of both *Of Empire* and *Of Usury* that merchants are the 'vena porta', that is, the gate vein to the liver, Joabin is essential for the maintenance of the health of the body politic.[55] Indeed, in *Of Usury* it is not usurers' Jewishness that Bacon attacks but rather the non-regulation of usury which 'in process of time breeds a public poverty'.[56] In this essay Bacon proposes just such a strategy to regulate usury, so that 'the tooth be grinded, that it bite not too much.' In fact he writes, 'to speak of the abolishing of usury is idle: all states have ever had it, in one kind or rate or other. So as that opinion must be sent to Utopia.'[57] Bacon refers here to More's *Utopia* where, since there was no private property, there could be no usury. Such a reference is ironic; in the *New Atlantis* the figure of the Jewish merchant Joabin can be seen as Bacon's attempt to show the benefits of a regulated usury system in practice. Bensalem is a Christian society despite the presence of Joabin and contemporary fears that the tolerance of usury will result in a society becoming 'judaize[d]'.[58]

However, though it seems that the explicit aim of the character of Joabin is to show the harmony and profit Christian toleration of Jews can engender, as we have seen, the text is unable to maintain this positive representation. Bacon attempts to represent Joabin as Christianised but marks of his Jewishness still persist. For example, Joabin's description of Bensalem's chastity, which he contrasts with European sexual voracity, can be read in the light of his Jewishness. Ostensibly, Bensalem's emphasis upon chastity and the 'natural concupiscence' of marriage, which Joabin uses to condemn the 'meretricious embracements', 'stews' and 'dissolute houses' common in Europe, seems to be undiluted praise of the New Atlantan state (477). However, in *Of Marriage and Single Life* Bacon's support of marriage is rather more equivocal. He writes, 'He that hath wife and children hath given hostages to fortune, for they are impediments to great enterprises, either of virtue or mischief.'[59] It becomes clear that marriage is a form of social control more suited to some social groups than others. Marriage is represented as a corrective for the lower orders since 'wife and children are a kind of discipline of humanity', but it is not a panacea as 'the best works, and of greatest merit for the public, have proceeded from the unmarried or childless men.'[60] The advocation of marriage as social control for the masses, but not necessarily the elite, revealed here can also be seen in the *New Atlantis*. Joabin is circumcised; in other words, his sexual desires have been curbed by trimming his foreskin because, as the gloss to Genesis 17.11 in the Geneva Bible outlines, the 'privy part is circumcised to show that all that is begotten of man is corrupt and must be mortified'.[61] In his New Year's Day sermon about the Feast of Circumcision (1624) John Donne also ruminates on the connection between circumcision and sexual desire. Donne argues that 'this rebellious part is the root of all sin,' and that the privy member 'need[s] this stigmatical mark of circumcision to be imprinted upon it' to prevent Abraham's descendants from 'degenerat[ing] from the nobility of their race'.[62] Joabin's circumcision thus acts as an impediment to sexual desire – specifically Jewish sexual desire – in the same way that marriage is intended to control the lower social orders. Joabin's Jewishness and his descriptions of Bensalemite marriage practices amongst the general population are both representations of groups in need of social control. In other words, elite Christians – for example, the Fathers of Salomon's House and members of the English Protestant nobility like Bacon – do not need to be controlled in the same way since they are the performers of 'great enterprises'.[63] According to Bacon, these groups should remain unmarried in order to promote the interests of their respective governments more effectively. Consequently, though it initially seems that New Atlantan concupiscence is unequivocally recommended as an example to be learnt from by Europe, in fact it is selective in its application. Lower-class Christians can be sexually and socially controlled by marriage in the same way that Joabin's circumcision – though it marks him as indelibly alien – curbs Jewish sexual desire. Jews, then, need two restraints placed upon them. They need to be 'disciplined' by marriage in the same way as non-elite Christians, yet the regulated sexual outlet of marriage is not enough to control Jewish appetites. To control Joabin effectively, circumcision as well as marriage is needed.

It is clear, then, that Bacon has evolved a hierarchical theory of social control which is revealed here through descriptions of marriage and sexual practice. It is no surprise that elite Christians

– men like Bacon – occupy pole position. However, it is note-worthy that, though this text ostensibly aims to lessen the differ-ences between Jews and Christians through its representation of the Christianised-Jew Joabin, the *New Atlantis* confirms racial difference. The fact that Bacon's Jew needs marriage and circum-cision to 'discipline' him means that circumcision is simultane-ously an essential tool to ensure harmony in a Christian state and a mark of an alien culture. In effect the Jew can never fully turn Christian.

In the *New Atlantis* Joabin is not treasonable, but the threat of such treachery is present. The lessons Bacon believed needed to be learnt from the histories of Lopez and Warbeck are thus visited upon Joabin. In order to ensure that Joabin does not – like Lopez and, to an extent, Warbeck – become treasonable through the failure of state monitoring policies, in the *New Atlantis* the circumcision of Jews is practised to maintain social control and segregation. The alien nature the sign of circum-cision represents to a Christian culture prevents Joabin's com-plete assimilation into New Atlantan society. Just as Bacon evolves a dual attitude to colonial expansion in this text depending upon whether such activities are European or New Atlantan in origin, his representation of Jewishness is similarly double-voiced. On the one hand, the character Joabin shows the benefits of policies of Jewish–Christian toleration and assimilation which might in the future be achieved in England. On the other, the differences signalled by Joabin's Jewishness need to be maintained because, once they are eroded (as in the cases of Lopez and Warbeck), it becomes much harder for any government to distinguish Jew from Christian, or malcontent from faithful subject.

This essay has attempted to show the practical and ideological difficulties of 'speak[ing] plain' that Bacon encountered in the *New Atlantis*. We have identified the covert criticism Bacon levelled at James I. Indeed, the fact that Bacon's dissatisfaction was articulated obliquely should come as no surprise since for a counsellor not to make his advice palatable by sugaring the pill was political, often literal, suicide. Given the uncertainty of the patronage system and the powerlessness, or worse, of those that failed to please their patron, in the *New Atlantis* the monarch was unlikely to be the target of direct criticism.

We have also noted the social, political, and cultural contradictions of early seventeenth-century England reflected in the *New Atlantis*. Though this text recommends travel for the increase in knowledge it will engender, it is also riven by a fear that new knowledge will have a culturally destabilising effect. Consequently, we see a scientocracy in operation that insists on sole control over the filtering of new knowledge into the wider society. The *New Atlantis* is just as inconsistent in its representation of Jewishness. In the fictive world of the *New Atlantis*, Bacon attempts to show the value of Christian toleration and assimilation of Jews, but keeps returning to stereotypical Christian assumptions about Jewishness which maintain difference. Indeed, as my analysis of Bacon's representations of colonialism and Jewishness in the *New Atlantis* has revealed, it was quite possible for Bacon simultaneously to represent issues of colonialism and issues of Jewishness positively and negatively. Hence the *New Atlantis* does not 'speak plain' about these issues because the culture of Bacon's time was itself so divided concerning the benefits and drawbacks of policies of colonial endeavour and Jewish toleration. Bacon's opinions concerning England's monarch are deliberately, indeed pragmatically, obfuscated by the text. However, the text's representations of colonialism and Jewishness fail to 'speak plain' in another way. Due to the social inconsistencies inherent to Bacon's time, any kind of unequivocal statement about such subjects was impossible. Like Salomon's House, the *New Atlantis* does not, indeed cannot, easily divulge its secrets.

## Notes

For helpful critical readings of earlier drafts of this essay I would like to thank the following: Eliane Glaser, Andrew Hadfield, Paulina Kewes, Sarah Prescott, and Diane Watt.

1  Brian Vickers (ed.), *Francis Bacon: A Critical Edition of the Major Works* (Oxford, Oxford University Press, 1996), pp. 457–89 (p. 382). All subsequent references to Bacon's *The Advancement of Learning*, *Essays*, and *New Atlantis* are to this edition. Page references to *New Atlantis* will follow quotation in brackets.

2  *The Advancement of Learning*, p. 122.

3  *Essays*, p. 407.

4  On the dating of this text see Lisa Jardine and Alan Stewart, *Hostage to*

*Fortune: The Troubled Life of Francis Bacon* (London, Victor Gollancz, 1998), p. 476.

5  Richard Hakluyt, *The Principal Navigation, Voyages, Traffiques and Discoveries of the English Nation*, 12 vols. (London, J. M. Dent, 1927–1928). On Hakluyt's text, see Richard Helgerson, *Forms of Nationhood: The Elizabethan Writing of England* (Chicago, University of Chicago Press, 1992), pp. 107–47.

6  For further details see Carole Shammas, 'English commercial development and American colonisation', in K. R. Andrews, N. P. Canny and P. E. H. Hair (eds), *The Westward Enterprise: English Activities in Ireland, the Atlantic and America, 1480–1650* (Liverpool, Liverpool University Press, 1978), pp. 151–74; Brian Dietz, 'England's overseas trade in the reign of James I', in Alan G. R. Smith (ed.), *The Reign of James VI and I* (London, Macmillan, 1973), pp. 106–22.

7  See Louis B. Wright, 'Colonial developments in the reign of James I', in *The Reign of James I and VI*, pp. 123–39 (pp. 128–35); A. D. Innes, *The Maritime and Colonial Expansion of England under the Stuarts, 1603–1714* (London, Sampson Low, 1931), pp. 81–124; William Robert Scott, *The Constitution and Finance of English, Scottish and Irish Join-Stock Companies to 1720*, 3 vols (Cambridge, Cambridge University Press, 1910–12), vol. I, pp. 130–1.

8  See Michael Zuckerman, 'Identity in British America: unease in Eden', in Nicholas Canny and Anthony Pagden (eds), *Colonial Identity in the Atlantic World, 1500–1800*, (Princeton, Princeton University Press, 1987), pp. 115–59; and Nicholas Canny, 'The permissive frontier: the problem of social control in English settlements in Ireland and Virginia 1550–1650', in *The Westward Enterprise*, pp. 17–45. For a discussion of particular examples of ideal and degenerate representations of America see Claire Jowitt, 'Old worlds and new worlds: renaissance voyages of discovery', unpublished PhD dissertation, University of Southampton, 1996, pp. 159–73.

9  Thomas More, *Utopia*, trans. Paul Turner (Harmondsworth, Penguin, 1965); Johann Valentin Andreae, *Christianopolis*, ed. Felix Held (New York, Oxford University Press, 1916); Tommaso Campanella, *Civitas Solis*, trans. William J. Gilstrap, in G. Negley and J. Max Patrick (eds), *The Quest for Utopia: An Anthology of Imaginary Societies*, 2nd edn (College Park, Maryland, McGrath Publishing, 1971), pp. 181–207. On utopianism see J. C. Davis, *Utopia and the Ideal Society* (Cambridge, Cambridge University Press, 1981); Mary Baine Campbell, *The Witness and the Other World: Exotic European Travel Writing, 400–1600* (Ithaca, Cornell University Press, 1988); Amy Boesky, *Founding Fictions: Utopias in Early Modern England* (Athens and London, University of Georgia Press, 1996).

10  See Edward Surtz and J. H. Hexter (eds), *Utopia* (New Haven, Yale University Press, 1965), pp. i–xxxii.

11  On Plato's geography see J. A. Stewart, *The Myths of Plato* (London, Macmillan & Co, 1905), pp. 457–69.

12  On de Gomara's text see William Brandon, *New Worlds for Old: Reports from the New World and their Effect on the Development of Social Thought in Europe, 1500–1800* (Athens, Ohio, Ohio University Press, 1986), pp. 40–3.

13  See John Bakeless, *America as Seen by its First Explorers* (New York, Dover Publications, 1989), pp. 9–225.

14  See Leo Bagrow and R. A. Skelton, *History of Cartography*, 2nd edn (London, C. A. Watts, 1964), p. 193; Simon Berthon and Andrew Robinson, *The Shape of the World* (London, George Philip, 1991), pp. 81–100; John Goss, *The Mapping of North America: Three Centuries of Map-Making 1500–1860* (Secaucus, New Jersey, Wellfleet Press, 1990).

15  See Jerry Brotton, *Trading Territories: Mapping the Early Modern World* (London, Reaktion Books, 1997).

16  See Ruddolf Wittkower, 'Marvels of the East: a study in the history of monsters', *Journal of the Warburg and Courtauld Institutes*, 5 (1942), 159–97; Campbell, *The Witness and the Other World*, pp. 47–86; Robert Ralston Cawley, *Unpathed Waters: Studies in the Influence of the Voyages on Elizabethan Literature* (London, Frank Cass & Co. Ltd, 1967), p. 104.

17  Bacon, *Instauratio Magna* (London, 1620), frontispiece.

18  See John Steadman, 'Beyond Hercules: Francis Bacon and the scientist as hero', in *Studies in the Literary Imagination*, 4 (1971), 3–47; Claire Jowitt, 'Old worlds and new worlds', pp. 87–106.

19  Davis, *Utopia and the Ideal Society*, pp. 47 8.

20  Jerome Turler, *The Traveiller*, ed. D. E. Baughan (Gainseville, Florida, Scholars Fascimiles and Reprints, 1951), sig A3v.

21  More, *Utopia*, p. 84. For a similar reading, see Mary W. Helms, *Ulysses' Sail: An Ethnographic Odyssey of Power, Knowledge and Geographical Distance* (Princeton, Princeton University Press, 1988), p. 66.

22  See Wayne Franklin, *Discoverers, Explorers, Settlers? The Diligent Writers of Early America* (Chicago, Chicago University Press, 1979), p. 12.

23  See Anthony Pagden (ed.), *The Languages of Political Theory in Early Modern Europe*, (Cambridge, Cambridge University Press, 1987), pp. 79–98.

24  See Jeffrey Knapp, *An Empire Nowhere: England, America, and Literature from Utopia to The Tempest* (Berkeley, University of California Press, 1992); Andrew Hadfield, *Literature, Travel and Colonial Writing in the English Renaissance* (Oxford, Clarendon Press, 1999), pp. 69–133.

25  See J. H. Elliot, *The Old World and the New 1492–1650* (Cambridge, Cambridge University Press, 1991), pp. 30–1, 58–62.

26  Vickers (ed.), *Francis Bacon*, p. 786.

27  See Smith, *The Reign of James VI and I*, pp. 15–8; Simon L. Adams, 'The Protestant cause: religious alliance with the European Calvinist communities as a political issue in England, 1585–1630', unpublished D. Phil, Oxford, 1972.

28  See Dietz, 'England's overseas trade', p. 118.

29  *Ibid.*, p. 111.

30  See Astrid Friis, *Alderman Cockaygne's Project and the Cloth Trade* (Copenhagen, Levin & Munksgaard, 1927), p. 145.

31  See Jardine and Stewart, *Hostage to Fortune*, pp. 444–72.

32  Cited by Jardine and Stewart, *Hostage to Fortune*, p. 448. Other writers of the time also connected James I with Solomon: see, for example, John Carpenter, *Schelomoncham or King Solomon His Solace* (London, John Windes, 1606), sigs A6r, B3v.

33  See Howard B. White, *Peace Among the Willows: The Political Philosophy of Francis Bacon* (The Hague, Martinus Nijhoff, 1968), pp. 45–57.

34  Bacon, *History of the Reign of King Henry VII*, ed. Brian Vickers (Cambridge, Cambridge University Press, 1998), pp. 156–8.

35  See Lewis Feuer, 'Francis Bacon and the Jews', *Transactions of the Jewish Historical Society of England*, 29 (1982–6), 1–25.

36  See David Katz, *The Jews in the History of England, 1485–1850* (Oxford, Clarendon, 1996), pp. 1–106.

37  For further details see James Shapiro, *Shakespeare and the Jews* (New York, Columbia University Press, 1996).

38  See Christopher Hill, 'Till the conversion of the Jews', *Collected Essays*, 2 vols, (Amherst, University of Massachusetts Press, 1965), vol. II, pp. 269–300.

39  2 Samuel 3: 29; 1 Kings 2: 33.

40  *The Works of Francis Bacon*, ed. J. Spedding, R. L. Heath and Douglas Denon Ellis, 14 vols, (London, Longman, 1857–74), vol. VIII, p. 278.

41  Bacon, *Works*, vol. VIII, p. 278.

42  On Lopez see Katz, *The Jews*, pp. 49–106.

43  Bacon, *Works*, vol. VIII, p. 278.

44  See Katz, *The Jews*, p. 91.

45  Bacon, *Works*, vol. VIII, pp. 286–7.

46  Bacon, *History of the Reign*, p. 97.

47  See Ian Arthurson, *The Perkin Warbeck Conspiracy 1491–1499* (Stroud, Alan Sutton, 1994), pp. 25–42.

48  Bacon, *History of the Reign*, p. 97.

49  *Ibid.*, p. 97.

50  *Ibid.*, p. 102.

51  *Ibid.*, p. 96. See also Galit Hasan-Rokem and Alan Dundes, *The Wandering Jew: Essays in the Interpretation of a Christian Legend* (Bloomington, University of Indiana Press, 1986).

52  Bacon, *History of the Reign*, p. 99.

53  *Ibid.*, p. 96.

54  *Ibid.*, p. 108.

55  Bacon, *Essays*, pp. 379, 422.

56  *Ibid.*, p. 422.

57  *Ibid.*, pp. 422–3.

58  *Ibid.*, p. 421. See also Thomas Pie, *Usuries Spright Conjured* (London, Melchisech Bradwood, 1604), sig D2r; and see Shapiro, *Shakespeare and the Jews*, p. 98–100.

59  Bacon, *Essays*, p. 353.

60  *Ibid.*, p. 353.

61  See James Shapiro, *Shakespeare and the Jews*, pp. 117–21; Daniel Boyarin, *A Radical Jew: Paul and the Politics of Identity* (Berkeley, University of California Press, 1994), pp. 1–38.

62  John Donne, 'A Sermon Preached at Saint Dunstan's Upon New-Year's Day, 1624', *Sermons*, eds George R. Potter and Evelyn M. Simpson, 10 vols. (Berkeley, University of California Press, 1953–1962), vol. VI, pp. 190–2.

63  Bacon, *Essays*, p. 353.

# 8

# 'Strange things so probably told': gender, sexual difference and knowledge in Bacon's *New Atlantis*

## KATE AUGHTERSON

### I

Let us establish a chaste and lawful marriage between mind and nature, with the divine mercy as bridewoman.[1]

I am come in very truth leading to you Nature with all her children to bind her to your service and make her your slave ... so may I succeed in my only earthly wish, namely to stretch the deplorably narrow limits of man's dominion over the universe to their promised bounds.[2]

The human mind in studying nature becomes big under the impact of things, and brings forth a teeming brood of errors.[3]

Man, being the servant and interpreter of nature can do and understand so much and so much only as he has observed in fact or in thought of the course of nature ... nature to be commanded must be obeyed.[4]

Bacon's persistent use of gendered and sexualised metaphors in his scientific and philosophical writings is undeniable: but there is disagreement amongst critics over the significance of these metaphors. Baconian science has been accused of naturalising the discourse of science as one in which the proper object of scientific enquiry, nature, was feminised as a sexual object to be invaded, enquired into and dominated by masculine science.[5] Feminist critics argue that the separation of the object of enquiry (nature/ feminine/other) and subject (scientist/masculine/self) aided the development of a technological society in which an ethics of ecology (humankind as an integral part of nature) became philosophically and imaginably impossible.[6]

But Bacon uses sexualised and gendered metaphors in a more complex way than critical history allows. Was he really the 'founding father'[7] of a binary epistemology that linked reason, masculinity and knowledge in contradistinction to feeling, femininity and matter? The metaphors of chaste marriages and legitimate children certainly invoke the discourse of seventeenth-century patriarchy, but it is noticeable that the description of marriage is one of mutuality and equity ('nature to be commanded must be obeyed'). Bacon's utopian text, the *New Atlantis,* is both a literal representation and an allegorical figuration of Bacon's ideal society. Both sexual difference and gender are prominent literal and allegorical signifiers within the tale, and are therefore central to any interpretation of the text and to Bacon's epistemology. Concepts of sexual difference and gender in the *New Atlantis* inform and mark the way he asks us to think about science: but both the way of knowing and the object of knowledge do not subsist in a hierarchical gendered opposition. Instead, sexual difference and gender are both more equitable, more ethical and more fluid signifiers of our relationship with the natural world than has generally been recognised.

This essay raises four theoretical issues about the *New Atlantis,* Bacon's epistemology and its link to gender and sexual difference. First, a utopia is a description of an ideal society:[8] if gender and sexual difference are central to Bacon's new epistemology, this should be textually transparent. Second, more complex analyses of the utopian genre suggest that the utopian text betrays a dialectical relationship to its originating society and ideology. Jameson, for example, argues:

> all genuine utopias betray a complicated apparatus which is designed to 'neutralise' the topical allusion, at the same time that it produces and reinforces it.[9]

Utopian texts demonstrate rhetorically and narrationally their originating ideological contradictions and debates by displacing them into a fictional no-where. This, in turn, offers ways of re-thinking these ideologies. In other words, utopian fiction simul-taneously displaces and asserts its critique of contemporary power relations and structures. The *New Atlantis*, then, should demonstrate this dialectical relationship to both its topical sources and its proposed ideal society.[10] Jameson's approach, however, offers an additional and fruitful avenue of thought, leading us to consider to what extent gender and sexual differ-ence in the *New Atlantis* may 'neutralise' radical scientific proposals, or be key to the topical critique of contemporary ideology. Third, gender is a key signifier of difference and status in the early modern period, marshalled and manipulated by writers grappling with concepts of difference and status in fields other than those of gender and sexuality. Consequently, representations of gender and sexual difference also narrate and challenge power structures, including those of dominant epistemologies.[11] Fourth, given that gender representations are implicated in power structures, the utopian genre, by creating a 'neutral' place from which to view its originating culture, is a key genre through which contemporary gender ideology and its link with Bacon's reformulation of epistemology is displayed and displaced.

This essay aims to re-historicise the marshalling of gender in the *New Atlantis* and to argue that an understanding of Bacon's use and manipulation of the utopian genre helps re-articulate the gendering of his epistemology. As a consequence of our theor-etical approach, there are some key questions to ask about gender and sexual difference in the *New Atlantis*. To what extent are gender and sexual difference presented in normative terms within the text and how do they relate to contemporary writings about, and contests over, gender? Do they, for example, contest Jacobean political norms? Does utopian discourse reconfigure gender and sexual difference, and in what ways does the *New Atlantis* shed a different light on the epistemological and gendered paradigm described by his critics?[12]

Sexual difference and gender are displayed, both literally and allegorically, within the fable: yet such images are carefully placed rhetorically, structurally and symbolically. Bacon asks us to renew our ways of looking at the world, and both sexual difference and gender are part of this re-visioning. This essay will first argue that the structural placing of gender issues crucially determines our interpretations, and then assess Bacon's literal and symbolic use of gender difference in the light of his utopian discourse.

## II

There are two discernible and interlinking tripartite structures to the fable: the sequential linear narrative structure and the thematic content. The linear structure moves us gradually closer to the centre of the island's meaning:[13] the travellers' arrival told through the narrator's eyes; the island's history and relationship with the outside world narrated by the Governor; finally, the island's customs, narrated directly through the narrator's experience, conversations with Joabin, and the words of the Father of Salomon's House. The tripartite thematic structure displays the relations between the island and the outside world; the marital, familial and sexual habits and structures of the island; and an account of Salomon's House and the new science. Linear and thematic structures are carefully ordered to manipulate and initiate the reader. The reading time of the fable traces the reader's and narrator's gradual movement from exclusion to inclusion in the new world. The narrator, men and reader are first confined in the liminal position of the Strangers' House and access knowledge only through the narration of past history, before being permitted to move into present experience and future possibilities. Grammatical tenses mimic this movement through time, from past historic, through the present tense to the future.

The thematic structure moves on a parallel axis: from an understanding of the island and the outside world; to knowledge of familial structures, including those of gender and sexual difference; and, finally, to knowledge of the work of Salomon's House. Bacon's discussion of gender and sexual difference is significantly placed. It follows the readers' initiation; it precedes an account of the scientific praxis; and it acts as a metonymic signifier for the whole social and political organisation of Bensalem's civic society. Why does Bacon structure our encounter with gender thus? A close reading of the opening section will provide some answers.

When the travellers first reach the island events are re-
counted through the eyes of the narrator in a straightforward
and lucid style, which nevertheless belies the strange contents.
The events and people described are inversions of both European
habits and of travellers' tales of the new world, intermixed with
the standard motifs of early travel writing. Utopian otherness is
not portrayed simply as an inverted world: it combines inversions
of generic conventions (of travel writing, scientific discovery,
and political philosophy) with conventions signifying in an
expected way. This juxtaposition of the unexpected with the
expected, the unknown with the known, is a rhetorical ploy
typical of the first part of the fable's tripartite structure. There
are eight reversals in the opening section, each of which restruc-
ture our view on the world. The first four inversions are: the
'wilderness' which provides 'salvation',[14] a reversal with both
Biblical and travelogue precedent; the discovered land being a
'fair city', rather than uninhabited and undeveloped, an inversion
recognised by readers familiar with More's *Utopia*; the initial
absence of an ascribed gender to the 'undiscovered' land, which
conventionally would be identified as female;[15] the description of
the islanders, who are dressed in European style and speak
Greek, Latin, Spanish and Hebrew (458), and thus inverts the
conventional travelogue's depiction of native peoples.

Bacon uses a consistent rhetorical technique for these inversions: travelogue narrative conventions, followed by a shift of
perspective through purportive new eye-witness evidence. The
reader becomes a participant in changes of perception and
taxonomy. The third and fourth inversions act as a commentary
on the first two: they displace the 'othering' of the new world,
not by assimilating its description to European conceptions and
conventions, or asserting an imperial and epistemological hierarchy,[16] but by placing the visitors (and hence readers) in the
subordinated position. We are estranged from our habitual hierarchical taxonomy of and in the new world. It is not 'nature' that
provides salvation, as it does in the travelogues, but 'culture'.
However, this is a culture displaced from time, European history
and conventions. Two of these inversions are *topoi* found in
More's *Utopia* and Plato's *Timaeus*, but the unnamed and un-
gendered land is Bacon's innovation, read in juxtaposition to the

normative symbolism of the new world as natural paradise. Hence, there are two contradictory representations of the nature/ culture opposition, from which gender and sexuality are conspicuously and unusually absent.

The next four inversions also encourage a critique of Western imperial and gendered hierarchies. The sailors' offer of merchandise to the islanders is rejected (458), a conventional utopian inversion of the exchange economy of European merchants and an inversion of contemporary descriptions of native Americans as eager to trade for trifles.[17] This double generic inversion acts as both an acknowledgement and critique of contemporary economic and representational practice. The critique emerges not from simple inversion of binary opposites, but the discovery of a neutral space which is only defined by double negatives. It is not-Europe and not-the-New-World. Thus, this space does not participate in the imperial construction of 'otherness' as foreign, dangerous and feminised. The destabilising of settled and Western identity continues in the subsequent inversions. The Bensalemites are also Christians, thus inverting and appropriating Christian history from both Europe and the New World, and also disturbing conventional accounts of Christian teleology and identity. Europeans are placed in The Strangers' House and defined as 'other', creating two mutually exclusive conceptual hierarchies: the conventional one of Europeans versus new world inhabitants and the utopian textual one of Bensalemites versus Europeans. The gift of oranges that heal represents the islanders' superior medical knowledge and practice ('beyond both the old world and the new' [461]), and destabilises European conceptions of knowledge.

These inversions reconfigure emergent early modern Western assumptions and discourses about territory, economics, identity, Christian history, the natural world, and practical science. Bacon places travelogue and utopian discourses into a dialogic relationship. The 'real' interrogates the utopian and vice versa, so as to construct a sceptical reading position which disturbs conventional binary accounts of the world, and sceptically re-visions 'others'. By reversing and displacing contemporary imperial discourse and its concomitant epistemology (Europe/civilisation versus new world/primitivism), Bacon exposes its contingent historicity as well as its inadequacy. Western customs, habits of thought and perceptions are de-naturalised. It is only after this that we hear about Bensalem directly from its inhabitants, as we shall see in a moment. Having repositioned his readers, Bacon ensures a continued displacement of both Western and Bensalemite discourses throughout the second and third parts of the fable. This is a key intellectual strategy, and has major implications for thinking about gender.

### III

The second part of the fable names the island, its mission and its history, and uses images and metaphors with connotations of gender and sexual difference. These narrations continue the utopian and generic reversals of the first part of the fable, re-emphasising European practices as inverted reference points. Gendered and sexual metaphors are explicit in the name of the island, the articulation of an epistemology and the description of the Governor.

The name of the island is a double departure from convention. It is named by the inhabitants rather than the Europeans, and the name is not feminine: Bensalem signifies 'the perfect son'. By masculinising what is usually female (the land), Bacon continues to displace the Euro-centric construction of the relationship of man to land, and additionally asserts the island's impenetrable status. Furthermore, the masculine island bears a typological relationship to Christ, the other perfect son. Through the direct revelation of Christianity, Bacon posits an unmediated and unbroken genealogical connection between God, fathers and sons. The image of the birthing God and father, source of all knowledge and production, is an enduring myth in Western philosophy and culture. It is also one which defines masculinity by excluding the significance of female procreativity and power.[18] However, this initial gendering of the island and its productive capacities as solely masculine is qualified and challenged in the third part of the fable, to which I shall turn later.

Bacon explicitly confirms the articulation of a non-Western, but nonetheless hierarchical epistemology: the subject knower is Bensalem, the object of knowledge is the rest of the world: 'we know well … the … world, and are ourselves unknown' (463). The College of the Six Days' Works, which symbolises the island's epistemological practice and theory, describes its purpose as: 'the finding out of the true nature of all things' (230). The objects of knowledge are open to Bensalem, but they are not explicitly feminised. Rather, the place that is usually feminised (the new world), is re-gendered as masculine, and becomes subject rather than object; while the object(s) of knowledge, which include Europe and its customs, as well as nature, are not explicitly gendered. Bacon's positioning of a sceptical reader asks us to reject conventional binary oppositions, including that of a feminised, subjugated nature.

The relationship between Governor and visitors is self-consciously didactic (described by the narrator as 'parent-like' (463)). Familial relationships are thence symbolically central to the *New Atlantis,* first introduced through the visitors' perceptions of their welcome. This confirms a system of relationships in which the newcomers are supplicants, positioned as children in need of nurturing and educating. The metaphor of visitors and readers as children continues subtextually throughout the fable, echoing Bacon's varying uses of the birth metaphor cited at the beginning of this essay. At this stage, the parental symbol is not specifically patriarchal.

In summary, then, the first part of the fable offers a revisioning of Euro-centrism via an inductive reading experience[19] which sets up a neutral place from which we as sceptical readers revalue and critique Western ideologies and epistemologies. The fable's second part provides a history, a set of external relationships, and systems of belief for that island, which are inversions of European traditions. Where gendered allegories or metaphors are used, the text explicitly denies them a conventional meaning. Gender is used non-normatively at this stage; but it is masculinity (not femininity) which is re-figured in the second part of the fable. In the light of these non-normative significations, let us now turn to consider how gender and sexual difference are represented in the rest of the fable.

## IV

In the last part of the fable the narrator describes three experiences at length: his attendance at 'the feast of the family'; a conversation with Joabin about Judaism, Christianity, and chastity and marriage customs in Bensalem and Europe; and the lecture by the Father of Salomon's House on its work and philosophy. Two out of three of the directly narrated experiences focus both explicitly and allegorically on gender and sexuality. The description of the sexual division of labour at the feast and the apparent allegorical functions of the gendered symbols have exact cultural parallels in Jacobean political thought and praxis, most notably, the interlinked contemporary discourses of patriarchy and chastity. Many critics argue that the feast of the family is a patriarchal model and proof that Bacon legitimises the domination of nature via patriarchal allegory.[20] However, this argument ignores several key points, as we shall see.

Having been positioned as sceptics, we are reminded to read the feast in the context of both its position in the fable and intertextually. It is in the light of this revisioning that readers should re-examine the familial and social structures in Bensalem in the context of both the *New Atlantis*, and of contemporary accounts of familial patriarchy. The narrator's first directly experienced description is that of an event: the Feast of the Family. It functions as both a description of a utopian practice and as a resonating social symbol. By considering these separately, we can see that Bacon both advocates a Jacobean patriarchal model and supersedes it.

Let us first consider the feast as a literal embodiment of Bacon's utopian social organisation. The feast is an overt celebration of patriarchal productivity, provided by the state for the family of a man who has thirty children 'descended of his body' (473). The power and position of the father as head of household is paramount. He holds court for two days prior to the feast, where he:

> sitteth in consultation concerning the good estate of the family. There, if there be any discords or suits between any of the family, they are compounded and appeased. There, if any of the family be distressed or decayed, order is taken for their relief and competent means to live. There, if any be subject to vice, or take ill courses, they are reproved and censured. So likewise direction is given touching marriages and the courses of life which any of them should take, with divers other the like orders and advices. The governor assisteth, to the end to put in execution by his public

authority the decrees and order of the Tirsan, if they should be disobeyed: though that seldom needeth, such reverence and obedience they give to the order of nature. The Tirsan doth also then ever choose one man from amongst his sons to live in house with him: who is called ever after the Son of the Vine. (473)

This patriarchal unit differs from contemporary Jacobean models in several ways. This extended family looks more like a feudal model than a bourgeois patriarchal unit.[21] Moreover, in contrast to James I's version of patriarchalism, Bacon here inverts the relationship between family and national political authority. In *The True Law of Free Monarchies* James I wrote:

> By the law of nature the king becomes a natural father to all his lieges at his coronation, And the father, of his fatherly duty, is bound to care for the nourishing, education and virtuous government of his children: even so is the king bound to care for all his subjects. (1603 ed., Fo.B3v)

James I's patriarchal theory entails absolute, if nurturing, monarchical authority, and concomitant obedience from subjects to monarch. By contrast, Bacon's father has central authority and is assisted by the Governor. Patriarchalism is naturalised ('reverence and obedience to the order of nature') and privatised; but the family dominates the state.[22] Analogies between family and state emerged in the late sixteenth century, arguably as new protestant theories of fatherhood evolved, and political defences of absolutism were required. Contemporary patriarchal theory used the family as a metaphor to explain and justify absolute loyalty to monarch, to aid political centralisation as regional loyalties dispersed and to bolster social hierarchies in an era of social change.

Bacon's inversion of patriarchal absolutism is ignored by critics who argue that the feast is paradigmatic of his patriarchal and masculinist theory of knowledge.[23] The discourse surrounding the father in the *New Atlantis* echoes contemporary patriarchal theory, but Bacon alters the political balance between individual and state.

Other features of the description of the festival significantly raise questions about gender and sexual difference. There is both a gendered division of labour and a hierarchy of value placed on

sons over daughters. The Tirsan sits under a canopy, wrought by
'some of the daughters of the family', and he parades forth 'with
all his generation or lineage, the males before him and the females
following him' (473). The mother is physically unseen:

> if there be a mother from whose body the whole lineage is
> descended, there is a traverse placed in a loft above on the right
> hand of the chair, with a privy door, and a carved window of glass,
> leaded with gold and blue; where she sitteth but is not seen. (473)

The children stand about the room 'in order of their years without difference of sex', while a herald delivers a scroll in which
the Tirsan is granted revenue, honour and 'points of exemption
… for propagation of his subjects' (474), and then delivers an
ornamental bunch of enamelled grapes, decorated differentially:

> if the males of the family be the greater number, the grapes are
> enamelled purple with a little sun set on the top; if the females,
> then they are enamelled into a greenish-yellow, with a crescent on
> the top. (474)

The Tirsan's primary heir is male, but age, not gender, orders the
children's place in the festival. Both daughters and sons are
given a symbolic value in the state's gift to the family as moon
and suns respectively. The food is served by the sons, while the
daughters stand at the edge of the room, followed by a celebration of hymns praising,

> Adam and Noah and Abraham; whereof the former two peopled
> the world and the last was the Father of the Faithful; concluding
> ever with a thanksgiving for the nativity of our Saviour, in whose
> birth the births of all are only blessed. (475)

Fatherhood, sons, faith and procreation are intertwined. Finally,
the Tirsan blesses each of his children, usually in age order again,
and delivers a special jewel to one or two of his sons if 'of
eminent virtue' (475).

   In this description, reproductive labour is explicitly acknowledged as central to the economic and political well-being of the
state, and the source of that reproduction is figured publicly as
masculine. The mother, though present, is hidden, and while
daughters are given some public recognition and role, male
success is measured by the production of sons.

However, the allegorical and symbolic resonances of the feast modify this interpretation. Bacon makes it clear that, like other early modern festivals, the feast functions symbolically as an icon of natural social stability and harmony. The narrator's description delineates it as both natural and symbolic: 'a most natural, pious and reverend custom it is, shewing that nation to be compounded of all goodness' (472). This self-proclaimed naturalism reminds us that the binary opposition between culture and nature has earlier been transgressed, and then proleptically suggests a new nature, paradigmatic of the ethos of Bensalem society.

The absence of the mother, the symbolic icons associated with the father, and the primacy given to sons, project a fantasy of masculine generative power. Fertility is central to this celebration through the icon of the family. Most critics argue that Bacon appropriates the parental role solely to the figure of the father, figuring fertile power as masculine and metonymically linking this to the 'Fathers' of Salomon's House and their knowledge about and power over the natural world.[24]

Any reading of the symbolic function of the family, however, must analyse the representation of the mother. She is veiled from sight, sitting to the right of the father, but can see. This absent presence demands an allegorical reading. The figure of the veiled woman, particularly at a festive ritual which celebrates the production of children, is resonant of the contemporary ceremony of women's churching after childbirth.[25] Cressy argues that this ritual was a Church ceremony of thanksgiving for the survival and health of mother and child, marking the return of the mother to her community, and a collective celebration of maternity, and not a rite of purification. The celebratory interpretation and use of this ritual may be seen as part of a contemporary protestant revaluation of marriage and motherhood, in which maternal influence was seen as equal but different to that of the paternal.[26]

Both the formal significance and actual events of this ceremony are echoed in Bacon's feast. The parallel draws attention to the fact that here the mother is never unveiled, remaining in a liminal position. She is not reincorporated into the community of the family. Instead, it is the father whose fertility and place in the community is publicly celebrated and marked. Here, then, is further iconic evidence of Bacon's appropriation of fertility and its customs to masculine power. However, there are two further attributes given to the hidden mother which counterbalance, but do not erase, this interpretation. They thence offer us a third way of interpreting Bacon's familial images.

The mother is placed on the right of the father, which explicitly places the mother's relationship to the father typologically parallel to both the scriptural representation of the relationship between Christ and God, as well as between the Church and God: 'hereafter shall ye see the Son of man sitting on the right hand of power' (Matthew, 26: 64). Scriptural and theological accounts of the relationship between God and his people often figure it as one of marriage, in which the Church was allegorised as female bride to male God. This explicitly gendered and sexualised relationship symbolises bodily and spiritual unity and a reinforcement of patriarchal authority. Nevertheless, Bacon's appropriation of this image is less clear because at all points the image of the mother continues to signify an individual female in addition to any allegorical function. At one and the same time she is mother, Christ, and people: fertility, saviour, and faith. While at a literal level she is excluded from incorporation into the festival of the family, at an allegorical level her association with Christ and with Church renders her equal with God the Father. The tradition of representing a feminised Christ and of God as both mother and father is one which has been marginalised in the patriarchal Hebraic tradition.[27] Lancelot Andrewes, who helped translate the 1611 Authorised Version of the Bible, frequently used combined images of the maternal and paternal to describe God:

> [God has …] that faithfulness that is in a mother towards her children, for as a woman cannot but pity her own child and the son of her womb, so the Lord will not forget his own people. [28]

Bacon's maternal figure is radically both masculine and feminine. The father is celebrated for fertility through a festival which echoes but extends contemporary churching rituals for women. Thus the superficial clarity of hierarchical gender roles, explicit in the literal events of the festival and the function of the father, is rendered indeterminate by a symbolic reading of the place and representation of the mother.

The second remarkable feature about the representation of the mother, which counterbalances the apparent patriarchalism of the festival, is of her as seeing but unseen. This figuration of sight replicates the earlier description by the Governor of the Stranger's House of how Bensalem is hidden from the rest of the world, but knows and can see the world. This model for new knowledge, in which relationships between Europe and the new world, culture and nature are inverted and displaced, parallels a veiled, productive mother. Knowledge, and, moreover, the Baconian ideal empirical knowledge of observation, is therefore allegorically figured as being held by the hidden mother, as it is by the hidden island.

Theories of the patriarchal subordination of women's labour argue that ownership and acknowledgement of female authority in reproduction is displaced and erased by the economics of our Western gender–sex system, in which female sexuality and childbirth are regulated by a normalised heterosexual system of marriage. Women are only legitimated when passed between father and husband, thereby simultaneously establishing masculine 'ownership' to progeny and female subjection to this system.[29] Feminist theorists argue that such a sex–gender system is a patriarchal compensation for men's own alienation from reproduction, and that this alienation has underpinned man's urge to master nature.[30]

Bacon displays figuratively the manner in which reproductive labour is alienated from men and in which women are subordinated. Yet by elucidating this for a reader, already positioned as sceptical, Bacon refuses to naturalise and erase the ideological construction of woman as invisibly and accidentally reproductive. In figuring forth the mother as veiled but present, and disturbing conventional binary relationships between nature and culture, Bacon's text *resists* conformity to a fantasy of male parturition. This device is comparable to the magical re-presentation of Hermione in *The Winter's Tale*, interpreted by critics as *both* a fantasy of masculine productivity and as a liberating restoration of an equity between male and female in reproduction.[31] Additionally, by inverting conventions, and feasting masculine fertility, Bacon also critiques European humanist masculine alienation from reproduction.

The Baconian parallel between children and technology offers an additional symbolic frame for sexual reproduction in Bensalem. Bacon's name for useful scientific experiments elsewhere

in his writings as 'experiments of fruit' is literalised in naming
the father's sons and daughters as 'vines', and illustrated by
technological advances celebrated and used by the Bensalemites.
The metaphor of legitimate (re)production links Joabin's
discussion of chastity to the account of useful scientific experiments in Salomon's House. In *Valerius Terminus*, an early
summary of his ideas, Bacon wrote:

> Knowledge that tendeth but to satisfaction is but as a courtesan,
> which is for pleasure and not for fruit or generation.[32]

Knowledge as female is a conventional renaissance symbol.[33] By
contrast, in Bensalem, the symbol of productive sexuality belongs
to both sexes: woman is not demonised or divided (although she
is isolated). Thus Bacon's fruitful fable acquires the best of both
worlds: social structures which acknowledge and celebrate male
fertility, whilst symbolically and allegorically nodding at female
influences. Let us now turn to the other account of gender and
sexual difference in the fable: the narrator's conversation with
Joabin.

V

This dialogue acts as both a direct and an indirect interpretation
of the festival: directly, in response to the narrator's request for
elucidation, and indirectly, because Joabin's comments on European marriage and familial customs are a counterpoint to the utopian
inversions of the feast. The narrator asks for Joabin's views:

> I had never heard of a solemnity wherein nature did so much
> preside. And because propagation of families proceedeth from the
> nuptial copulation, I desired to know of him what laws and
> customs they had concerning marriage; and whether they kept
> marriage well; and whether they were tied to one wife? (476)

Joabin's answer reads:

> You shall understand that there is not under the heavens so chaste
> a nation as this of Bensalem; nor so free from all pollution or
> foulness. It is the virgin of the world ... the Spirit of Chastity ... For
> there is nothing amongst mortal men more fair and admirable than
> the chaste minds of this people. Know therefore, that with them
> there are no stews, no dissolute houses, no courtesans, nor anything

of that kind. Nay they wonder (in detestation) at you in Europe
which permit such things. They say ye have put marriage out of
office: for marriage is ordained a remedy for unlawful concupiscence; and natural concupiscence seemeth as a spur to marriage.
But when men have at hand a remedy more agreeable to their corrupt
will, marriage is almost expulsed. And therefore there are with you
seen infinite men that marry not, but chuse rather a libertine and
impure single life, than to be yoked in marriage; and many that do
marry, marry late, when the prime and strength of their years is
past. And when they do marry, what is marriage to them, but a
very bargain; wherein is sought alliance, or portion, or reputation,
with some desire (almost indifferent) of issues; and not the faithful
nuptial union of man and wife that was first instituted. (476–7)

Read allegorically, sterility lies with European traditions (figured
as the courtesan) and fecundity with those of Bacon's New World
(figured as Bensalem, the virgin of the world), an image replica-
ting that of *Valerius Terminus*. Read literally, Bacon articulates a
radical critique of sexual double standards. I shall return to this
point in a moment.

However, in the context of generic reversals, the reader is
encouraged to venture further interpretations. Bacon reintro-
duces the gendering of land: Bensalem, having been figured as
the perfect son, is now 'the virgin of the world'. He invokes
Elizabethan discourses about Virginia. Yet Bensalem's chastity is
not constructed as Ralegh's Guiana or Harriot's Virginia was: it
does not represent an invitation to plunder, invade and possess.
In contrast, it is an image of chastity as both inviolable and reproductive: an image resonant, rather, of those linked to Elizabeth I,
whose link to chastity paradoxically invoked dominion over
others rather than subjection to them.[34] Bacon's image also echoes
Spenser's Britomart in book III of *The Faerie Queene*, where chastity symbolises marital union and reproduction in a protestant
revision of marriage. At this late stage in the fable Bacon uses the
conventional image of 'virgin land', but we have learned the
island has its own history and culture: as a result definitions and
concepts of virgin land are radically inverted and reformed. His
island claims the image of chastity as one with real meaning: the
land is not a blank canvas, inviting invasion, nor is it open to it,
but will invite selected strangers to visit. This re-appropriation
of the discourse of virgin land combines images of masculinity

and femininity: Ben-salem, the perfect son, is also the virgin of
the world. Here, then, gender is recognised by the text as central
to the discourse of imperial knowledge. But it is then manipulated to aid the displacement from present ways of thinking, as
well as to suggest that domination of land and nature does *not*
produce legitimate knowledge.

Bacon's utilisation of chastity as a positive symbol is the
grounds for his lengthy critique of contemporary sexual customs,
the only explicit comment the fable makes on European mores.
This is further evidence that Bacon places gender and sexual
difference as central organising metaphors in his utopian discourse. Joabin's commentary on European habits reads like a
protestant sermon on marriage,[35] whose ideals are only realised in
Bensalem. In Joabin's description, European practice is represented as the opposite to Bensalem's ideal, in its economic and
political manipulation of marriage, its use of courtesans, 'delight
in meretricious embracements', adultery, 'deflowering of virgins',
and 'masculine love' (477). The objects of Bacon's critique un-
cannily echo those voiced by feminists, in particular the double
sexual standard and the organisation of sexual behaviour solely
by the yardstick of masculine libertinism.

In an Arcadia human desires are moderate and simplified,
but satisfied and, in addition, humanity and nature are integrated,[36] a vision present in *Valerius Terminus*, where the new
epistemological world is described as being:

> a restitution and reinvesting ... of man to the sovereignty and
> power (for whensoever he shall be able to call the creatures by their
> true names he shall again command them) which he had in his first
> state of creation.[37]

Many features of Bensalem, including the Adam and Eve pools,
echo this prelapsarian motif. In *The Refutation of Philosophies* ('a
chaste and lawful marriage') Bacon also uses protestant marriage
theory as a metaphor for the integration of man and nature. What
he advocates, then, is not domination, but a sustainable, integrated ecology. He uses the protestant re-articulation of masculinity
as chaste husbandry in an equitable marriage as his ideal model
of self-restraint, social order and a concomitant social structure
which enables true knowledge and the practice of true science. [38]

Chastity, then, in the *New Atlantis* becomes a metonymic signifier for both the necessary self-restraint, which will maintain social and political order, and for the union between scientist and nature. Chastity is not desexed: rather, it applies necessarily and equally to both sexes. Bacon's continued emphasis on the 'natural' customs of Bensalem, in contrast to the 'unnatural' ones of Europe, elides the articulation of Bensalem's advanced technological culture with a proclaimed rediscovery of nature and the natural. Contemporary discourses of sexuality and chastity, and their transformation in Bensalem, are the pivot for this paradoxical epistemological realignment of nature *with* technology. It is now possible to reconsider whether this realignment really does replicate the models of a patriarchal objectivist masculine epistemology.

Before the reader is finally introduced to the inventions and knowledge of Salomon's House, there is another fusion of gender difference: the narrator figures himself and his repositioning through a parallel with a woman:

> I would say to him [Joabin], as the widow of Sarepta said to Elias, that he was come to bring to memory our sins and that I confess the righteousness of Bensalem was greater than the righteousness of Europe. (478)

This reference is to the story in 1 Kings 17:8–24 where a poor widow takes in and feeds Elijah. When her son takes ill and dies, she repents of her sins, and in acknowledgement of her penitence, Elijah brings the son back to life. The narrator thus acknowledges his own submissive and erroneous position, figuring himself as a widow whose progeny have yet the potential to be resurrected.

It is only now, at the point of this personal, gender transformation and acknowledged radical openness to the future, that the narrator is admitted to the knowledge of Salomon's House. We and the narrator are figured as children to the text and to knowledge itself, which is both mother and father. Bacon writes of the necessity of re-figuring our relationship to nature thus in *Valerius Terminus*:

> It is no less true in this human kingdom of knowledge than in God's kingdom of heaven, that no man shall enter into it except he become first as a little child.[39]

The Father of Solomon's House opens his revelation parentally:

> God bless thee, my son, I will give thee the greatest jewel I have.
> For I will impart unto thee, for the love of God and men, a relation
> of the true state of Salomon's House. (480)

The narrator and reader, through a series of initiations and slowly
changing perceptions and understandings, may now encounter a
survey of technological innovations and experiments for the
revelation of 'the knowledge of causes and secret motions of
things, and the enlarging of the bounds of human empire to the
effecting of all things possible' (480). Included in these descriptions are accounts of mines, experiments on refrigeration, water
purification, artificial weather systems, medicines, foods, and
selective plant breeding. Animal experiments are described thus:

> Of beasts and birds ... for dissections and trials; that thereby we
> may take light what may be wrought upon the body of man, ... we
> try all poisons and other medicines upon them, as well of chirugery
> as physic. By art likewise we make them taller than their kind is;
> and contrariwise dwarf them and stay their growth; we make them
> more fruitful and bearing than their kind is, and contrariwise
> barren and not generative. (482)

Bacon articulates the new experimental philosophy in which
human knowledge, wealth and health dominate over earth and
animals. But the ethics of such dominion have been clearly
delineated by the earlier part of the fable where a chaste and
equitable union is proposed. Although Bacon advocates animal
experimentation, which today we might question, there is no
evidence of the language of rape and the kind of domination
claimed by Merchant.[40]

Nevertheless, there is much here that is still patriarchal. The
paternal relationship of the narrator to the Father of Salomon's
House, narrator to listener, knower to unknowing, is clear. Transmission of knowledge is figured through masculine primo-
geniture, symbolically represented in the Feast of the Family. But
this model of transmission does not fully encompass the insertion
of gender and sexual difference into models of knowledge in the
*New Atlantis*. The fable ends doubly open-ended: the Father of
Salomon's House grants permission for the narrator to dissem-
inate the new knowledge and the work itself was published as

'not perfected'. Bacon's island offers itself as a closed and patriarchal society, the archetypal image of the classical masculine body which Bakhtin characterises as symbolic of the new politics and science of the seventeenth century.[41] Yet, like Bensalem itself, the body of the text does lie open to those who are willing to pass through its tests of purity and understand its transformations. The veiled woman (and island) is both the object of knowledge and knowledge itself. Bacon continues the ancient tradition of feminising knowledge, but simultaneously figures it as masculine.

Bacon uses gender and sexual difference as a way of signalling several important epistemological points. In particular, the *New Atlantis* shows: the necessity of articulating an ethics of *legitimate* knowledge; the acknowledgement of a respectful and mutual relationship between nature and humans; the placing of productivity and utility within an ethical configuration; and the bisexuality of scientific knowledge and practice.

If we return to the questions asked at the beginning of this essay, it is possible to see how Bacon has used gender and sexual difference to redefine knowledge. Bacon's gendered images both display and exceed the normative at key symbolic points, and act both to unsettle the reader's prejudices and to model a new epistemology. Such images clearly contest contemporary imperial and epistemological assumptions, particularly in the signifiers of knowledge and chastity.

Furthermore, sexual difference is reconfigured in Bacon's utopian vision. Birth and rebirth are a major metaphorical subtext. The island is refigured as a two-sexed child: the perfect son and the chaste daughter, who will pass on the legitimate line and way of knowledge, in contradistinction to that practised in Europe. Both the way of knowing and its products are figured as bisexual: denying a binary gendered epistemology, and advocating transgression to achieve new knowledge and new ways of knowing.[42] The open-ended text offers itself to all reborn readers, male or female. This image of our relationship to nature suggests that Bacon's new scientist may, in his or her role reversals, and equal respect for both the natural world and technology, remind us more of Harraway's cyborg,[43] than the masculinist ideologue described by many ecofeminists. This reading of the *New*

*Atlantis* offers a way of enabling us to re-articulate the legacy of Baconian science for the twenty-first century.

## Notes

1 Francis Bacon, *The Refutation of Philosophies*, in B. Farrington (ed.) *The Philosophy of Francis Bacon* (Chicago, Chicago University Press, 1966), p. 131.

2 Francis Bacon, *The Masculine Birth of Time*, in Farrington (ed.), *The Philosophy*, p. 62.

3 *Ibid.* p. 70.

4 Francis Bacon, *Novum Organum,* aphorisms I and III, in *The Works of Francis Bacon*, ed. James Spedding, Robert Leslie Ellis and Douglas Denon Heath, 14 volumes (London, Longman, 1857–74), vol. IV, p. 47.

5 For example, Mark Breitenberg, *Anxious Masculinity in Early Modern England* (Cambridge, Cambridge University Press, 1996), pp. 69–96; Carolyn Merchant, *The Death of Nature: Women, Ecology and the Scientific Revolution* (San Francisco, Harper and Row, 1980), pp. 164–90; Maria Mies and Vandana Shiva, *Ecofeminism* (London and New York, Zed Books, 1993), pp. 13–20; Valerie Plumwood, *Feminisms and the Mastery of Nature* (London, Routledge, 1993); Londa Schiebinger, *The Mind has No Sex?: Women in the Origins of Modern Science* (Cambridge, Mass., Harvard University Press, 1989), pp. 119–59. In solitary contrast, Iddo Landau, 'Feminist criticisms of metaphors in Bacon's philosophy of science', *Philosophy*, 73 (1998), 47–61, demonstrates how critics cite Bacon selectively, and argues that his philosophy is not a hierarchical sexist epistemology.

6 See Susan Bordo, 'The Cartesian masculinization of science', *Signs*, 11 (1986), 439–56; Brian Easlea, *Science and Sexual Oppression: Patriarchy's Confrontation with Women and Nature* (London, Weidenfeld and Nicholson, 1981); Evelyn Fox Keller, *Feminism and Science* (Oxford, Oxford University Press, 1996), pp. 1–40; Genevieve Lloyd, *The Man of Reason: 'Male' and 'Female' in Western Philosophy* (London, Routledge, 1994), pp. 1–15; and Merchant, *The Death*, Chapter 5.

7 Merchant, *The Death*, p. xx; Mies and Shiva, *Ecofeminism*, p. 18.

8 See J. C. Davis, *Utopia and the Ideal Society* (Cambridge, Cambridge University Press, 1979), pp. 1–10, 36–40, 106–37.

9 Frederic Jameson, 'Of islands and trenches: naturalisation and the production of utopian discourse', *Diacritics*, 7 (1977), 2–21. See also Denise Albanese, 'The *New Atlantis* and the uses of utopia', *English Literary History*, 57 (1990), 503–28.

10 See Charles Whitney, *Francis Bacon and Modernity* (New Haven, Yale University Press, 1986); Jerry Weinberger, 'Science and rule in Bacon's utopia: an introduction to the reading of *New Atlantis*', *American Political Science Review*, 70 (1976), 865–85, and *Science, Faith and Politics: Bacon and the Utopian Roots of the Modern Age* (Ithaca, Cornell University Press, 1985).

11  See, Joan Wallach Scott, *Gender and the Politics of History* (New York, Columbia University Press, 1988), pp. 42–5; S. Amussen, *An Ordered Society: Gender and Class in Early Modern England* (Oxford, Basil Blackwell, 1988); P. Stallybrass, 'Patriarchal territories: the body enclosed', in M. Ferguson, M. Quilligan and Nancy J. Vickers (eds), *Re-Writing the Renaissance* (Chicago, Chicago University Press, 1986), pp. 127–42); and David Underdown, *Revel, Riot and Rebellion: Popular Politics and Culture in England 1603–1660* (Oxford, Oxford University Press, 1985).

12  See notes 5 and 6.

13  This is an elaboration of Davis, *Utopia*, p. 107.

14  Francis Bacon, in Brian Vickers (ed.), *Francis Bacon: A Critical Edition of the Major Works* (Oxford, Oxford University Press, 1996), pp. 457–89 (pp. 457, 463). All subsequent references to *New Atlantis* come from this edition and are given in parenthesis in the text.

15  Newly discovered land was graced with a feminised European name: America, Virginia, Guiana. The ideology behind such naming is clear in Ralegh's plea to Queen Elizabeth to fund his exploration of Guiana: 'Guiana is a country that hath yet her maidenhead: never sacked, turned, nor wrought; the face of the earth hath not been torn, nor the virtue and salt of the soil spent by manurance; the graves have not been opened for gold; the mines not broken with sledges; nor the images pulled down out of their temples' (*The Discovery of ... Guiana*, London, 1595, fo.99). New World land usually signified an invitation to possession: gender is used both to convey and justify this signification, and to justify a gendered, racial and epistemological hierarchy. See Richard Burt and J. Archer (eds), *Enclosure Acts: Sexuality, Property and Culture in Early Modern England* (Ithaca, Cornell University Press, 1993); Annette Kolodny, *The Lay of the Land: Metaphor as Experience and History in American Life and Letters* (Chapel Hill, University of North Carolina Press, 1975); Peter Mason, *Deconstructing America: Representations of the Other* (London, Routledge, 1990), Chapter 1); and Adrian Louis Montrose, 'The work of gender in the discourse of discovery', *Representations*, 33 (1991), 1–41.

16  These were the two available discursive conventions, see J. H. Elliot, *The Old World and the New* (Cambridge, Cambridge University Press, 1970) ; S. Greenblatt, *Marvellous Possessions: The Wonder of the New World* (Oxford, Oxford University Press, 1991); P. Hulme, 'Hurricanes in the Caribees: the constitution of the discourse of English colonialism', in Francis Barker *et al.* (eds), *1642: Literature and Power in the Seventeenth Century, Proceedings of the Essex Conference on the Sociology of Literature July 1980* (Colchester, Hewitt Photo-Lith, 1981); W. E. Washburn, 'The meaning of "discovery" in the fifteenth and sixteenth centuries', *American Historical Review*, 68 (1962), 1–21.

17  For example, Thomas Harriot's *A Brief and True Report of the New Found Land of Virginia* (London, 1588); Robert Gray's *A Good Speed to Virginia* (London, 1608); Walter Ralegh's *The Discovery of the Large, Beautiful and Rich Empire of Guiana* (London, 1596).

18  See Breitenburg, *Anxious Masculinity*, pp. 76–96 and Merchant, *The Death*, Chapter 5. Feminist critiques of male parturition fantasies include, Renate Blumenfeld-Kosinski, *Not of Woman Born: Representations of Caesarean Birth in Medieval and Renaissance Culture* (Ithaca, Cornell University Press, 1990); Terry Castle, 'La'bring bards: birth topoi and English poetics', *Journal of English and Germanic Philology*, 78 (1979), 193–208; Susan Friedman, 'Creativity and the childbirth metaphor: gender difference in literary discourse', *Feminist Studies*, 13 (1987), 49–82; Adrienne Rich, *Of Woman Born: Motherhood as Experience and Institution* (London, Virago, 1977), pp. 56–83.

19  See Stanley Fish, '"Georgics of the mind": the experience of reading Bacon's *Essays*', in *Self-Consuming Artefacts: The Experience of Seventeenth-Century Literature* (Berkeley: University of California Press, 1972), pp. 28–155; Charles Whitney, *Francis Bacon and Modernity* (New Haven, Yale University Press, 1986); see also Kate Aughterson, '"The waking vision": reference in the *New Atlantis*', *Renaissance Quarterly*, 45 (1992), 119–39.

20  For example, H. B. White, *Peace Among the Willows: The Political Philosophy of Francis Bacon* (The Hague, Elsevier, 1968), pp. 166–89; Merchant, *The Death*, pp. 180–6.

21  Davis, *Utopia*, p. 113.

22  See Gordon Schochet, *Patriarchalism in Political Thought* (Oxford, Basil Blackwell, 1976), Chapter 1.

23  Merchant, *The Death*, pp. 180–4.

24  See *ibid.*, Chapters 1 and 2; White, *Peace*, pp. 166–89.

25  See Patricia Crawford, 'The construction and experience of maternity in seventeenth-century England', in Valerie Fildes (ed.), *Women as Mothers in Pre-industrial England* (London, Routledge, 1990), pp. 3–38 and David Cressy, *Birth, Marriage and Death: Ritual, religion and the Life-Cycle in Tudor and Stuart England* (Oxford, Oxford University Press, 1997), pp. 197–230.

26  See Kathleen Davies, 'Continuity and change in literary advice on marriage', in R. Outhwaite (ed.), *Marriage and Society: Studies in the Social History of Marriage* (New York, St. Martin's Press, 1981), pp. 58–80; Margaret Ezell, *The Patriarch's Wife: Literary Evidence and the History of the Family* (Chapel Hill, University of Carolina Press, 1987); C. H. and K. George, *The Protestant Mind of the English Reformation* (Princeton, N. J, Princeton University Press, 1961), pp. 260–84; Linda Fitz, 'What says the married woman? Marriage theory and feminism in the English renaissance', *Mosaic*, 13 (1980), 1–22; Lawrence Stone, *The Family, Sex and Marriage 1500–1800* (London, Weidenfeld and Nicholson, 1977), pp. 217–41.

27  See David Leverenz, *The Language of Puritan Feeling: An Exploration in Literature, Psychology and Social History* (New Brunswick, N. J., Rutgers University Press, 1980) and Deborah Shuger, 'Nursing Fathers: Patriarchy as a Cultural Ideal', in Deborah Shugar (ed.), *Habits of Thought in the English Renaissance* (Berkeley, University of California Press, 1990), pp. 218–49.

28  *The Works of Lancelot Andrewes*, ed. J. P. Wilson and James Bliss, 11 vols, Library of Anglo-Catholic Theology (Oxford, Oxford University Press,

1854), vol. 4, p. 272.

29 Mary O'Brien, *The Politics of Reproduction* (London, Routledge, Paul Kegan, 1981); Gayle Rubin, 'The traffic in women, notes on the "political economy" of sex', in Rayner Reiter (ed.), *Toward an Anthropology of Women* (New York and London, Monthly Review Press, 1975), pp. 157–210.

30 O'Brien, *The Politics*, Chapter 1; Michelle Stanworth, 'Reproductive technologies and the deconstruction of motherhood', in M. Stanworth (ed.), *Reproductive Technologies: Gender, Motherhood and medicine* (Cambridge, Polity Press, 1987), pp. 10–35.

31 For the former reading, see Richard Wilson, 'Observations on English bodies: licensing maternity in Shakespeare's late plays', in Archer and Burt (eds), *Enclosure Acts*, pp. 121–50. For the latter reading, see Janet Adelman, *Suffocating Mothers: Fantasies of Maternal Origin in Shakespeare's Plays, Hamlet to The Tempest* (London, Routledge, 1992), pp. 220–38.

32 Bacon, *Works*, vol. III, p. 222.

33 Phillipa Berry, *Of Chastity and Power: Elizabethan Literature and the Unmarried Queen* (London, Routledge, 1989), pp. 9–37 and Schiebinger, *The Mind*, pp. 119–59.

34 See Berry, *Of Chastity*, pp. 1–8 ; Frances Yates, *Astraea: The Imperial Theme in the Sixteenth Century* (London, Routledge and Kegan Paul, 1975).

35 For example, the *Homily on Matrimony* or *Of Whoredom and Adultery;* or William Whately's *A Bride Bush* (London, 1617).

36 Davis, *Utopia*, p. 24.

37 Bacon, *Works*, vol. III, p. 222.

38 See Mary Fissell, 'Gender and reproduction: representing reproduction in early modern England', *Gender and History*, 7 (1995), 433–57; George, *The Protestant Mind;* Lorna Hutson, *The Usurer's Daughter: Male Friendship and Fictions of Women in Sixteenth-Century England* (London, Routledge, 1994), Chapter 1; Leverenz, *The Language of Puritan Feeling*, Chapter 1.

39 Bacon, *Works*, vol. III, p. 224.

40 See Merchant, *The Death*, pp. 164–90.

41 Peter Stallybrass, 'Patriarchal territories', in M. Ferguson, M. Quilligan and Nancy J. Vickers (eds), *Rewriting*, pp. 123–42.

42 Evelyn Fox Keller notes that the science proposed by Bacon is more like 'an hermaphroditical birth' in 'Baconian science: an hermaphroditical birth', *Philosophical Forum* 11 (1980), 299–308, and gives a more sophisticated reading of Bacon's metaphors than Merchant.

43 Donna Harraway, 'A cyborg manifesto: science, technology and socialist-feminism in the 1980s', *Socialist Review* (1980), 65–108.

# 9

# Censorship and the institution of knowledge in Bacon's *New Atlantis*

## SIMON WORTHAM

I

Critical readers of Bacon's *New Atlantis* have often drawn attention to the complex relationship between, on the one hand, the production and dissemination of enlightened scientific knowledge in Bensalem – and, indeed, the forms of social community for which it implicitly provides a model – and, on the other, the secret or concealed *conditions* of this very same process of production. For example, Robert K. Faulkner in *Francis Bacon and the Project of Progress* notes that, while 'every official performs his function [and] everyone does what he is ordered,' nevertheless 'all this order is the more remarkable since the relation of king, city, nation, state, and scientist is not clarified. The order that orders ... is hidden.'[1] Jerry Weinberger, meanwhile, argues that Bensalemite 'science is shrouded in secrecy, denying the possibility of full enlightenment.' Such secrecy surrounding the activities which contribute to the production of scientific knowledge Weinberger reads in terms of, as he sees it, Bacon's idea that 'the politics of science must be secret and retired because only the most resolute souls will be willing to embrace such a world with full knowledge of its moral risks and dangers.'[2] What these critics would appear to suggest, then, is that the production of various sorts of ground-breaking scientific knowledge and enlightened social relationships remain dependent, at bottom, upon a supplementary dose of censorship that simply cannot be dispensed with if the project of the Bensalemites is to persist and thrive. For readers of Bacon and students of the early modern period in England more generally, the *New Atlantis* therefore unavoidably raises questions concerning the relationship between censorship and knowledge, insofar as this relationship actually comes to structure and define the possibilities for any advancement of learning of the sort that is imagined to take place in the formal, institutional space of an ideal academy such as Salomon's House.

One of the places where questions of censorship have been raised most interestingly in recent times is in Renaissance studies. For example, Richard Burt, in his book *Licensed by Authority: Ben Jonson and the Discourses of Censorship*,[3] has attempted to rethink the problem of censorship in the early modern period in ways that call into question some of the conceptions and assumptions concerning censorship that have typically underpinned supposedly more 'radical' critiques of the workings of power and authority in sixteenth- and early seventeenth-century England. In particular, Burt describes an 'ahistorical, moral definition of censorship' (censorship as a repressive, external threat to essential freedoms) that has been adopted by 'political critics' working on the early modern period (particularly British cultural materialists), which 'makes available in the Renaissance a certain essentially moral notion of critical opposition'. 'By extension,' argues Burt, 'a similar kind of critical opposition becomes available in the present.'[4] This situation may well have come about, as Robert Young has noted, because cultural materialism as a broadly leftist critical practice has pretty much supplanted or displaced the dialectical or 'historical' materialism it inherits, such that 'a form of reflection theory' has been reasserted, through which 'history has become a mirror in which contemporary political priorities have been substituted for the former certain ground of Marxist analysis.'[5] By extension of his or her reading of the Renaissance in terms of 'moral' definitions of censorship, then, Burt goes on to contend that the political critic 'can be seen to oppose at once the professionalism and the formalism of a supposedly apolitical literary criticism and the postmodern (now post-Reaganite and post-Thatcherite) state. Thus censorship and criticism become self-identical terms that can be juxtaposed in a stable opposition; the critic is "opposed" to censorship.'[6]

Of course, cultural materialists must oppose and expose, too, reactionary standpoints on Renaissance literature and culture by showing them to be politically motivated, thus revealing their ostensible apoliticism as an ideological smokescreen. As the foreword to *Political Shakespeare* puts it, cultural materialism 'does not, like much established literary criticism, attempt to mystify its perspective as the natural, obvious or right interpretation of an allegedly given textual fact'.[7] Yet to distinguish itself from these positions, political criticism has often been forced to repeat the mystificatory stance of truth, reference and legality (note the legalistic tone of 'allegedly') which it typically criticises in its opponents. Thus, in order to contest Nigel Lawson's conservative reading of *Troilus*, for example, Margot Heinemann, in *Political Shakespeare*, argues that the ex-Chancellor presents his quotations 'wholly out of dramatic context' which she then goes on properly to retrieve.[8] As Robert Young puts it, this kind of manoeuvre in fact attempts to 'reground the link between representation and reference that has been questioned by the semiotics of the last twenty [now more than thirty] years'.[9] In suggesting that her position is more 'true' to its object (and her understanding of a dramatic excerpt more 'true' to its context) than is Lawson's, Heinemann produces a mystificatory reading, 'the right interpretation of an allegedly given textual fact'. Similarly, Walter Cohen in his essay 'Political criticism of Shakespeare' stresses the demythologising power of political criticism, but then becomes trapped in a position where he is compelled to insist that the left-wing 'partisanship' of contemporary 'political writing on Shakespeare' is 'not only compatible with but also necessary to a commitment to objectivity and scholarship'.[10] This in fact realigns radical critique with oppressive ideology, which tries to represent its politics, 'partisanship', as 'true'. Cohen's backsliding into 'objectivity and scholarship' signals at once a retreat from reactionary 'false politics' and a return to the politically disinterested, judicial image of the intellectual on which, according to cultural materialism, those politics are founded. It is indeed within the very process of differentiation between two opposable 'positions' that an uncanny identity emerges. Thus, censorship (or right-wing 'misreading') and (leftist) criticism cannot, to borrow Burt's language, be 'juxtaposed in a stable opposition', since 'political' criticism can often only legitimate and sustain itself as radically oppositional (or, as it were, 'free') by way of a forceful repression of its own 'politics' or, in other words, by censorship of itself.

Burt's *Licensed by Authority* argues against any clear-cut distinction between criticism and censorship, poetic liberty and licensed poetry, within the multiple and dispersed, and often equivocal and contradictory, spaces and conditions of the court and market during the early seventeenth century. Here, following Bourdieu's sense that the acquisition and formation of cultural capital (the market) depends on 'a *compromise* between the *expressive interest* and a *censorship* constituted by the very structure of the field in which discourse is produced',[11] Burt argues that Renaissance panegyric 'involves neither willing submission to courtly tact nor open defiance of it but a mixture of both ... a neurotic compromise between the desire to fit in and the desire to express the censored material'.[12]

Such broadened and non-oppositional conceptions of censorship, in which the 'negative, repressive function is ... only one of the many regulatory mechanisms',[13] and of criticism, which can be seen to legitimate as well as delegitimate both the writer and the court, are by no means exclusive to Burt's book. Richard Dutton's *Mastering the Revels*, for example, concludes that 'the position of the Master of the Revels, jealously protecting court privileges as much as he sought to suppress "dangerous matter", made him as much a friend of the actors as their overlord. The stability that his office gave to an exchange of meaning in the early modern theatrical market-place clearly played a part in fostering the unique vitality of the drama of the period'.[14] Annabel Patterson similarly emphasises this 'productive' aspect of censorship, noting that 'it is to censorship that we in part owe our very concept of "literature"';[15] while others such as Janet Clare, Kevin Sharpe and Steven Mullaney have contributed to an ongoing and lively reconsideration of the complex interplay between censorship and licence insofar as it concerns the field of Renaissance studies.[16] Such studies provide a useful context in which to return, with questions of knowledge and censorship in mind, to Bacon's *New Atlantis*.

Before so doing, and given that a discussion of some contemporary critical trends and debates has been taken to frame an approach to Bacon's text, it is perhaps worth making a – necessarily very brief – comment on the question of historical difference and relationship that inevitably surrounds any such project of re-reading. While it is important not to repeat the kind of 'reflectionism' that Robert Young associates with some cultural materialist strategies of reading, whereby the past functions rather straightforwardly as a platform for larger arguments of topical relevance, nevertheless it seems to me equally problematic to position the *New Atlantis* historically according to crude notions of epoch or chronological pastness, since such ostensibly stable conceptions of time (and indeed place) are themselves rendered uncertain in the text by the *uncanny* relation of Bensalem to Europe and, by extension, to the values of progress and linearity that begin to emerge on the cusp (or on just the other side) of Enlightenment. This uncanny relationship upsets the designation of a self-identical point of origin or ground on which rest traditional notions of historical time and historical difference (themselves allied to those nascent Enlightenment values). However, as a text that is in many ways in flux, in transition or in some other sense 'at sea', the *New Atlantis* may be of interest to the contemporary reader in that it seems possible to locate Bacon's text within the interstitial space of a shift from 'premodern' to 'modern' types of legitimation, a shift that Lyotard discusses extensively in his account of the postmodern condition. In *Lyotard: Writing the Event*, Geoffrey Bennington states that 'Lyotard suggests a change from a sort of classical and premodern science which produced narratives for seeking legitimisation in an origin or ground, a first principle or a transcendental authority, to "modern" forms of legitimation based on consensus … [this] type of legitimation allows for the possibility that the discussion of experts can lead to an improvement in the rules for speaking truth, and that this improvement can be projected into a future under the sign of progress.'[17] This transitional phase resonates with the shift from deduction to induction, from similitude to Cartesian separation and classification, from sameness to difference, that can be located at the horizon of the early modern period and, more particularly, identified with Bacon himself. Reading (and locating historically) the *New Atlantis* in the interstices of these forms of legitimation, in a space of contestation and struggle between the authority of a ground and the concerns of the present with its politics of future use—value, it is not surprising that the text itself raises questions of historical method, taking us beyond simple 'either/or' choices of sameness/difference.

## II

According to Rawley, Bacon's secretary, the 'fable' of the *New Atlantis*[18] was devised by its author so as to 'exhibit therein a model or description of a college instituted for the interpreting of nature and the producing of great and marvellous works for the benefit of men, under the name of Salomon's House' (36). Salomon's House exemplifies in ideal terms the advancement of learning, in the context both of academic principle and institutional practice. As B. H. G. Wormald has put it, as well as providing 'a framework of directing axioms conducive to learning's advancement', the *New Atlantis* is Bacon's 'vision of an institution established by government for furthering natural philosophy/science'.[19] As a source of enlightenment, discovery and invention, Salomon's House is, to borrow Burt's phrase, licensed by authority: it is created and officially sanctioned by royal act (58); and the Father of Salomon's House, who imparts to the European visitors 'the true state' – the foundations, instruments, functions and ordinances – of the institution, is himself described as arriving, almost regally, 'in state' (69). The close connections between the state and the academy are underlined, then, through reference to the authority of the House of Salomon's officials; but also the authority of the institution is reflected in the orderliness that everywhere characterises its activities. As a research institute, it supports the study of, among other things, the natural sciences, mathematics and geometry, philosophy, medicine, the mechanical arts, and optics and acoustics. The description offered by the Father of the means and ends of these pursuits is given in terms of an extremely lengthy and well-ordered identificatory and classificatory grouping and listing of the various faculties and functions within the academy, bordering on the facile, so that the almost legalistic monologism of the Father's speech can be taken to reflect the legality as well as the orderliness of the institution. Indeed, since it tells us so little that might really be interesting (about scientific ethics, for example, or the precise terms of the relationship between state and academy) the Father's account of the 'true state' of Salomon's House is characterised by an absence of interlinearity to which, we might imagine, all censors aspire, alerting us to the possibility that the revelation to which we are brought in the concluding section of the *New Atlantis* may be communicated in the very language of censorship.

The orderliness of the institution's academic disciplines is matched by that of the conduct of its officials. As we have already seen, Robert K. Faulkner remarks that 'every official performs his function [and] everyone does what he is ordered'. However, as he goes on to point out, 'all this order is the more remarkable since the relation of king, city, nation, state, and scientist is not clarified. The order that orders ... is hidden'.[20] It is generally recognised that this utopian domain of enlightened knowledge, declaring itself dedicated to '*Light*: to have *light*' (59), is founded upon such concealment, although critics disagree as to exactly what is being concealed. Recall how Jerry Weinberger notes that Bensalemite 'science is shrouded in secrecy, denying the possibility of full enlightenment', attributing this to Bacon's sense that 'the politics of science must be secret and retired because only the most resolute souls will be willing to embrace such a world with full knowledge of its moral risks and dangers.'[21] From this point of view, any consideration of the ethical implications and responsibilities of science and learning must therefore be censored in order for enlightenment, advancement and progress to continue apace. In contrast, Faulkner reads the *New Atlantis* in the context of what he sees as Bacon's belief that the 'science of government is a thing secret and reserved, to be handled with reverence and even in silence.'[22] According to this analysis, it is the governing social and material contexts and conditions rather than the moral implications of the academy's activities that must remain invisible: a different sort of politics of science. This is backed up by Faulkner's contention that the very processes of production underlying the achievements of Salomon's House and Bensalem generally are concealed. He states, 'we are plied with a promise of pleasant affluence, but any system of painful industry and production is kept well behind the scenes'.[23] Indeed, the catalogue offered by the Father of Salomon's House of its faculties and functions barely touches upon the labours of production involved (we are occasionally told *what* is done, but rarely *how* it is done), so that science and knowledge are described, as it were, within the rhetorical terms of commodity fetishism, in which the means to the end are hidden from view.

This difficulty of saying exactly what is concealed in the *New Atlantis*, either at the social or textual level, arises partly out of the problem of identifying something that is not, in any apparent way, there. Absence can, of course, be defined simply in an oppositional relationship to presence, but (as we shall see in the *New Atlantis*) what is present is itself a matter of interpretation or reading, and, as such, cross-cut by effects of uncertainty, ambiguity or a certain sort of slipperiness. Thus, the identificatory strategies of an oppositional logic of presence/absence are undermined by the 'otherness' or internal difference of what is present. Indeed, Bensalem, as both an exemplary 'model' and a 'secret conclave' (51) exists, in Freudian terms, in an *uncanny* relation to the positivistic knowledge, progress and plenitude that gains importance on the way to a nascent European-Enlightenment project, representing simultaneously 'what is familiar and agreeable' and 'what is concealed and kept out of sight'.[24] In these terms, the polarities and boundaries of known/unknown, visible/invisible, outside/inside collapse into more complex and undecidable formations epitomised by the non self identical doubleness of Europe/Bensalem. The *New Atlantis* is both a beacon of previously undiscovered wisdom and truth and, as Bacon puts it, 'a mirror in the world worthy to hold men's eyes' (60): both subject and object, self and other.

Thus, it would seem that critics and readers of the *New Atlantis* are placed in the same boat as the European visitors themselves. That is, these critics become, as it were, knowledgeably ignorant, just as the European voyagers become, as it were, ignorantly knowledgeable, of Bensalemite learning and society. The journey of the Europeans towards revelation, like that of the critic towards understanding, is beset at every turn – even, as we have seen, at the end – by limitations, confinements and prohibitions, as if such constraints were less an obstacle to than a *condition of* enlightenment. A host of terms are laid down before the strangers can come ashore, including the restriction of numbers allowed to enter Bensalem, and the taking of an oath prior to the 'license to come on land' (40). They are 'sent to, and brought to the Stranger's House' (41) or, in other words, escorted along predetermined routes. They are subjected to an initial period of quarantine in 'chambers' and 'cells' in which are continually present 'six people appointed to attend you, for any business you may have abroad' (42). Whether or not these officials are intermediaries or guards, their job is clearly to forcibly prevent contaminatory contact between the Bensalemites and the Europeans. Here, we find that the utopian space of enlightenment is a protected and protective zone, quick to enforce its borders against real and symbolic threats of infection. However, the brick walls that keep the strangers *in* are also presented as a means of ensuring undisturbed freedom. They are assured, 'do not think yourselves restrained, but rather left to your rest and ease' (42), and subsequently spend 'three days joyfully and without care' (44). In this sense, the boundary that materially divides the Europeans and the Bensalemites is itself symbolically subverted and transgressed the moment it is enforced, since the freedoms of both are guaranteed by the prohibitory borders of both, opening out the suggestion of an identity or parallel state that contradicts images of hermetically closed non-contact and difference.

It is worth looking more closely at the way in which the enlightenment offered by the Bensalemites is, as Weinberger puts it, 'shrouded in secrecy'.[25] Revelation is made in the rather conspiratorial manner of exclusive, private conversations. The officer of Salomon's House encountered initially by the Europeans desires, we are told, 'to speak with some few of us, whereupon only six of us stayed, and the rest avoided the room' (44). The interview with the Father of Salomon's House is described in terms of 'private access' and 'private conference with one that ye shall choose'; and, prior to his disclosure, all other company departs and even the pages are 'warned' from the room (70–1). Moreover, the special privilege of revealed wisdom is highlighted by reference to 'the laws of secrecy which we have for our travellers' (46) and through the affirmation that Bensalem is founded on 'fundamental laws' comprising 'interdicts and prohibitions which we have touching the entrance of strangers'. Furthermore, just as things start to get interesting, the speaker is invariably called away rather abruptly by a mysterious messenger (49, 68). Some critics have interpreted these interruptions as evidence of Bensalemite surveillance and self-censorship,[26] yet they do not seem to inhibit, at a later stage, further scenes of revelation which dynamise and propel the structure of the narrative itself. Flying in the face of critical assertions that Bensalemite secrecy masks the organising principles and infrastructural pith of their society, these shenanigans (the orchestration of private conversations, the sense of exclusive revelation, even of clandestine liaison) might therefore appear to be little more than an elaborate way of convincing the strangers that Bensalemites have juicy secrets to share! From this point of view, Bensalemite secrecy does not constitute a form of repression operating at the threshold of enlightenment, but enacts a kind of 'productive' censorship, in which the controlled management and manipulation of what is apparently unsaid and unrevealed lends meaning, value and authority to what *is* said and discovered. Correspondingly, from this perspective, we move from Faulkner's contention that 'the order that orders ... is hidden' (repression) to Lyotard's 'problematic of legitimation' of modern science, in which the non-transcendental legality of the law problematises dreams of unearthing ultimate proofs of prior truths, but also prompts enlightenment fantasies of improvement, development, progress, under the sign of a future (production).[27]

On beginning the instruction of the strangers, the officer of Salomon's House states that there are 'some things I may tell you, which I think you will not be unwilling to hear' (44). The commencement of Bensalemite disclosure is couched in delightfully interlinear terms: reading between the lines, the implication is, of course, that there are other things that may not be told, and which in any case the Europeans would be unwilling to hear. Weinberger argues that the subject of this 'unsaid' is itself prohibitory restraint: 'if Bensalemite law and policy are consistent, strangers unwilling to stay, or those judged unfit to stay, must have been restrained by force or killed. This doubtless the sailors would not have been willing to hear.'[28] However, the idea that the officer's speech censors (or is censored) is not consistent with the interlinearity of the phrasing found here. The sophisticated twists and turns of syntax produce, as Paul de Man has put it,

'negative knowledge about the reliability of linguistic utter-
ances',[29] encouraging interrogative reading. Thus, the censorship
found by Weinberger in the official's statement actually produces a kind of enlightenment. Although it is possible to read
into the official's remarks a sinister and foreboding sense of
limitation, we can also interpret what he says as an act of entice-
ment rather than prohibition – though no less disingenuous,
perhaps – urging the listener to believe that there is more to
know beyond the threshold of what is said, and thus sustaining
the very project of enlightenment.

At another point, the officer says 'because he that knoweth
least is fittest to ask questions, it is more reason, for the enter-
tainment of the time, that ye ask me questions, than that I ask
you' (46). This proposition might immediately raise suspicion:
'ask me anything you like' isn't the same as 'I'll tell you everything I know.' Indeed, granting the freedom to ask ingeniously
shifts the onus from the expert official to the unknowledgeable
questioner, to the extent that it may be seen to provide an ideal
opportunity to neglect a mass of information. This leaves the
Europeans no grounds for complaint about suppression since no
prior limitations have been placed on the questioning. Yet it is
precisely the absence of these limitations, in the sense of a fixed
context of discussion, that limits what will become known.
Reading between the lines, it seems that – within the particular
formation of enlightenment found here – limits and parameters
are an essential precondition if knowledge is to be optimised.
From another perspective, however, the idea of an almost bottom-
less pit of hitherto undiscovered knowledge responsive to any
question whatsoever (although attainable only by the fixing of
contextualising limits) encourages the unknown to be sifted *ad
infinitum*; so that once again it is indispensably within the context of boundaries (known/unknown, visible/invisible, inside/
outside), albeit the crossing and relocating of them, that we find
the enabling conditions of the enlightenment project.

## III

The problem of enlightenment in the *New Atlantis* rests, then, on
whether truth is or can be divined in a prior relation to knowledge,

or whether knowledge – as a complex formation of linguistic encounters and propositions – represents truth into being. We are told early on that Bensalem has been founded on Christian revelation. A mile out to sea, a 'great pillar of light' topped by a 'large cross of light' appears 'about twenty years after the ascension of our Saviour' to the 'people of the city'. For a while, this revelation remains shrouded in mystery, as the sign conveys no message as such. However, one of the wise men of the society of Salomon's House is at hand and, 'having awhile attentively and devoutly viewed and contemplated the pillar and cross', he prays to God that interpretation will be forthcoming. While all others remain miraculously transfixed, the wise man alone is permitted to approach the pillar of light, and delivered to him is an 'arc or chest' in which is found a 'book' containing 'all the canonical books of the Old and New Testament' as well as a 'Letter' bringing the good news of salvation from St Bartholomew (47–8). This scene lies at the origins of a symbolic interplay which runs throughout the *New Atlantis*, between the spiritual 'light' of Christianity and the project of enlightenment founded by the House of Salomon, suggesting that its advancement of learning is divinely sanctioned and illuminates a transcendental signified. Thus, unsurprisingly, the wondrous meaning of the 'great pillar of light' becomes apparent foremost to the 'house or college' (in the shape of the representative figure of the wise man) which is 'the very eye of this kingdom' (48).

However, the relation between Christian 'light' and scientific enlightenment becomes problematic at the very moment the analogy between the two hardens. A few pages later, we are told that Salomon's House is itself the 'lanthorn' or light of Bensalem (58). It is not simply that this doubling and displacement of the source of illumination might appear heretical. More importantly, the 'eye' that sees is itself the 'light' that illuminates. In what Christopher Pye describes as the 'Renaissance theory of sight beams',[30] the eye is the *agent* of what it perceives, and indeed in the pageant poetry written to celebrate James I's accession, the king himself is represented simultaneously as the ultimate source of light, a sun, and a self-illuminating, all-seeing eye.[31] The currency of such contemporary ideas can be traced elsewhere in the *New Atlantis*. Although we are told that Bensalem is a copious source of 'light', it remains 'hidden and unseen to others', while the less enlightened Old World is nevertheless 'open and in a light' to Bensalemite travellers (51). This apparent reversal of the scenes of illumination and darkness in fact attributes the presence or absence of 'light' to the subject rather than the object, the seeing eye rather than the thing viewed. Such configurations seem to align more with Bacon's views on poetry than with his views on science. Quoting from *The Advancement of Learning*, Faulkner states: 'According to Bacon … poetry is … a rational management of invented illusion to help satisfy real desire. Poets do not divine an ideal or feel the sublime. They incline to "submit the shows of things to the desires of the mind"'.[32] The emphasis within Bacon's concept of poetic vision on subjectivity and sense-impression clearly foreshadows certain strands of eighteenth-century philosophical discourse, but most interestingly this view of poetry as the conscious manipulation of consciousness advocates rationalism without recourse to pre-existing 'truth'. Poetry's self-reflexivity seems, however, to be present in Bensalemite science: Salomon's House is both the eye that sees and the light that illuminates. Indeed, it is possible to re-read the scene of Christian revelation in the *New Atlantis* in light of Bacon's conception of poetic vision: that is, in aligning Christianity and science as compatible belief systems or narratives and thus satisfying spiritual and secular needs simultaneously, the spectacle serves to 'submit the shows of things to the desires of the mind'. Thus, Faulkner casts doubt on the miraculous pillar of light, drawing attention to the theatrical staginess of the scene of revelation (we are told 'the boats stood all as in a theatre' (47)), and noting, in the Father's description of Salomon's House, 'the scientist's ability "to represent all manner of reflections, refractions, and multiplications of visual beams of objects," and to represent also all manner of "false apparitions, impostures and illusions"'.[33] Indeed, the Father reveals that the Bensalemite science of optics has enabled its proponents to produce artificially 'all delusions and deceits of the sight in figures' as well as unnaturally vivid views of 'objects far off; as in the heaven and remote places'. 'We make artificial rain-bows, halos, and circles of light', he goes on, before concluding with a description of the 'houses of deceits of the senses' within Salomon's

House itself (78–80). We can only conclude from this irony that, as Faulkner puts it, 'Bacon thinks divinations but artificial light, imaginings like all suppositions of divinity.'[34] Thus, it is not that Salomon's House provides an exemplary, model college in which natural or divine phenomena might be discovered and exhibited; rather, revelation is, in Bourdieu's terms, 'the very structure of the field' in which the 'rational management of invented illusion' can take place so as to 'satisfy real desire', either that of the Bensalemites or the Europeans. And, of course, 'the very structure of the field in which discourse is produced and circulated' constitutes Bourdieu's definition of censorship. Here, however, we are alerted by the fact that it simultaneously constitutes a definition of enlightenment.

## IV

Since, as Faulkner puts it, divination in fact represents the 'rational management of invented illusion',[35] it follows that censorship, as the 'structure of the field' in which it takes place, is enacted non-repressively, as it were, on disclosures that have no primordial unity or transcendental grounding. The revelation of the 'Book' that accompanies the miraculous 'light' of Christianity is, however, presented as being instantaneously and transcendentally complete. It contains not only the portions of the Bible written by AD 20 but also 'some other books which were not at that time written', yet which are 'nevertheless in the Book' (49). In Faulkner's terms, the productive process – the labour and temporality of writing – once again appears to have been concealed or repressed, within the fetishised spectacle of a spontaneous text, both unique and fully finished. From this kind of perspective, the wholeness of the Book is itself a product of repressive exclusions.

As if to confirm the unity of the Book, its reception is characterised by the absence of interlinearity, since by 'a great miracle' similar to 'that of the Apostles in the original Gift of Tongues' the various peoples of Bensalem – 'Hebrews, Persians and Indians, besides the natives' – are all able to read the Book and Letter 'as if they had been written in his own language' (49). This constitutes a kind of reverse Babel-effect in which cultural, religious and

linguistic fragmentation is miraculously overcome and restored
within a monological moment of absolute certainty and harmony.
What would appear to be a reclamation of a prior wholeness,
both of the text and of the people, is achieved, then, at the ex-
pense of any slippage between the lines. Translational ambiguity
is entirely dispensed with: just as the productive processes of
writing are omitted, so the labour of translation is also redundant
and, indeed, even the effort of reading seems to be discounted,
since the meaning of the text becomes instantly and unequivocally apparent to all present. This absence of interlinearity
suggests, once again, a definition of censorship. But here we find
censorship − within the terms of a repressive hypothesis, the
harbinger of violence and danger to the project of enlightenment
− (co)operating at the very moment of overcoming a castrating
severance or fragmentation of the Word and the Nation. The
damage done to a repressive hypothesis by this paradoxical state
of affairs is compounded, since such censorship cannot be said to
excise or suppress an earlier or more complete original: the Book
we are dealing with is the ultimate prior text, or otherwise it is
part of the 'invented illusion' brought into being by the event
itself. Here, denied the lag or gap that it requires between a
primary and secondary 'object', this theory of repression runs
into trouble: the originality of the Book, its unfaltering continuity
with the moment, its non-concealment of anything, is indisput-
able either way and yet, paradoxically, it is subjected to a kind of
censorship. This forces us once again to rethink conventional
notions of censorship as blemish, and therefore, by extension,
paradoxically unsettles an oppositional image of knowledge as
purity at the very moment it would seem, superficially at least, to
confirm it.

Both the text and the society of the *New Atlantis* seem to
revolve around the production and circulation of 'little scrolls of
parchment' (38) which, embodying the authority of the Christian–
Bensalemite order, continually reinvoke the scene of revelation
of the Book and the Letter. On their first encounter with the
Bensalemites, the Europeans are not spoken to, but read to from
such a scroll, 'written in Hebrew, and in ancient Greek, and in
good Latin of the School'; that is, in universally legible language,
not unlike the miraculous Book itself. However, the scroll

welcomes or 'includes' only to 'prohibit' and exclude its audience: 'Land ye not, none of you' it commands (38). Content and context are here antagonistically fused, as the prohibitory message is delivered within an enticing gesture of openness, greeting, legibility. A similar scroll of 'shining yellow parchment' is indispensable within the ritual of the Tirsan feast, given to honour the father of the family who can boast 'thirty persons descended of his body alive together'. This scroll is the King's Charter, containing 'gift of revenew, and many privileges, exemptions and points of honour' (60–2). The scroll thus simultaneously rewards and regulates generation, since breeding, it is suggested, is mainly a means to achieve financial security: thus, those who marry for 'alliance, or portion' (dowry) are 'almost indifferent ... of issue' (67). By conferring large amounts of money on the family as a whole, the scroll effectively limits what it celebrates, ingeniously controlling at the same time as glorifying population, and in the process offering freedoms to its beneficiaries which turn out, simultaneously, to be restrictions. Similarly, when the Father of Salomon's House conveys to the unnamed narrator of the *New Atlantis* the substance of the final portions of the text, he does so with his blessing and largess, giving 'leave to publish it' as well as 'about two thousand ducats, for a bounty' (83). If such plenitude is intended to signal the ripe finishedness and full presence of the text, then nevertheless we have already seen how the monologic purity of the Father's descriptions contains, as a pre condition, a host of limitations, restrictions and prohibitions. As I have suggested, these serve not so much to conceal an 'inner' truth, as critics of the *New Atlantis* would have it, as to suggest unfinishedness, that there is more to know. From this perspective, a finished text would seem to be wholly dependent on its unfinishedness, perhaps offering a key to the question of why Rawley inscribes at the end of the *New Atlantis* '[THE REST WAS NOT PERFECTED]', even though, as Faulkner points out, Bacon must have considered it ready for publication to have translated it into Latin, the universal language (the language of the book), before his death (321).[36]

Thus, in the context of the institutionalisation and systematised circulation of writing underlined here by the powerful ties between academy and state found in Bensalem, these examples show once more how openness, freedom from obligation, and textual originality remain inseparable from the forms of censorship, regulation and restraint that in fact produce them. The borders between freedom and prohibition, knowledge and censorship, inside and outside, are radically unstable within the space and vision of the institution, collapsing these supposed oppositions into more complex and indeterminate formations characterised by, for example, the non-self-identical doubleness, the uncanny twinning, of Europe/Bensalem. However, in relation to questions of the limitations placed on the production of knowledge within this academy, it is also suggested that, while such boundaries can never seem to be stabilised, their very indeterminacy and fluidity is precisely what sustains the project of such enlightenment. The masquerade of secrecy in Bensalem achieves this canny effect: no matter how far the frontiers of knowledge are pushed back, there's always more to know just over the threshold. As we have seen, then, it is the absence of limitations that limits what can become 'known', while the positioning of boundaries, particularly shifting and thus incessant ones, remains vital in the crossing or journey towards enlightened knowledge.

## Notes

1  Robert K. Faulkner, *Francis Bacon and the Project of Progress* (Maryland, Rowman and Littlefield, 1993), p. 248.

2  Jerry Weinberger, 'Introduction' to Francis Bacon, *New Atlantis and The Great Instauration*, ed. Jerry Weinberger (Wheeling, Illinois, Harlan Davidson, 1980, revised edn, 1989), p. xxxii.

3  Richard Burt, *Licensed by Authority: Ben Jonson and the Discourses of Censorship* (Ithaca and London, Cornell University Press, 1993).

4  *Ibid.*, p. 152.

5  Robert Young, *White Mythologies: Writing, History and the West* (London, Routledge, 1990), p. 89.

6  Burt, *Licensed by Authority*, pp. 152–3.

7  Jonathan Dollimore and Alan Sinfield, 'Foreword', in Jonathan Dollimore and Alan Sinfield (eds), *Political Shakespeare: New Essays in Cultural Materialism* (Manchester, Manchester University Press, 1985).

8  Margot Heinemann, 'How Brecht read Shakespeare', in *Political Shakespeare*, p. 203.

9  Robert Young, 'The politics of "the politics of literary theory"', *OLR*, 10 (1988) 132.

10 Walter Cohen, 'Political criticism of Shakespeare', in Jean Howard and Marion O' Connor (eds), *Shakespeare Reproduced: The Text in History and Ideology* (London, Methuen, 1987), p. 20.

11 See Pierre Bourdieu, 'Censorship and the imposition of form', in *Language and Symbolic Power*, ed. and intro. John B. Thompson, trans. Gino Raymond and Matthew Adamson (Oxford, Basil Blackwell, 1991), p. 137.

12 Burt, *Licensed by Authority*, p. 11.

13 *Ibid.*, p. 13.

14 Richard Dutton, *Mastering the Revels: The Regulation and Censorship of English Renaissance Drama* (London, Macmillan, 1991), p. 248.

15 Annabel Patterson, *Censorship and Interpretation: The Conditions of Writing and Reading in Early Modern England* (Madison, Wisconsin, University of Wisconsin Press, 1984), p. 4.

16 Janet Clare, *Art Made Tongue-Tied by Authority: Elizabethan and Jacobean Censorship* (Manchester, Manchester University Press, 1990); Kevin Sharpe, *Criticism and Compliment: The Politics of Literature in the England of Charles I* (Cambridge, Cambridge University Press, 1987); Steven Mullaney, *The Place of the Stage: License, Play and Power in Renaissance England* (Chicago, University of Chicago Press, 1987).

17 Geoffrey Bennington, *Lyotard: Writing the Event* (Manchester, Manchester University Press, 1988), p. 115.

18 Francis Bacon, *New Atlantis and The Great Instauration*, ed. Jerry Weinberger (Wheeling, Illinois, Harlan Davidson, 1980, revised edn, 1989). All further references will be given in the main body of the text.

19 B. H. G. Wormald, *Francis Bacon: History, Politics and Science, 1561–1626* (Cambridge, Cambridge University Press, 1993), p. 235.

20 Faulkner, *Francis Bacon*, p. 248.

21 Weinberger, 'Introduction', p. xxxii.

22 Faulkner, *Francis Bacon*, p. 235.

23 *Ibid.*, p. 246.

24 Sigmund Freud, 'The Uncanny', *The Penguin Freud Library Volume 14: Art and Literature*, ed. Albert Dickson (London, Penguin, 1985), p. 345.

25 Weinberger, 'Introduction', p. xxxii.

26 Faulkner, for example, notes that the officer of Salomon's House 'waxes enthusiastic and didactic about Bensalem's salvation from infidelity, through the "apostolical and miraculous evangelism of St. Bartholomew." A messenger interrupts him when he pauses. When he returns, the topic is the marvel of Bensalem as unknown knower, and our governor–priest smiles at the suggestion that Bensalem benefits from supernatural spirits. Does someone listen and direct from behind the scenes?' (245–6). Later on, Faulkner remarks that 'the priest is interrupted by a messenger just after

he waxes evangelical, and is called away; we are later told of devices for
transmitting sounds in pipes and lines' (249).

27  Lyotard writes: 'Scientific knowledge cannot know and make known that
it is the true knowledge without resorting to the other, narrative, kind of
knowledge, which from its point of view is no knowledge at all. Without
such recourse it would be in the position of presupposing its own validity
and would be stooping to what it condemns: begging the question, pro-
ceeding on prejudice' (*The Postmodern Condition* (Manchester, Manchester
University Press, 1984), p. 29). Yet it is in relation to this passage that
Bennington discusses Lyotard's concept of a shift from premodern to modern
forms of scientific legitimation which allow for consensual discussion among
experts leading to improvements in the rules for speaking the truth, 'projected into a future under the sign of progress' (Bennington, *Lyotard*, p. 115).

28  Weinberger, 'Introduction', p. xvi.

29  See Paul de Man, 'The resistance to theory', in *The Resistance to Theory*
(Minneapolis, University of Minnesota Press, 1986), pp. 10–11.

30  Christopher Pye, 'The sovereign, the theater, and the kingdome of dark-
nesse: Hobbes and the spectacle of power', in Stephen Greenblatt (ed.),
*Representing the English Renaissance* (California, University of California
Press, 1988), p. 295.

31  Pye's article touches upon the solar imagery of early modern power, but
for a fuller discussion of this in relation to the literature of James I's
accession, see Simon Wortham, 'Sovereign counterfeits: the trial of the
pyx', *Renaissance Quarterly*, 49.2 (Summer 1996) 334–59.

32  Faulkner, *Francis Bacon*, p. 237.

33  *Ibid.*, p. 243.

34  *Ibid.*, p. 239.

35  *Ibid.*, p. 237.

36  The *New Atlantis* is indeed open-ended and, as it were, unfinished at both
ends, since the text commences by joining the Europeans in mid-voyage.
Kate Aughterson, in '"The waking vision": reference in the *New Atlantis*',
*Renaissance Quarterly*, 45.1 (Spring 1992) 119–39, argues that the opening
passage, beginning, 'We sailed from Peru, (where we had continued by the
space of one whole year)', comprises 'simple vocabulary', 'accurate geographical directions' and a straightforward fit between syntactic and temporal
sequence, which epitomises an 'apparently closed system of determining
referents' (122). Aughterson thereby suggests that, apparently, 'no
reference is unfixed or floating' (122), yet the irony of this metaphorical
representation of reference as 'unfloating' is that the opening sequence of
the *New Atlantis* is about a voyage at sea! Moreover, the description of the
Europeans as having 'continued' awhile in Peru carries the sense of
ongoingness, impermanence, flux. Thus, Aughterson concludes that
'metaphoric "open-endedness"' arises out of the seemingly 'closed system'
(122): to some extent, this parallels my argument about the inseparable
relation of censorship and freedom or enlightenment in the *New Atlantis*.

# Notes on contributors

KATE AUGHTERSON is a Senior Lecturer in the School of English at the University of Central England, specialising in the sixteenth and seventeenth centuries. Her publications include articles on Francis Bacon; *Renaissance Woman: Constructions of Femininity in England* (London, 1995); *The English Renaissance: An Anthology of Sources and Documents* (London, 1998); *Webster: The Tragedies* (2001); and *Aphra Behn: The Comedies* (forthcoming). She is currently working on an edition of renaissance mothers' advice books.

DAVID COLCLOUGH is a Lecturer in English at Queen Mary, University of London, England. He has published on early modern scientific writing and is working on a book about freedom of speech in early Stuart England. He is editing the *New Atlantis* for *The Oxford Francis Bacon*.

SARAH HUTTON is Reader in Renaissance and Seventeenth-Century Studies at Middlesex University, England. Her publications include *Platonism and the English Imagination*, edited with Anne Baldwin (Cambridge, 1994); *Women, Science and Medicine 1550–1700*, edited with Lynette Hunter (Stroud, 1997); a new edition of Ralph Cudworth, *Treatise Concerning Eternal and Immutable Morality* (Cambridge, 1996); and a revised edition of *The Conway Letters*, ed. M. H. Nicolson (Oxford, 1992). She is a consultant to the 'Feminism and Enlightenment' research project, organised by Barbara Taylor, and research associate on the Newton Papers Project. She is Director of International Archives in the History of Ideas.

CLAIRE JOWITT is a Lecturer in Renaissance Literature at University of Wales, Aberystwyth. Her book *Travel Drama and Gender Politics 1589–1642: Real and Imagined Worlds* is forthcoming with Manchester University Press. She has edited a special issue of the journal *Women's Writing* (Spring, 2002) and *The Arts of Seventeenth-Century Science* (Aldershot, 2002). She has published a range of articles on women's writing, Jewish-Christian relations and gender and travel, in journals including *The Seventeenth Century* (1995), *Connotations* (1997), *Women's Writing* (1997), *Reformation* (1999), *Prose Studies* (1999) and *Parergon* (2001), *Renaissance Studies* (2002). She is currently working on a book on representations of Jews, pirates and Turks in early modern drama.

BRONWEN PRICE is a Principal Lecturer in English at Portsmouth University, England. She has published a range of essays and articles on seventeenth-century literature, most recently on Margaret Cavendish (*Literature and History*, 1998; Cambridge, 1996), Katherine Philips (Ashgate, 2001), Women's Poetry 1550-1700 (Blackwell, 2002) and An Collins (*Women's Writing*, 2002). She is currently working on a book on early modern women's poetry.

PAUL SALZMAN is a Senior Lecturer in English at La Trobe University, Melbourne, Australia. He has recently completed *Literary Culture in Jacobean England: Reading 1621* (Palgrave) and is currently working on a history of the transmission and reception of the work of eight early modern women writers. He has published widely in the area of early modern prose fiction, including *English Prose Fiction 1558-1700* (Oxford, 1985) and editions of sixteenth- and seventeenth-century fiction for Oxford World's Classics. He has recently edited a collection of essays with Jo Wallwork entitled *Women Writing 1550–1750* (Meridian, 2001).

RICHARD SERJEANTSON is a Fellow of Trinity College, Cambridge, and currently holds a three-year Assistant Lectureship in the Faculty of History at Cambridge, where he teaches the history of political thought and the history of science. His research interests lie broadly in early modern intellectual history; he is author of 'The passions and animal language, 1540–1700' (*Journal of the History of Ideas*, 2001) and has edited *Generall Learning* by Meric Casaubon (Cambridge, 1999). He is also the author of the forthcoming essay on 'Proof and Persuasion' in the sixteenth- and seventeenth-century volume of the *Cambridge History of Science*.

JERRY WEINBERGER is a Professor in the Department of Political Science at Michigan State University, USA. He is Director of the LeFrak Forum, and Co-Director of the Symposium on Science, Reason, and Modern Democracy, both at Michigan State University. Professor Weinberger is the author of *Science, Faith, and Politics: Francis Bacon and the Utopian Roots of the Modern Age* (Cornell University Press, 1985) and *Francis Bacon: The History of the Reign of King Henry the Seventh – a new edition with introduction, annotation and interpretive essay* (Cornell University Press, 1996). He is also editor of the *New Atlantis and The Great Instauration* (Wheeling, Illinois, 1980, revised 1989). He is presently writing a book on the political thought of Benjamin Franklin.

SIMON WORTHAM is a Principal Lecturer in English at Portsmouth University, England. He is the author of *Rethinking the University: Leverage and Deconstruction* (Manchester University Press, 1999), and has written numerous articles in a variety of journals, both on seventeenth-century literature and on issues of literary and critical theory. He jointly edited *Angelaki* 2.2 on the special topic of 'Authorizing culture' and also edited the second issue of the electronic journal *Culture Machine* (http://culturemachine.tees.ac.uk) on 'The university culture machine'. He is currently working on a collection of essays to be published by Stanford University Press, provisionally entitled *Samuel Weber: Technics and Deconstruction*.

# Select bibliography

## Editions

*The Works of Francis Bacon*, ed. James Spedding, Robert Leslie Ellis and Douglas Denon Heath, 14 vols (London, Longman, 1857–74).

*The Oxford Francis Bacon*, ed. Graham Rees, Lisa Jardine, Michael Kiernan, Julian Martin, Marta Fattori, Michael Edwards *et al.*, 15 vols forthcoming (Oxford, Clarendon Press, 1996–).

*Francis Bacon: A Critical Edition of the Major Works*, ed. Brian Vickers, Oxford Authors series (Oxford and New York, Oxford University Press, 1996).

*New Atlantis and The Great Instauration*, ed. Jerry Weinberger (Wheeling, Illinois, Harlan Davidson, 1980, revised edn 1989).

*Three Early Modern Utopias: Thomas More, Utopia; Francis Bacon, New Atlantis; Henry Neville, The Isle of Pines*, ed. Susan Bruce (Oxford and New York, Oxford University Press, 1999).

*Sir Francis Bacon: La Nouvelle Atlantide*, trans. Michèle Le Doeuff and Margaret Llasera (Paris, Flammarion, 1995).

## Biographies

Jardine, Lisa and Alan Stewart, *Hostage to Fortune: The Troubled Life of Francis Bacon* (London, Victor Gollancz, 1998).

Mathews, Nieves, *Francis Bacon: The History of a Character Assassination* (New Haven and London, Yale University Press, 1996.

## Critical Studies

Achinstein, Sharon, 'How to be a progressive without looking like one: history and knowledge in Bacon's *New Atlantis*', *CLIO*, 17:3 (Spring 1988), 249–64.

Adams, Robert P., 'The social responsibilities of science in *Utopia, New Atlantis* and after', *Journal of the History of Ideas*, 10 (1949), 374–98.

Albanese, Denise, 'The *New Atlantis* and the uses of utopia', *English Literary History*, 57:3 (Autumn 1990), 503–28.

Aughterson, Kate, '"The waking vision": reference in the *New Atlantis*', *Renaissance Quarterly*, 45:1 (Spring 1992), 119–39.

Bierman, Judah, '*New Atlantis* revisited', *Studies in the Literary Imagination*, 4:1 (1971), 121–41.

Blodgett, Eleanor Dickinson, 'Bacon's *New Atlantis* and Campanella's *Civitas Solis*: a study in relationships', *Publications of the Modern Languages Association*, 46:3 (September 1931), 763–80.

Boesky, Amy, 'Bacon's *New Atlantis* and the laboratory of prose', in Elizabeth
    Fowler and Roland Greene (eds), *The Project of Prose in Early Modern
    Europe and the New World* (Cambridge, Cambridge University Press, 1997),
    pp. 138–53.
——, *Founding Fictions: Utopias in Early Modern England* (Athens and London,
    University of Georgia Press, 1996).
Box, Ian, *The Social Thought of Francis Bacon: Studies in the History of Philo-
    sophy*, vol. 10 (Lewiston, The Edwin Mellen Press, 1989).
Bruce, Susan, 'Virgins of the world and feasts of the family: sex and the social
    order in two renaissance utopias', in Neil Rhodes (ed.), *English Renaissance
    Prose: History, Language and Politics* (Tempe, MRTS, 1997), pp. 125–46.
Davis, J. C., *Utopia and the Ideal Society: A Study of English Utopian Writing
    1516–1700* (Cambridge, Cambridge University Press, 1981).
Demers, Patricia, 'Bacon's allegory of science: the theatre of the *New Atlantis*',
    *Journal of the Rocky Mountain Medieval and Renaissance Association*, 4
    (1983), 135–48.
Elliott, Simon M., 'Bacon's *New Atlantis*: the kingdom of God and man', *Christ-
    ianity and Literature*, 38:1 (Autumn 1988), 43–61.
Faulkner, Robert K., *Francis Bacon and the Project of Progress* (Maryland, Row-
    man and Littlefield, 1993).
Flannery, Kathryn, 'Models of reading: seventeenth-century productions of
    Bacon's Texts', *Critical Approaches to Medieval and Renaissance Texts*, 5
    (1989), 111–33.
Gibson, R. W., *Francis Bacon: A Bibliography of his Works and of Baconiana to
    the Year 1750* (Oxford, The Scrivener Press, 1950).
Innes, David C., 'Bacon's *New Atlantis*: the Christian hope and the modern
    hope', *Interpretation*, 22:1 (Autumn 1994), 3-37.
Leary, John E., *Francis Bacon and the Politics of Science* (Ames, Iowa State
    University Press, 1994).
Martin, Julian, *Francis Bacon, the State, and the Reform of Natural Philosophy*
    (Cambridge, Cambridge University Press, 1992).
Matar, N. I., 'The sources of Joabin's speech in Francis Bacon's *New Atlantis*',
    *Notes and Queries*, 41:1 (March 1994), 75–8.
McCutcheon, Elizabeth, 'Bacon and the cherubim: an iconographical reading of
    the *New Atlantis*', *English Literary Renaissance*, 2:3 (Autumn 1972), 334–55.
Peltonen, Markku (ed.), *The Cambridge Companion to Bacon* (Cambridge, Cam-
    bridge University Press, 1996).
Pérez-Ramos, Antonio, *Francis Bacon's Idea of Science and the Maker's Know-
    ledge Tradition* (Oxford, Clarendon Press, 1988).
Quinton, Anthony, *Francis Bacon*, Past Master series (Oxford, Oxford Uni-
    versity Press, 1980).
Renaker, David, 'A miracle of engineering: the conversion of Bensalem in Francis
    Bacon's *New Atlantis*', *Studies in Philology*, 87:2 (Spring 1990), 181–93.
Sessions, William A. (ed.), *Francis Bacon's Legacy of Texts: 'The Art of Discovery
    Grows with Discovery'* (New York, AMS, 1990).
——, *Francis Bacon Revisited*, Twayne's English Authors series (New York,
    Twayne and London, Prentice Hall, 1996).
Solomon, Julie R. '"To know, to fly, to conjure": situating Baconian science at

the juncture of early modern modes of reading', *Renaissance Quarterly*, 44:3 (Autumn 1991), 513–58.

Urbach, Peter, *Francis Bacon's Philosophy of Science: An Account and a Reappraisal* (La Salle, Illinois, Open Court, 1987).

Vickers, Brian (ed.), *Essential Articles for the Study of Francis Bacon* (Hamdon, Archon Press, 1968, rpt. London, Sidgwick and Jackson, 1972).

Webster, Charles, *The Great Instauration: Science, Medicine and Reform, 1626–1660* (London, Duckworth and co., 1975).

Weinberger, Jerry, 'Science and rule in Bacon's utopia: an introduction to the reading of the *New Atlantis*', *American Political Science Review*, 70 (1976), 865–85.

——, *Science, Faith, and Politics: Francis Bacon and the Utopian Roots of the Modern Age* (Ithaca and London, Cornell University Press, 1985).

White, Howard B., *Peace Among the Willows: The Political Philosophy of Francis Bacon* (The Hague, Martinus Nijhoff, 1968).

Whitney, Charles, *Francis Bacon and Modernity* (New Haven, Yale University Press, 1986).

Wormald, B. H. G., *Francis Bacon: History, Politics and Science, 1561–1626* (Cambridge, Cambridge University Press, 1993).

Zagorin, Perez, *Francis Bacon* (Princeton, New Jersey, Princeton University Press, 1998).

Zetterberg, J. Peter, 'Echoes of nature in Solomon's House', *Journal of the History of Ideas*, 43:2 (April–June 1982), 179–93.

# Index